Les Bourgeois Gentilshommes

An Essay on the Definition of Elites in Renaissance France

George Huppert

Les Bourgeois Gentilshommes

The University of Chicago
Chicago and London

George Huppert is Professor of
History at the University of Illinois
at Chicago Circle.

The University of Chicago Press,
Chicago 60637
The University of Chicago Press,
Ltd., London

Printed in the United States of
America
81 80 79 78 77   9 8 7 6 5 4 3 2 1

Library of Congress Cataloging in Publication Data

Huppert, George, 1934–
    Les bourgeois gentilshommes.

    Includes index.
    1. Upper classes—France—History.   2. Elite (Social
sciences)—France—History.   3. France—History—
16th century.   I. Title.
HN425.H86   301.44′2   76-22954
ISBN 0-226-36099-7

lh 1/16

L. L. H., in memoriam

Ce n'est rien que foiblesse particuliere qui nous faict contenter de ce que d'autres ou que nous mesmes avons trouvé en cette chasse de cognoissance; un plus habile ne s'en contentera pas. Il y a toujours place pour un suyvant, ouy et pour nous mesmes, et route par ailleurs.

Montaigne

Contents

Acknowledgments

I do not wish to go so far as to say, in the conventional manner, that this book could never have been written without the spiritual support of a host of friends and colleagues too large to enumerate. I feel no need to express astonishment at the disproportion between my own feeble means and the implied splendor of the final achievement. This is an ordinary, workmanlike book, precisely the sort of book to be expected from its author. No great sacrifices were incurred in the course of writing it. If anything, the author is sorry to see the book out of his hands. He is, to tell the awful truth, considering a sequel.

Having admitted as much, it gives me pleasure, nonetheless, to acknowledge the provocative conversations which took place over the years and which may have helped to shape my course, if only indirectly. Fernand Braudel, Hans Baron, Bill Bouwsma, Emmanuel Le Roy Ladurie, Jean Glénisson, Natalie Davis, among others, helped me a great deal. A special thanks must be reserved to Denis Richet, who challenged me in conversation and graciously allowed me to use and cite his excellent unpublished monograph on the Séguier family. Roland Mousnier cannot be left unmentioned, even if our brief encounters took on an adversary tone. Debra Qureshi typed and retyped the manuscript, corrected it, cleaned it up—in a word—edited it. My thanks go to her.

The Social Science Research Council made it possible for me to make an early exploration of provincial archives in 1970. The Research Board of the University of Illinois paid for the microfilming of a good many documents in subsequent years. Finally, the John Simon Guggenheim Memorial Foundation gave me the greatest gift of all: a full year of uninterrupted research time in Paris. To all these I offer my gratitude.

1   *Introduction*

I should like to start by explaining why I choose to describe this weighty volume as an essay. It is an essay in the French and original sense of the word. Such an essay is an inquiry which follows from the question, What do I know? when it is applied to a particular subject and when it is answered, Nothing. In the course of this essay we shall be asking questions so basic that it may be difficult to imagine that historians can entertain doubts about them. They appear to be classic questions. At least it can be said of them that they were answered, long ago, in classic works. When Tocqueville or Marx, for example, spoke of preindustrial society in Europe, and more particularly in France, they retained the ancient words "nobility" and "bourgeoisie" on the assumption that these words could be used to describe social groups from the thirteenth to the eighteenth centuries. We continue to speak of the nobility in France, the *noblesse,* as an elite of birth which ruled the kingdom until its collapse. We speak of the bourgeoisie as a secondary elite defined not by birth but by wealth acquired in commerce and industry. This abstract vision of two elites was cast in a lasting mold by the polemics of the French Revolution.

Working historians of all persuasions have long been uncomfortable with these categories. The more we have found out about the social structure of the *ancien régime,* the more difficult it has become to fit our discoveries into the old mold.[1] Quite simply, no two historians agree on what they mean by "bourgeois" and "noble."[2] Nor is there any agreement on the nature of these two categories. Are they social classes, in Marx's sense? Are they what contemporaries had described as "orders"? The heart of the problem has been our failure to explain what we know to be true, namely, that there was considerable movement between social groups. Wealthy merchant families found their way into the seemingly closed world of the hereditary nobility, the *gentilshommes.* According to contemporaries, such a transformation was necessarily of a miraculous nature since the status of *gentilshommes* was by definition a matter of birth. The wealthiest merchant families abandoned commerce, *marchandise,* and invested their capital in land, education, and royal offices. Having achieved this much, they began to claim a status superior to that of their ancestors. Were they on the road to becoming *gentilshommes?* Mousnier, in his writing on the officeholders, wrestles with this question. We find him speaking of the *officiers* as "a new social class intermediary between the merchant-bourgeoisie and the nobility of the sword."[3] The most prominent *officier* families, he suggests, "appear to have left the Third Estate."[4] Left it? To go where? The *gentilshommes* refused to accept them as their equals.[5] What becomes of the *officiers* then? Do they form a new social class[6] or a new order?[7] If this is true, we are cautioned, such an order exists only de facto, it has no legal standing. Besides, the *officiers,* in the end, go back to their own order.[8] Which is what, exactly? This kind of confusion is entirely warranted by the sources. Contemporaries were incapable of giving clear answers to such questions.

The kind of clarity imposed on the past in the name of Marxism is of no help here. One can ignore all the talk of orders and estates and still end up with an equally useless scheme according to which two social classes, the "nobility" and the "bourgeoisie," face each other, each defined by its "mode of production." Quite aside from the difficulty inherent in defining a "feudal mode of production" and of finding sixteenth-century bourgeois who will fit Marx's definition, the fundamental problem remains unsolved.[9] We still have no way of explaining social mobility, we still do not know what to do with the *officiers,* whom we cannot dismiss as a marginal group. Their wealth, their political power, their sheer numbers do not permit it.[10]

The *ancien régime* is characterized by the existence of families which deny that they are bourgeois, insist that they are "living nobly," and complain about being treated as inferiors by the *gentilshommes.* For the sake of convenience we have spoken of these families as if they were defined merely by officeholding. Actually, in recent years, we have moved further. We have reached the point of defining solidarities within this social group which extend far beyond the occupational function of officeholding.

What is to be done with these families? We can hardly ignore them, since they, and not the merchant-bourgeois, are the real challengers to the power of the *gentilshommes*.[11] A distinguished Marxist historian would exclude the *officiers* from the bourgeoisie. Another equally distinguished and equally Marxist scholar pleads with his colleagues to find room for the *officiers*—and others "living nobly"—among the bourgeoisie.[12] No agreement is reached. In the face of this utter confusion,[13] one of the most learned historians of our generation is ready to capitulate entirely: the nobility, in France, is simply composed of "the rich and the powerful at any given time."[14]

Do we know nothing, then? We have amassed an almost indigestible heap of information, but we seem to be at a loss when it comes to making sense of our knowledge.[15] We are condemned to remain forever perplexed if we cannot reconcile the conflicting evidence presented in specialist monographs. Mousnier finds that it is exceedingly difficult to become a *gentilhomme*—and so does Lefebvre. Goubert, on the contrary, seems to conclude that anyone willing to bear the expense can usurp the status of a *gentilhomme*. Mousnier draws his conclusions from a study of Normandy around 1600, Lefebvre writes about the Orléans region in the late eighteenth century, and Goubert covers the Beauvaisis around 1690.[16] Is it not reasonable to assume that the rhythm of usurpation may have varied in the course of several centuries—to say nothing of the possibility of regional variations?

We shall inquire into usurpation as it was practiced in the sixteenth century. If we are to believe contemporary sources—and the modern literature as well—this choice should allow us to observe the brutal contrast between a period of great mobility—or easy usurpation—and a period of drastic contraction which appears to set in immediately afterward. At first the grandsons or great-grandsons of merchant (*marchand*) bourgeois are said to be turning into *gentilshommes* in droves. Later such persons continue, perhaps, to rise above their station—their *estat, condition,* or *qualité*—but they no longer become *gentilshommes*. We shall attempt to test these propositions. Should they prove to be plausible, it may be practical to speak of two distinct problems: rising beyond the status of merchant-bourgeois on the one hand, being accepted as a *gentilhomme* on the other.

It will prove easy enough to answer the question: How does one leave *marchandise* behind? We shall do this at some length. The question, How does one become a *gentilhomme*? is far more difficult to answer. The purist would say that one cannot become a *gentilhomme*, one has to be born one. A second, more accommodating, answer is that the king has the power to ennoble a commoner, to turn a *roturier* into an *anobli*. To be sure, the crown did perform this costly social miracle on occasion. The number of *anoblis* was always small,[17] though, and the esteem in which such "parchment nobles" were held by *gentilshommes de race* was never high.[18] How then did usurpation occur in periods of large-scale social mobility? The answer given by contemporary observers was to speak, discreetly or furiously, of tacit ennoblement, *anoblissement taisible*. This is the process, surely, which ought to hold our attention.

In subjecting tacit ennoblement to our scrutiny we shall perforce be describing two related but nonetheless distinct processes—and this may lead to occasional confusion. We shall be hearing, on the one hand, of merchant-bourgeois who leave their *condition* behind and whose descendants are allowed to assume "tacitly" the status of *gentilshommes* by various means of "arriving."[19] The destination of other successful families of merchant-bourgeois origin often appears to be deflected. They succeed in "living nobly" without becoming identified with the *gentilshommes*. This second group will hold our attention throughout this essay. In the late sixteenth century in particular, the evidence of contemporary sources forces the historian to view this group not merely as a herd of usurpers arrested in their migration from *roture* to *noblesse* but as a large, powerful, and vocal category of families who claim that they are neither bourgeois nor *gentilshommes* but something both different and better.

The formidable presence of these families was the most notable and explosive subject of political argument at the time. They were accused of rising above their station by merchants who envied their swift progress toward tax exemption and other spectacular privileges. They were scorned and hated by *gentilshommes* who contemplated their rapacious sweep of noble fiefs with justified fear. The newcomers were not satisfied with the ownership of fiefs, or seigneuries, once held by *gentilshommes*. Equipped with capital and with law degrees, they purchased offices and so acquired control over the administration of the kingdom at all levels.

The holding of office has often been the most visible mark of these families. We shall see, however, that in the sixteenth century, office does not, in and of itself, change their *condition*. Neither does the possession of fiefs—in and of itself. It is, rather, the combination of a number of ingredients, carefully amalgamated, which makes for "living nobly." The recipe is not quite the same as that which leads to the usurpation of *gentilhomme* status, although in both cases the family propels itself beyond the bourgeois *condition*.

Our inquiry may lead us to the suggestion that merchant-bourgeois dissatisfied with their *condition* were not necessarily dreaming of becoming *gentilshommes,* like Molière's Monsieur Jourdain. We may discover that in the sixteenth century such men were more likely looking up to the ideal of "living nobly" defined in this essay, an ideal utterly at variance with the way of life of the *gentilshommes de race.* We may hence be led to the conclusion that the *ancien régime* harbored, discreetly, a newer elite, side by side with the military and commercial elites of medieval origin.

2

"In France there are two kinds of persons: the first kind are nobles; the second kind are *roturiers,* or nonnobles. These two categories encompass all the inhabitants of the kingdom, whether clergy, magistrates, military men . . . or others . . . of whatever estate, quality, or condition they may be."[1]

This is the starting point of serious social analysis in the sixteenth century. We can dispense with the confusing tradition of speaking of three orders or estates: the clergy is not a social group. French society *grosso modo* is composed of two kinds of people; that is what the jurists tell us.

The real question for them is, Who is noble? And further, What is nobility? And finally, How can a commoner achieve it? As we prepare to follow the jurists in their attempts to answer these questions, we must realize that their testimony proceeds from a vested interest. They are, to a man, lobbying for a position which favors them, their families, their alliances—in short, their social class.

Social class? What else shall we call it? Not one of our respected legal authorities is recognized as a *gentilhomme,* and not one admits to being a mere bourgeois. They are the sons or grandsons or great-grandsons of merchants. They are themselves capitalists, money-lenders, usurers. They belong to a profession, the law, whose social status is ill defined. In the exercise of this profession they receive salaries and fees for work performed. They do not seek glory on the battlefield or diversion in hunting or conspicuous spending. In all these respects they fail to meet the test of the nobility. On the other hand, they are not directly engaged in commerce. They enjoy fiscal privileges theoretically beyond the reach of commoners, and they own noble fiefs and country estates.

What are they? Noble or not? That is, of course, the question which preoccupies them and their clients.

Among the jurists, Loyseau is a very good choice as the star witness in this inquiry,[2] not only because he is obviously much read and respected—the same could be said for Bacquet, for example[3]—and not only because he writes well, succinctly, with clarity and style, but, I think, chiefly because of the timing of his treatise *Des Ordres*, which was published in 1613 at a moment when class lines were hardening.

Thirty years earlier, when Bacquet was writing, it was still preferable to let sleeping dogs lie. There was no need to make extravagant claims for social mobility. One was satisfied to let confusions stand as long as the practical means for arriving at tax exemption and quasi-noble status were freely available. Thus Bacquet could afford to be a purist on the one hand (*in dubio* one presumes a man *roturier*), while on the other hand he shows himself comfortably indulgent toward commoners who chose the *taisible* route (that is, tacit, extralegal, by means other than royal letters patent) to tax exemption: "It is enough if the witnesses testify to having known his father and grandfather" and "observed them to have lived nobly." He adds, shrewdly, with apparent innocence: "It would be best if the witnesses were *gentilshommes* by birth, royal *officiers*, or other people of quality rather than simple merchants."[4] A plausible enough recommendation, even if one does not raise an eyebrow at the casual putting-together of *gentilshommes* by birth (*de race*), royal *officiers*, and other *gens de qualité* as if they were all equal. The real point here would not have escaped contemporary readers: in effect, it was sufficient for some rich lawyer to get four or five of his cronies in office to swear that his father and grandfather had always "lived nobly"—that is, without working and without being subject to the *taille*. The whole matter could be handled discreetly and quickly, in the judge's chambers. What the taxpayers did not know would not hurt them. And should they eventually find out that another wealthy citizen's name had been quietly removed from the tax rolls, they could sue. But where would it get them? "The judges will be the last to care and will declare them *gentilshommes* on the spot, they themselves having relatives of the same kind and only too glad to set the stage to usurp in their turn someday."[5]

Bacquet is straightforward enough on issues which are technical matters of law. The very important question of the payment of the *francs-fiefs* tax, for instance. This tax was exacted from commoners who held noble lands. Here Bacquet does not equivocate: "Royal *officiers* who are neither noble by birth nor legally ennobled are subject to the payment of the *francs-fiefs* tax." This is a blow to the notion that royal office ennobles the holder. Bacquet is quite firm on this: even *baillis, prevosts, lieutenants generaux* or *particuliers, conseillers presidiaux, esleus, advocats du roy*—all are subject to the *francs-fiefs* tax if their family is not noble by birth or ennobled by royal act. Where is the catch? We find it, quite simply, in Bacquet's liberal definition of what it takes to be declared noble, as seen a moment ago. He sticks to the letter of the law—and subverts its spirit.[6]

In 1582 we may still be in the heyday of tacit ennoblement. Bacquet could allow that offices did not confer nobility as long as he made nobility so easy to acquire tacitly that any *officier* worth his salt would have contrived this little trick before buying his office. What Bacquet has in mind, I would deduce, were I reading him in 1582, is that all persons having succeeded in acquiring the honorific title of *noble homme*—and all that this implies in social position—could count themselves noble in the eyes of the law, if not in the eyes of the local *gentilshommes*.[7]

Bacquet is writing at a time when confusion reigns, when usurpation is the rule,[8] when "you cannot trust coats of arms or family names."[9] Attacks against this state of affairs soon grew violent. Written from the point of view of those left behind by the meteoric rise of the new class (Tabourot) or from the point of view of those who feared its approach (du Fail), these polemics changed nothing. Other forces were at work: to leave bourgeoisie behind seemed to be becoming more difficult as the ranks of the fiscally privileged became ludicrously crowded—two crowded, perhaps, for the economy to support. Those who came along too late to join the world of privilege were forced to stand by helplessly. Their fury, it has been argued, made the wars of the League possible.[10] And Loyseau's treatise on orders is a declaration of war aimed at the *gentilshommes*.[11]

Loyseau's predecessors could speak well of the *gentilshommes* because they saw themselves and their kind tacitly included—or at least not explicitly rejected—by the old elite. We have seen Bacquet's very relaxed rules for gaining tacit admission to noble status. Thierriat's were even more relaxed. Where Bacquet had spoken of witnesses, without specifying their number, Thierriat heads toward a minimum requirement: four witnesses will suffice. Where Bacquet had specified that the witnesses must declare that they had known the father and grandfather of the candidate, Thierriat waives this requirement. It is enough for him if the witnesses have heard about the noble reputation of parents and grandparents.[12] Is it any wonder that Thierriat is able to heap praise upon the *nobles de race*?[13] He feels himself so much a part of this elite that he does not hesitate to adopt the title of *escuyer*. And, although he writes as if from the point of view of the old nobility ("the judicial offices are for the most part out of our hands, and occupied by rich *roturiers*") he is candid enough to admit, in addressing himself to his noble patron, that "I am not of those who can say that they are children of the land." He makes a distinction between his own kind of nobility and that of the nobility of birth: "You and others, truly nobles by birth from race to race and lineage to lineage."[14]

Thierriat in 1605 still indulged in calculated confusion, but enough time had passed since Bacquet's formulations that one could no longer be confident that a bourgeois could be made into a *gentilhomme* by the discreet court procedures outlined earlier. While all the theorists had agreed that there were in France two kinds of nobility, the usual formulation, as in Bacquet, had been to speak of *nobles de race* and *anoblis* only.

This formulation, standard in the sixteenth century, deliberately begged the only two questions which really mattered, namely, were ennobled persons (the *anoblis*) as noble as those who were noble by birth? Was official ennoblement by the crown really the only way for a *roturier* to become noble?

The jurists knew that to seek official ennoblement by the crown was not only expensive but was said to be ineffective. Even phony *gentils-hommes* were laughing at the expense of the *anoblis,* whom they called "parchment gentlemen."[15] What the sixteenth-century jurists were carefully not saying is that legions of wealthy commoners were acquiring, tacitly, a kind of nobility at least as good as that of the crown's *anoblis*.

The assumption of the earlier jurists, flattering to their readers, was that new nobles—either the official sort or the tacit variety—were to be considered equal to the *nobles de race*. By 1605 such a position was too unrealistic.

"The question is whether wealth ennobles," asks Thierriat. His answer is characteristic: "Wealth is a vile thing and vileness cannot give nobility, which is a dignity"—but "it is a firm base from which one can arrive at nobility," because "he who is rich can exempt himself from the mechanical arts." He adds, righteously, "But that the rich should become noble without either virtue or the prince's grant—that is an abuse." He may hem and haw when it comes to the question of whether wealth opens the way to the real nobility of the *gentilshommes*. But "that wealth is a means for acceding to *Noblesse Politique:* that is evident, it happens every day."[16]

Here we have it, in 1605: a clear capitulation, long in the making. Thierriat admits that there exists a political or civil nobility, which is composed of rich commoners who are at the same time officeholders and form "a middling estate between the nobility and the people: through this middling estate," he adds, optimistically, "they accede eventually to nobility." Thierriat's three-class structure of (1) *gentilshommes,* (2) a "civil nobility," which included those who had received *anoblissement exprès* as well as those who used *moyens taisibles,* and, finally, (3) *roturiers,* or commoners—this is an admission of defeat. Thierriat is resigned to second-class status for the new class, at least temporarily.[17]

Loyseau is writing several years later. The class lines have hardened further, the polemics have become more heated. There is no question in 1613 of joining the old nobility without fuss. The battle is lost. No need to hide one's feelings any longer. So it is that in Loyseau's book we meet the clearest example of class consciousness and class hatred from the point of view of the civil nobility. Loyseau argues, halfheartedly, that the various sorts of ennoblements "purge the blood and the posterity of the *anobli* of all taint of *roture* and transform his *qualité* and *dignité* so entirely that it is quite as if his race had always been noble." But he admits that this transformation is "more fiction than truth" and comments upon the obvious, namely, that Frenchmen avidly "hide the beginnings of their nobility."[18]

The chief conflict, he explains, is between "the *gentilshommes faisant profession des armes*" on the one hand and the *"noblesse de ville"* (urban nobility) on the other. Whereas the first have always tried to distinguish themselves from the second, the urban nobility has always tried to mix with the *gentilshommes* and "become confused with them." This can be seen, he points out, in the custom of the most notable inhabitants of cities ("plus honnestes habitans des villes") of styling themselves *"nobles hommes."* As a result the *gentilshommes* have begun to feel contempt for the title *noble homme* and have resorted instead to using the title *escuyer.*[19]

Loyseau is full of rancor at the sight of the arrogance of the old nobility. He despises the *gentilshommes*. He wishes they were dead. "If one were to take their claims seriously and grant them all the privileges they claim for themselves," he writes of the country nobles, the *gentilshommes des champs* (prudently excluding the great noblemen of the court from his scorn), "it would become necessary to compose a special set of laws for them, nay, set aside for their use a separate country in this world and a separate paradise in the next—for the insolence of these little country *gentilshommes* is so extreme that it just isn't possible to live in peace with them: they are savage animals."[20] Loyseau's rage is that of his class. He cannot restrain himself when speaking of these *"traisneurs d'espée,"* those sword-dragging parasites, this French nobility, "the most violent and insolent in the world." He tells us bitterly that he is grateful to Divine Providence, which appears to have arranged for the French nobles to kill each other off—as is true in nature, he observes, among certain harmful kinds of animals.[21]

Let us stop here and consider carefully. This respected and influential jurist would exterminate *gentilshommes* like rats. Can this same man believe in a hierarchy in which the *gentilshommes* hold the highest rank? The fundamental observation which needs to be made, if we are to understand Loyseau's thought, is that in 1600 there is no such thing as a generally agreed-upon theory of the nature of French society. I suppose this is a perfectly natural state of affairs. But historians and propagandists usually see order where contemporaries saw none. Just as the theoretical and ornamental aspects of chivalry were mostly nostalgic creations of an age which had no place for knights, so the society of orders described by the jurists is largely ornamental sociology. In Loyseau's vocabulary there are traditional words and phrases which echo earlier usages and legal treatises. Loyseau uses these at times in a customary way. At other times he gives them a different meaning or else coins his own usage and spells out his definition so as to be understood. Thus he will speak of the Third Estate as an *ordre* or *condition* or *espece distincte de personnes* and then go on to explain that within the Third Estate there are several *ordres*.[22] He is using a word like *ordre* very loosely. His attempts to fit all persons into some order, condition, or estate are full of contradictions. These contradictions reflect the social realities of his age, but they also, in part, proceed from deliberate obfuscation. The perspective of the *gentilshommes* was clear: if a person was known to have a bourgeois ancestor at any point in his past, he was not noble.[23] Within the ranks of the political nobility, such a view was heresy. It was spoken of mostly in private.

All of Loyseau's efforts tend in one direction: to graft a newly coalescing class onto the archaic theoretical structure of orders and estates. Where does his "urban nobility" belong? He knows that in one sense it is part of the Third Estate: in the sense, that is, of the seating arrangements at meetings of the Estates-General.[24]

He is willing to grant that the urban nobility should sit with the Third Estate,[25] although, interestingly enough, his opponents were not always agreed on this. Thus, in a speech addressed to the nobility of France in 1614, a *gentilhomme* is made to argue that there is a class of persons which has no business sitting with the Third Estate. He characterizes them as "another sort of persons, useless to the king and to the public." These "phony members of the Third Estate" have conspired to ruin the true nobility through their monopoly over officeholding, "which is the true beginning of the subversion of ancient noble families and the establishment of modern families which usurp and buy the *qualité*" ("status, position"). These sinister persons, according to our *gentilhomme*, have risen to power "to the detriment of the poor people" by making use of the "favor, relations, alliances, and understandings they have with the *officiers*, both of justice and finance." A specter was haunting the French nobility, that of a nameless class of persons who were taking over the kingdom.[26]

Loyseau speaks for this nameless class,[27] as had the jurists who preceded him. He places it modestly in the Third Estate, when it comes to precedence and honors due. When he speaks of its political power, of its juridical rights, and of its wealth, he abandons the traditional division into orders to seek a more practical framework for the description of French society. Here he is close to Thierriat, but with some very important differences. For Loyseau, the urban nobility consists principally of "honest bourgeois living off their *rentes*, especially those who are entitled to bear the *qualité* of *noble homme*."[28]

We have come a long way from the coyness of Thierriat and the discretion of Bacquet. Loyseau is not describing an elite of uncertain origin, distinguished by officeholding, ready to be noble. He writes instead of a very large group, the "most notable inhabitants of the towns." These men, retired from commerce and living off *rentes*, form a class which can be distinguished from the rest of the bourgeoisie by their use of the honorific title *"noble homme."* The *marchands* do not belong to this class. They bear the title of *"honorable homme"* or *"honneste personne"* or *"bourgeois"* of the town.[29]

Loyseau's chief thesis will be that the *noblesse des villes* and the *gentilshommes des champs*, despite their bitter antagonism, are equal in social standing.[30] He prepares the ground for this claim by stating what is essentially true: the first category may be lower in the esteem of public opinion, and, of course, the *gentilshommes des champs*, whose deplorable way of life will doom them to eventual extinction, may look down upon the new *nobles hommes;* but legally, the privileges they enjoy are about equal. Within this broad category of juridically equal persons he distinguishes between the real nobility of the *gentils-hommes* and the "honorary" nobility of the *noblesse de ville.*[31]

None of these distinctions of rank and dignity are more than tentative in Loyseau's mind. He tries to describe things as they are. He makes it clear that few—if any—of these matters have real standing in the law. "It would seem that the title of baron is the borderline," he writes. "As for the simple nobility, one might say that there is also an honorary kind." Do some very few royal offices actually ennoble the possessor? This claim is commonly made for the *conseillers* in the *parlements* and *chambres des comptes,* "although there is no specific edict to that effect," he acknowledges. "What should we say of those who have obtained letters of ennoblement? As for me, I would say that they should be ranked with the *gentilshommes* of birth."[32] Loyseau the sociologist is properly reluctant to come to hard-and-fast conclusions. When it comes to practical matters, such as tax exemption, the lawyer takes over in him: he may recognize "simple nobility" as an honorary rank, but he states candidly that those who are "commonly referred to as the *Noblesse des Villes,* have only the honorary title of *noble homme:* they are not exempt from the taille" by virtue of this honor.[33] Honorary titles such as *conseiller du roy* must not be mistaken for anything but an expensive decoration: "The title attributes no rights or privileges."[34] On the other hand, one must distinguish clearly between nobles of various sorts and those who are merely exempt of taille payments: this latter category can claim only a "demi-nobility."[35]

Most of the time Loyseau succeeds in maintaining a clear distinction between legal questions, on the one hand, which can be answered precisely by reference to edicts and precedents, and sociological questions, on the other hand, which resist this kind of solution. How does one distinguish between an urban elite of bourgeois origin and a rural elite of *gentilshommes* if both wear the same clothes, carry swords, exhibit coats of arms? Loyseau does not always have the answer to these difficult questions. His great merit is to admit that confusion is natural in these matters. He takes advantage of this confusion to buttress the claims of his own class, but he does so with a certain open-mindedness and with great ingenuity.

His comparison between the French bourgeois who are living nobly (*vivans noblement*) and the English gentry assuages his sociological curiosity—and it serves his insidious claims as well. "What is the English gentleman?" he asks. Citing Thomas Smith, he replies, "anyone who practices one of the liberal professions," or, even more broadly speaking, "anyone who can live comfortably off his income without resorting to manual labor, and has the appearance, the behaviour, the expenses of a gentleman." Such gentlemen, in England, squires or knights though they may be, are nevertheless counted as commoners, that is, they are represented in the House of Commons, which he compares to the Third Estate in France. Only the lords are considered really noble. They are the equivalent, as Loyseau sees it, of what he calls the high nobility in France. What Loyseau admires in English society, then, is the lack of distinction, within the gentry, between old families and new.

He poses the lawyer's question: "What would be the privileges of an English gentleman were he to come and reside in France? "I would not hold that such *anoblis* coming to reside in France ought to enjoy the privileges of nobility."[36] Unhesitatingly, Loyseau leads up to a definition of French society in which he allows room first of all for a small group of high nobles comparable to the English peerage. This court nobility owes its privileges to royal service. It is composed not so much of ancient feudal families as of the most powerful *officier* families in the kingdom. He goes so far as to claim that this high nobility "is not inherited . . . but personal, having been granted to a person because of his merit, as in knighthood . . . or because of his office or seigneurie." This highest dignity "follows the office or lordship perpetually."[37] The king, as Loyseau sees it—or pretends to see it—chooses chancellors, presidents, governors, bishops, and so on: these high dignitaries, while they perform the highest of royal functions, constitute a sort of peerage.

What is being denied here, by implication, is the principle of nobility as an inherited quality. The concept of nobility, as Loyseau wishes to understand it, becomes the very opposite of the commonly accepted one. Not that Loyseau's main purpose is to open careers to talent. His real concern is to diminish the importance of birth and to claim that bourgeois "living nobly" are not inferior in status to country *gentilshommes*. He rarefies the notion of nobility so that it remains limited to a galaxy of lords at court. He separates the rest of the *gentilshommes* from this high nobility in the most emphatic way: their status, he claims, is much closer to that of the honorary nobility of the towns than to the glory of the lords at court. In this perspective,

French society can be made to appear not so different from English society: a glittering peerage at the top, made up of men of great wealth and power; below, a large and amorphous collection of secondary elites, in which bourgeois *rentiers,* lawyers, physicians, financiers, and others enjoy a status almost indistinguishable from that of country squires of old family.

3
Contours and Solidarities

Let us step out of Loyseau's study to take a fresh look at what is going on. Loyseau was the chief *officier* in the town of Châteaudun. One could hardly be better placed to observe urban society. Châteaudun was a run-of-the-mill sort of town then, quite lacking in extraordinary features, with a population of at most ten thousand in the sixteenth century. Châteaudun occupies a piece of high ground dominating the small and not quite navigable Loir River to the southwest of Paris, between Chartres and Orléans. Not important enough to be the seat of a bishopric, overshadowed administratively by its more powerful neighbors, Châteaudun remained a mediocre place, utterly reliable in its typicality and, hence, understandably attractive to historians inclined to experimentation with quantitative methods. And so it happens that the same town which provided the elements of Loyseau's sociology served again, in the twentieth century, as the proving ground of a most ambitious and difficult inquiry, namely, the pioneering computer program designed by Marcel Couturier whose results were published in 1969.[1] The questions which Loyseau had asked—How is society organized? and How can one distinguish the various levels of status?—are also asked by Couturier. Using essentially the same kind of evidence, but more systematically and on a larger scale, Couturier, with the help of his computer, is often led to conclusions which substantially confirm those of Loyseau.

The town's governing group, Couturier discovers, is made up of the families using the epithet of honor *noble homme*, as Loyseau had told us. Couturier observes that the rate of endogamy (marriage within the group) within this category is nothing short of spectacular: before 1600 it reaches 85 percent and soon rises to 95 percent.[2] The *nobles hommes* of Châteaudun marry the daughters of other *nobles hommes*. Their marriages distinguish them, visibly, from the merchant class of *honorables hommes*. Their fortunes too are different: a *noble homme* fortune almost invariably includes the possession of a landed estate—a seigneurie.[3] The *nobles hommes* of Châteaudun usually possess university degrees and offices.[4] Of these offices, not a single one ennobles the holder—not even the highest office, that of *bailli*, exercised by Loyseau between 1600 and 1610. The catalogue of the *gentilshommes* of the district compiled in 1668 does not include a single *officier* of the *bailliage*. Nor are these *officiers* necessarily exempt from taxes.[5] The *nobles hommes* as a group are clearly defined: they are never confused with the *gentilshommes*, and they are fairly clearly marked off from the mere bourgeois through their education, their landholdings, and their possession of the more influential and expensive offices.

The *honorables hommes* are invariably wealthy enough not to work with their hands.[6] They may share one or more characteristics with the elite of *nobles hommes*. They may own a seigneurie, perhaps. But they lack the right combination of land, wealth, education, office, and marriage alliances to aspire to membership in the charmed circle of *noble homme* households.[7]

We shall have occasion to return to Châteaudun, but for the moment let us note the following facts, more amply and surely proven here than anywhere else. The lines which divide social groups in Châteaudun follow the use of epithets of honor in the private contracts and official papers:[8] the large mass of the population has none at all;[9] a small elite of merchants who have reached a certain level of wealth and real estate ownership have the epithet *honorable homme;* and, at the top, a tightly closed group of leading families, Loyseau's *noblesse des villes,* has the distinguishing epithet *noble homme.*

The group in question must not be confused with the occupational category of *officiers*—those whose professional function is linked to the *bailliage, élection,* or other administrative offices. There are 113 taxed households of *officiers* in Châteaudun, but a majority of these are headed by minor officeholders whose median wealth, education, and marriage patterns separate them from the *nobles hommes*. [10] In the boom years of the late sixteenth century, the leading families of Châteaudun were a little more open and more varied as a group; led by the foremost magistrates, the group also included a few of the richest merchants, physicians, and lawyers. All had this in common: landed wealth in the form of seigneuries. [11] Around the turn of the century, class lines grow rigid: *advocats* and *procureurs* who are sons of bourgeois *honorables hommes* find it close to impossible to join the elite, despite their degrees and their honorific epithets. [12] Keeping all this in mind, one can give a rough estimate of the size of the city's elite of *nobles hommes* as somewhere between fifty and one hundred households, which represents perhaps two hundred to four hundred individuals out of a total population of about ten thousand. [13]

A few of the wealthiest and most distinguished *noble homme* families may contract marriage alliances for their daughters with *gentilshommes*. But it remains clear that this is a group as profoundly set apart from the *gentilshommes* as it is set apart from the bourgeoisie, since 85 to 95 percent of the marriages are contracted within the category of *nobles hommes*. [14] The possession of university degrees sets the *nobles hommes* apart from both *gentilshommes* and bourgeois. So does their wealth. [15] And so does their choice of living quarters. In Châteaudun, 90 percent of them live crammed together in the central part of the old town. [16]

The society Couturier observes in Châteaudun, and which corresponds closely to Loyseau's observations, is a new society. The *nobles hommes* are a new class, entirely recruited from the bourgeoisie. Starting from a prosperous leather or cloth business and going through a transition stage characterized by the acquisition of seigneuries and of a law degree, a family reaches *noble homme* status, the proper marriage alliances, a new life style, and often office as well. This process takes two or three generations in the sixteenth century, when the sons of merchants frequently become *advocats*. [17] The entire life cycle of this social process is pretty much limited to a period beginning in the late fifteenth century and ending early in the seventeenth century. After that we are faced with a more rigid society. The new class no longer welcomes successful and educated bourgeois. It tends, rather, to build bridges toward the old nobility, to whom the fat dowries are more appealing than ever. [18]

At this point the reader will perhaps be prepared to grant the need for a new technical term. The existence of a class of people who are neither *gentilshommes* nor bourgeois—that is, people who are not merchant-bourgeois, *honorables hommes* on the one hand, and who do not appear in the catalogue of the nobility of the *bailliage* on the other hand—has been demonstrated in Châteaudun. We have noted, thanks to Couturier's work, a number of specific traits which characterize the class. And yet we have no name for the members of this class. We cannot describe them accurately as *officiers*, since most offices are held by men of lesser status, and officeholding is not an absolute requirement. The surest term might be that of *nobles hommes*, but there are quite a few *advocats* who are entitled to the epithet but lack the marriage alliances and other marks of membership in the new class. A further drawback of the term *noble homme* is that its meaning changes. Before the rise of the new class it may in fact have implied nobility of the older sort—and in time it was to lose its meaning altogether. What is more, epithets of honor do vary to some extent from region to region: *noble homme* does not mean in Provence quite what it means in the Loire Valley.

Clearly, once we are persuaded of the existence of an as yet unnamed class, we had best avoid misunderstandings altogether and give it a name. We could call it X, but this would be awkward. I propose to call it "gentry." The word is not without drawbacks. It does not have the purity of X, but the ambiguities which it may give rise to are not entirely unwelcome. Does it come close to suggesting a certain closeness to the *gentilshommes*? Or to the English gentry? We know that Loyseau, not without cause, did in fact intend these elective affinities. Let them stand. The main thing is that "gentry" is a new word in the vocabulary of French social history, almost unsullied by previous use. And we can now define it and invest it with precisely the meanings which we desire.

The same social class which we find solidly in charge of Châteaudun's destiny can be found everywhere in the kingdom. Amiens, the chief city of Picardy, north of Paris, is quite different from Châteaudun; for one thing, it is much bigger. But here, also, the city's life is dominated by a small and increasingly exclusive elite of landowners and officeholders. As in Châteaudun, this Amiens gentry is entirely recruited from the ranks of the bourgeoisie in the course of the sixteenth century—and here, too, it finds its aspirations toward nobility thwarted.[19] In Amiens, as in Châteaudun, the familiar pattern of reaching new status through the purchase of seigneuries and the acquisition of university degrees slows down in the seventeenth century. Here, too, the power, status, and wealth of the new class, once acquired, are never again lost. Deyon's study of the poor-tax records of 1625–35 reveals an economic pyramid in three stages. At the bottom is a large group of artisans and shopkeepers, taxed at three deniers. Above them is a middle class of merchant-bourgeois joined by the lesser *officiers* and *advocats*, taxed at twelve deniers. At the top, a small elite of *nobles hommes* taxed at twenty-four deniers; this group includes *officiers*, men "living nobly"—that is *rentiers* without occupation—six city councilors, and no merchants at all.[20]

The Amiens gentry lives in town and controls the municipal elections, as well as the political machinery of the *bailliage* and the tax system.[21] The old nobility of the *bailliage* lives in the country[22] and corresponds, on the whole, to Loyseau's portrait of the *gentilshommes des champs*. These *gentilshommes* are mostly poor and getting poorer, perpetually in debt to the rich *officiers* who buy up more and more of their lands. Meanwhile a few noble families of the first rank, possessors of very large estates, remain apart: it is with those that the richest gentry families will contract marriage alliances, eventually.[23]

In Amiens, then, as in Châteaudun, the characteristic feature of late sixteenth-century social history is the formation of a new urban elite of university-educated landowner-officials whose fortunes and social status mark them off both from the merchant-bourgeoisie, which they leave behind, and from the *gentilshommes*, whose world is closed to them for some time to come.

If we move from Amiens to Beauvais, we find an identical situation. Working with the 1696 tax records, Goubert analyzes a total of 2,562 households. The upper class is composed of 374 households belonging to the *bourgeoisie rentière*. Within this group, Goubert takes the 48 households assessed at fifty livres or higher and adds them to the 54 households exempt from taxation (because of royal or other privileges). The sum is a profile of what we may call the Beauvais gentry. This group of 100 or so households consists of the families whose names show up constantly on the honor rolls of Beauvais politics: the list of aldermen, mayors, judges in the *présidial*, in the *élection*, in the *grenier à sel*, and so on. (After the revolution of 1789, these same families will form the bulk of the buyers of *biens nationaux* in the region.)[24]

Goubert's study of Beauvais shows that gentry fortunes are different in character from bourgeois fortunes—another test available to us in determining social frontiers. Not only were the merchant fortunes smaller—they were, in Goubert's words, young, growing fortunes that consisted of stocked merchandise and outstanding loans. Real estate and *rentes* played a small part in merchant fortunes. In contrast, the gentry's wealth is old wealth, stabilized, and even sometimes declining. Typically, one-half of the capital invested is in land, one-quarter in *rentes,* and the remainder in the value of offices. In addition there will be two or three houses in the city, furniture, cash reserves, and always an important and expensive family library.[25]

To erase any doubts about the separation between the gentry and the merchant-bourgeoisie in Beauvais, one need only look at how these two elites express themselves in politics. In composing the *cahier de doléances* of the *bailliage* for the Estates-General of 1614, the local deputies from the Third Estate were unable to reconcile their differences. They finally presented two separate *cahiers,* one representing the interests of the merchant-bourgeoisie, whose politics gravitated around city hall, the other *cahier* expressing the point of view of the gentry led by the magistrates of the *bailliage.*[26]

The very same forces operated in Dijon, where the conflict between the gentry and the bourgeoisie was even more acrimonious. As Drouot notes, it seems almost banal to show that in Burgundy, as elsewhere, the *officiers* have established themselves as the leading social category.[27] This "social category, complex in its origins but homogeneous in its way of life,"[28] these wealthy families, whose imposing townhouses were grouped in the center of the city, "led an existence which defined an elite."[29] Despite the pretensions to nobility which marked the *officier* families in cities such as Dijon, one could say of the Dijon gentry that it participated in a feeling of solidarity which rose above such vanities: these families had a clear feeling of their common interest, they thought of themselves as a community, they had a kind of class consciousness.[30] Toward the end of the century, the Dijon gentry closed its doors to the ambitions of newly minted *advocats* of bourgeois parentage while cultivating its alliances with the nobility.[31] The gulf widened between the *"robe anoblie,* or in the process of being *anoblie,* and the representatives and the champions of the Third Estate."[32]

The Burgundian gentry appears especially successful in wresting power and land away from the old nobility.[33] It took over much of the church and controlled most political institutions, including the Estates meetings, the *chambres des élus,* and the *bailliages* and *présidiaux* as well as the *parlement* and the *chambre des comptes.*[34]

Dijon, a provincial capital with considerable autonomy, had a population of approximately 16,000 toward the end of the sixteenth century. Roupnel estimates that perhaps 40 percent of the population belonged to the world of the fiscally privileged. The list of *officiers* exempt from the taille in 1699 has 993 names. When you add 350 widows who also belong to this social and fiscal category—without, of course, exercising any offices—you are led to estimate that as many as 6,000 individuals out of a total population of about 22,000 are connected with office and exempt in some way.[35]

If we return to the sixteenth century, we probably get a more moderate figure, but it is clear that Dijon's social structure is top-heavy with an enormously powerful elite. The reason for this is not hard to find. Dijon's gentry is recruited not only from among the city's own bourgeoisie but also from the leading families of the other Burgundian towns. The most successful merchant families of Châlon, Autun, Saulieu, Beaune, Mâcon—and even of small places like Nuits—have Dijon in sight as their long-range objective. One can follow their patient climb through local offices in *présidial* and *bailliage* until they finally show up in the *parlement* at Dijon. The process often takes several generations.[36] Dijon, in other words, acts like a magnet for the wealth of the entire province: it is a small-scale Paris. And that explains the overwhelming, oppressive presence of the rich and privileged, whose imposing stone *hôtels* dominate the central parishes of a city still largely composed of wooden and thatch-roofed houses.[37]

In his profile of the Burgundian patriciate, Roupnel has no hesitation in speaking of it as a social class,' which, for lack of a better phrase, he resigns himself to calling the *bourgeoisie parlementaire*. While the possession of office is the most visible sign (visible, that is, to the historian, because the title of the office which gives the members of the class their specific character always accompanies a man's name in the records), Roupnel concludes that the social class in question is not quite the same thing as the group of families who hold offices. Offices, with very rare exceptions, did not confer nobility. Nor can it be maintained that the possession of office invested the purchaser with a new social status. As Roupnel observes, most of the families whose members acquire office in the *parlement* or *chambre des comptes* already possessed the social status which distinguished them from the mass of the bourgeoisie before the acquisition of the office! This status, quite clearly recognized by public opinion at the time, resides in the family's *qualité*. The *qualité* "of this social class whose contours—whose very name—are obscure to us" is linked specifically not so much to the possession of offices as to the possession of seigneuries. In Dijon, perhaps even more strikingly than elsewhere, this urban aristocracy which I call gentry is a class that was born in the city, resides in the city, but at the same time owns the land.[38] It is the possession of seigneuries, in Dijon as in Châteaudun, which separates the gentry from the bourgeoisie and precedes the acquisition of university degrees and offices. Marriage alliances will seal the success of the *familles,* or notable families.[39] The ranks are about to close.[40]

The pattern observed in large cities is repeated in very small towns: the social structure of Montmarand, with its 156 households in 1569, is in no essential way different from those of cities of several thousand households. Here too the *gentilshommes* are absent and the leadership is in the hands of two elites: at the top, the owners of office and land, living off their capital—and, below them, the *"bourgeois et marchands."*[41] In the small towns of the Poitou region studied by Raveau, we are once again confronted with the undeniable presence of a social class which rises above the bourgeoisie without quite reaching noble status—and once again we are in the presence of a new class, firmly constituted by the end of the century and about to cut its ties with the bourgeoisie.[42]

No matter how far we travel from the central regions of the kingdom, the gentry is there to meet us. We find it solidly entrenched in the most isolated hill towns of Provence[43] and beyond the frontiers of the kingdom as well. In the towns of the other Burgundy, as Lucien Febvre showed long ago, nothing is clearer than the rise to wealth and eminence of the new class, symbolized by the career of the Perrenot family.[44]

As we can see, the rise of a new class is the overwhelming fact of French social history in the sixteenth century. Why, then, has this phenomenon been hidden from sight for so long? The answer is not difficult: everything, from the start, has conspired to hide the obvious. First of all, the gentry moved heaven and earth to persuade public opinion that nothing had really changed, that there were still only two kinds of persons in France—nobles and commoners—and that *they* were noble. These claims rarely fooled contemporaries. But with the passage of time, as the sons and grandsons acquired noble relatives to be added to their noble estates, the ancestors found themselves retroactively ennobled in family legends and in carefully doctored documents. It takes the most uncompromising kind of skepticism to cut through these claims, hoary with age. But it is essential to do this. For unless we distinguish the old nobility from the new gentry, we shall understand nothing of the dynamics of French society.

4   *The Pursuit of Nobility*

The gentry aspires to noble status. Its wish is to be confused with the *gentilshommes*. So we are told by witnesses like Loyseau; and the evidence assembled in the regional studies of Goubert or Deyon also presents the gentry as a transitional class, barely emancipated from the taint of commerce and already impatient to slip into the role of *gentilshommes*. The time has come to introduce an inescapable and puzzling nuance: How seriously, how fully, can these men be said to wish themselves noble when they despise the *gentilshommes* and all they stand for?

We must ask whether these people really aspire to the way of life of the old nobility or whether they are merely after tax exemption and privilege. When success crowns the patient efforts of a family, when it finally adds the word *escuyer* to its name—and promptly erases all evidence of its previous status—does such a family move out of its town house, to join the *gentilshommes* in their rural setting? Does it take up a life of leisure? Do these new nobles go in for hunting, sumptuous entertainments, conspicuous spending, attendance at court? Do they choose military careers, fight duels, brawl in the streets? Do they abandon their frugal habits, their careful bookkeeping methods, their financial speculations? These are some of the questions to keep in mind as we take a closer look at the "treason of the bourgeoisie."

The testimony of those who fear the gentry's usurpations is plentiful.[1] The usurpation of nobility is "a disorder greatly injurious to this great province, where you will not see an authentic *gentilhomme de race* out of ten who pass for noble and occupy noble lands."[2] The *qualité* of these social climbers "changes gradually; they become *escuyers* and *gentilshommes* indirectly, that is to say, they usurp the title and the privileges with the passage of time, without giving proof of their valor—and under this pretext they escape being assessed for the tailles and other taxes."[3] Such mild descriptions of the obvious attract the reader's attention whenever he looks at the better-known published social commentaries of the time. Popular broadsides and posters attacked the parvenus more savagely, to the great amusement of most everyone.[4]

When Monsieur de Villeroy, one of the most powerful men in the kingdom, died in 1598, he had been *secrétaire d'état* for thirty years. His father had achieved the distinction of being made *chevalier* of the Order of Saint Michel. And yet, as L'Estoile noted in his diary, on the occasion of Villeroy's death, "public gossip has it that his grandfather was a fishmonger."[5] Public gossip was very close to the truth. Villeroy's grandfather, Nicolas de Neufville, was the first to abandon *marchandise.*

The wealth of the fish, cloth, and wine business, a number of seigneuries acquired in the course of three generations, an extremely profitable series of financial offices, the best kind of marriage alliances—including the Briçonnet and De Thou families—a Renaissance château rebuilt to his father's specifications, and an education at the Collège de Navarre—all this was Villeroy's inheritance. He was certainly noble in the eyes of the law, as his father had been before him. His discretion concerning his origins tells us that he was clearly not about to let people question his noble status.[6] Yet all that power and wealth, all those titles, did not suffice to fool public opinion. In the streets of Paris, and at court too, one knew Villeroy for what he was. One might fear Monsieur de Villeroy's power, but behind his back one made it clear that this little man was nothing but a scribbler who fought his battles with "paper, parchment and pen."[7] His was a paper knighthood.

It is not that the snobbism of the courtiers—or for that matter the snobbism of the masses—was founded on long memories or extraordinary expertise in genealogical matters. This was perhaps true a century later, when Saint-Simon amused himself by pointing out the dubious origins of the great. In the sixteenth century there was no need to be expert in heraldry, because the new nobles, however great they might be, were not yet disguised as *gentilshommes*. Their conversation, their dress, their habits all set them apart from the old nobility, whose privileges and status they wished to share or even surpass. Villeroy, who had been apprenticed to a royal secretary at sixteen "to learn writing," as one used to say; Villeroy, who married the daughter of a *secrétaire d'état* at eighteen; Villeroy, who began his professional career as royal secretary at twenty-four and spent his entire life working madly; Villeroy, *chevalier* though he was, remained always a man of paper, a calculating financial specialist. He led "the life of a very hard-working bourgeois of very regular habits."[8] There was no way to mistake him for a real nobleman.

In the sixteenth century, not even the greatest *parlementaire* families could pass for noble—in the true social rather than legal sense. The De Thou family, for instance, had long ago thrown a veil of discretion over their origins. They had achieved high offices, connections, and seigneuries; but when Augustin de Thou, seigneur de Bonneuil, *advocat au parlement*, took possession of his country estate near Paris, he found himself saddled with a lawsuit in which an aristocratic neighbor sought to prevent his moving in next door on the ground that he did not want the neighborhood tainted by the presence of "talem advocatum, ex humili plebe ortum."[9]

Such resistance only strengthened the resolve of the gentry. The effort, the money, the ingenuity and calculation which they expended in the course of their conquest of a higher status are truly admirable. Since these efforts necessarily involved fraud of one kind or another, we always find the process of metamorphosis assisted by notaries and publicists, themselves members of the social elite of their town and natural allies in this ritualized conspiracy.

Thus we find the biographer La Croix du Maine telling us that the poet Jacques Tahureau is a *gentilhomme* and that his mother's family, the Tiercelins, are a "tres noble & tres ancienne famille."[10] The poet's father, Jacques, no doubt *noble homme* and perhaps *escuyer* in local contracts, owned seigneuries; and he "lived nobly during thirty or forty years in full sight of the inhabitants of Jarzé on his estate of La Chevalerie, and he was held and reputed noble by the villagers."

But it was only in 1540 that the "ancient and noble" family of Tahureau claimed exemption from the taille for the first time, and this was granted to them in 1549.

Alas, Jacques Tahureau's brilliant social ascension was to be sabotaged by his son the poet, who married the daughter of an innkeeper.

Meanwhile, the poet's brother, *advocat* at the *parlement* of Paris, styled *escuyer* in the contracts, married the daughter of an *honorable homme* in 1556, and in 1584 the tax collectors challenged his claim to nobility.[11] As for Monsieur de la Croix du Maine, the complaisant biographer whom we shall meet again: if the truth be known, he was the son of plain Nicolas Grudé, bourgeois of Le Mans. The poet Pierre de Ronsard, whose family was taken to court for fraudulent use of the title *chevalier*, imagined himself to be descended from a mythical Marquis de Ronsart, "riche d'or et de gens, de villes et de terres," whose estates, he tells us, were located somewhere near the "icy Danube," "lower than Hungary, in a cold region."[12]

Modern biographers invariably tell us of Ronsard's nobility—and nobility, of a kind, it was. That is to say, the Ronsards (or Ronsart, Ronssart, Roussart) were prominent enough locally, owned a seigneurie, and managed to overcome the challenges to their claims in the course of the sixteenth century. (The more severe *recherches de noblesse* of 1666 gave them serious trouble.) They were surely not descended from an old feudal family. Still, in a way, the Ronsards really do seem more like *gentilshommes* than the Tahureaus, because their way of life is more noble. Whereas the Tahureaus keep making money, neither business nor office is much in evidence at the Ronsards. The poet's father not only took the title of *chevalier* but made his career as a courtier, as would his son Pierre. They passed for noble everywhere, I think, as the Tahureaus did not. The difference, here, lies more in the life style than in the antiquity of the family's prominence. And this noble style seems to involve a certain amount of obligatory genteel poverty, appropriate to the household of a *gentilhomme des champs*, a *simple gentilhomme*. Among great noblemen, *hauts et puissants seigneurs*, on the other hand, wealth and ostentation are not out of place. Thus, public opinion seems to have speculated and judged along fairly practical lines: if a *simple gentilhomme* is wealthy, there is something wrong.

Consider the Chevalier family, languishing in Périgueux, claiming nobility throughout the late sixteenth century, possessors of wealth, land, and office—but all, of course, on the reduced scale of a town which is far from being a metropolis. Having acquired the seigneurie of Puygombert, styled themselves *escuyer*, acquired the office of *conseiller* at the *présidial* court, and having built up a reasonable network of marriage alliances within the local *officier*-gentry circles, the Chevaliers nevertheless keep facing serious challenges, especially in the seventeenth century, when the gentry, here as elsewhere, becomes more exclusive.

As early as 1603 the widow of Jean Chevalier, *escuyer*, seigneur de Puygombert, is forced to submit an official document in which she refers to "certain marriage contracts, testaments, and other records concerning the families," which, according to her testimony, were assembled in 1594 by a notary for the purpose of furnishing proof of the family's ancient and noble ancestry. The Chevaliers' claim, which they press more and more stridently as they keep being challenged, revolves around a document of 1463 in which the first Chevalier is said to have given homage for the fief of Puygombert to the abbot of Brantôme. This document, of which innumerable copies were kept in the Chevalier family archives, was not taken seriously by the officials who conducted the various *recherches de noblesse*. It was a fundamental error of the Chevaliers' strategy to keep insisting on the authenticity of that document. Summoned to prove their nobility in 1666, they failed to comply. Belatedly they produced a nicely colored genealogy and a 42-page collection of documents, but the evidence did not convince the commission of inquiry and they were condemned to pay the standard fine of two thousand livres.

As if fighting the agents of the royal government were not enough trouble, the Chevaliers found themselves assaulted by the municipal government, which threatened to quarter soldiers in their house as if they were common inhabitants of Périgueux. Resourcefully (and at what price?), the Chevaliers managed to get the military commander to provide them with a written order protecting their house.[13] Rebuffed again and again by the royal commissioners, the Chevaliers seem to have been baffled. They had done everything right. Why were they refused? Very revealing in this respect, I think, is a single undated sheet of paper on which a Chevalier in an idle moment wrote down what preoccupied her. (I don't actually know why I thought the author was a woman when I saw the manuscript, but I must have had a reason.) Under the heading: "My relatives at the *présidial* court of Périgueux are ... ," she lists eleven current magistrates who are close relatives and six others more distantly related. There is something forlorn about this doodling.

In their efforts to help their case, the Chevaliers resorted to inept forgery. Among the succession of Chevaliers, seigneurs de Puymarteau, *escuyers*, who appear in the documents in unbroken series since 1463, we encounter suddenly, in the late sixteenth century, Georges Chevalier, seigneur de Puymarteau, resident of the town of Brantholme, who is styled *honorable homme*. This is a slip, because a few years later, in 1596, in another document, someone has taken the trouble to erase *honorable homme* and to substitue *escuyer* for it, clumsily, in a hand which does not match the rest of the document.[14] Alerted, one begins to look more closely at all the documents and soon finds wholesale falsification. Going back as far as 1532, we find *escuyer* obviously substituted for the original epithet.

It seems fairly certain, then, that the Chevaliers were not claiming nobility in 1532. When did they really buy the seigneurie? Most likely they grafted themselves onto another Chevalier family which may have been noble, probably died out, leaving no heirs, and had been seigneurs of Puymarteau. This is a familiar stratagem. In any case, the Chevaliers were not able to fool anyone, and their troubles were not over until 1711, when they were finally declared noble. This time they presented no documents earlier than 1541, and so they must have decided to change strategy. They also, perhaps, produced bribes. In the end, though, I would guess that the Chevaliers had such a difficult time persuading officials and public opinion of their nobility because they did not live nobly enough. I suspect that they never stopped being businessmen.

In Périgueux, it might be fatal to carry on the family business: nobility and commerce do not mix. But this dictum by no means applied as universally as one might think. Montaigne may define nobility as a "condition marked by leisure and in which one lives, as they say, off one's *rentes*,"[15] but in Provence commerce and nobility are not at all incompatible. The great merchant families of Marseille have no trouble reconciling their commercial activities with the attributes of nobility. The Albertas family, for instance, proceeds toward wealth and nobility in a stately two-front attack: Jean is a bourgeois of the small town of Apt in 1433; Baudon receives taille exemption for his lands in 1486; Surleon leases a galleon to the crown at the rate of 300 ducats monthly in 1495; Colin's nobility is attested to in court in 1526; Pierre is granted a royal license specifically permitting him to carry sword and dagger in the streets of Marseille in 1564; and, in 1577, once again, the lieutenant of the seneschal of Provence attests to the noble ancestry of Antoine, now styled *escuyer*. In 1588 Antoine is a deputy at the Estates meeting of Blois, where he sits with the nobility. In 1595 Antoine allows himself the luxury of buying the title of *gentilhomme ordinaire de la chambre*. In 1638 Pierre buys an office of *conseiller* in the *parlement* of Paris for 93,000 livres. All this time the Albertas continue their business. They are far from adopting the ideal of nobility founded on leisure. As late as 1673 an Albertas obtains a doctorate in law, hardly a distinction sought among noblemen and courtiers but valued by the gentry more highly than gilded crests.[16]

There is nothing unusual in Marseille about the Albertas' career.

The rich merchants of the city had legitimized their needs as early as 1566, when they obtained a royal ordinance permitting the nobles of Marseille to engage in commerce without *dérogeance*. Marseille itself is in no way exceptional. In Provence and along the Rhône Valley we find—as in Bourg-Saint-Andéol, for instance—that even the most prominent families, long secure in the possession of fiefs and titles, think nothing of keeping shop.[17] In nearby Villeneuve-de-Berg, the Desserres family provides a fine illustration of this region's slowness to recognize commerce as a demeaning activity. Originally farmers in the steep hill country close by, the Desserres were merchants and notaries in the fifteenth century. They owned one of the finest houses in Villeneuve, a big two-story house on the main shopping street, with four *boutiques* at street level. Jacques Desserres is already an important, rich, educated man when he enters the family cloth business in 1527. In 1532 he marries the daughter of an important notary of Bourg-Saint-Andéol, who contributes a dowry of 1,000 florins in cash in addition to land. Jacques's business continues to flourish; he is elected mayor in 1533. When his son Olivier returns from his university studies, he takes over the family business and is able to buy a seigneurie that the family had been eyeing for a long time, for 3,838 livres cash. This outlay makes it necessary to sell off a number of other, smaller properties—and probably prompts Olivier's marriage, a few months later, to the daughter of another rich bourgeois family, the Ancons. Olivier's father is dead by then, and the young couple settles into the family house with Olivier's widowed mother, where they keep the family cloth business going. Olivier, let us note, takes the title of *escuyer* in his marriage contract. Later in life he will become famous at court, and among the readers of his *Théâtre d'Agriculture*, as Olivier de Serres, seigneur du Pradel, and he will personify in his time and for later generations the very perfect type of the *gentilhomme de campagne*.[18]

The southern variant in status tests for nobility may be due to old urban traditions and legal concepts.[19] Another kind of regional variant, of which we find good examples in Normandy and perhaps more generally in busy Atlantic seaports, is that which is associated with a particularly highly developed economy. Here commercial fortunes are so rapidly made and are of such a size that sheer wealth and power play havoc with traditional social norms. The dimensions of usurpation in Normandy shocked contemporary observers. "The main trouble here," we read in one document of 1583, "is that for some time now the rich and opulent men who are by law subject to the taille have claimed exemption—for the most part by usurping the privilege of nobility."[20] The trouble gets worse. In 1620 we are told that "nowadays the most minor *officiers* . . . feel free to take the title of *escuyer*."[21] This "trouble" in the Norman seaports was already very much a reality in the fifteenth century.[22]

The early years of the sixteenth century were a time of happy chaos, when bourgeois became *gentilshommes* without half trying, like Raoul Bretel, merchant at Le Havre, who kept buying up fiefs in the surrounding country. At his death in 1556, he is described as "sieur de Vertot, bourgeois du Havre." Already lord of Vertot, Gremonville, and Saint-Rémy, he had found it natural to call himself *escuyer* on the occasion of his son's wedding in 1552, but he is so casual about this that he does not mind describing himself as *honorable homme* in a later contract. His son Raoul will live in a different world. Born in 1527, educated in Paris, furnished with a law degree and an office in the *parlement* at Rouen, he is called Monsieur de Saint-Rémy and even extracts an official document from the crown which declares his nobility in the most emphatic terms.[23]

Universally desired for its legal privileges, the *qualité* of being noble is supremely attractive to some—especially, of course, to families, like the Chevaliers of Périgueux, whose wealth, offices, lands, and local status combined are barely enough to justify their claim of not being bourgeois. The bourgeoisie dreams of nobility while the *gentilshommes* fear the usurpation of the gentry, who "are of no use to the commonwealth," "who are a fourth body politic which ruins the three others." "Let all these people who were made *gentilshommes de la chambre* for one hundred francs be stripped of their rank," writes the author of an anti-gentry pamphlet, who puts his words in the mouths of "six peasants." He wants to get rid of this "bewildering quantity of *officiers*;" he wishes to abolish the lawyers and all their cohorts, "this innumerable multitude of locusts"; he wishes to prevent social climbing: "Those who have their wives called *dames* although they are not descended from good and ancient houses must be forbidden to do so, on pain of corporal punishment"—and furthermore, noble titles such as *chevalier* must not be used in contracts except by authentic noblemen. As for noble fiefs and castles bought up by commoners, one must provide a way for the dispossessed noblemen to buy them back. All those who are not authentic noblemen, in fact, must be driven out of all government and judicial functions and chased away from the royal court, the *parlement* must have its power curbed, and, in short, the old nobility must be restored to leadership. For good measure, the Jews should be driven out of the kingdom.[24] This pamphlet, prepared in the heated atmosphere of the Estates-General meeting of 1614, lists

the grievances of the *gentilshommes des champs* together with those of
the minor bourgeoisie and adds some old peasant grievances as well.
The gentry is hated by all its victims, that is to say, by everyone:
expropriated feudal families, the peasantry forever in debt to them,
and, most of all, by the lesser bourgeoisie, those poorer relatives
whose hopes were being disappointed and who were finding the gate
to honors and riches closed in their faces.

The polemical literature which lists the grievances of the dispossessed nobility is often the work of bourgeois lawyers who are being
excluded by the gentry.[25]

The poet Jacques Tahureau writes about the gentry as a disappointed outsider. He describes the arrogance of the magistrates as
directed not only against bourgeois but also against *gentilshommes:*
"When an honest *gentilhomme* or other person, no matter how great a
lord he may be, finds himself in need of their good offices, and having
waited for a long time for the arrival of *Messieurs*, greets them ... you
will see *Monsieur de la robe rouge* ... walk past with such arrogance
and pride that, far from returning the salutation properly, he will
pretend not to have noticed the courteous greeting, and walk on, just
barely registering his presence."[26] Tahureau tells his readers that the
officier gentry have nothing but contempt for the old nobility's raison
d'être, the sword.[27]

And he may be right. The author of an anonymous pamphlet of
1608 that is written from a gentry perspective describes the feudal
nobility as a decadent class whose days are numbered and whose
interests would be best served by accepting the leadership of the
gentry. "Go on, boast about your ancestry, this is no virtue ... it is a
quality which does not belong to you." "Raise your painted escutch-
eons to the sky ... the glories they proclaim are surely not yours.
Neither Rome nor Thrace could match the valiance and wisdom of
your great ancestors," but, in our time, "you are degraded, you
breathe a life without life ... you are carried along and seduced by
interminable years of a languishing and enervating way of life." Having pointed out the sorry condition of this parasitical class, the writer
summons them to find new purpose in life: "Go back to your sources
and you will find that you were born to serve in the *parlements*."
Magnanimously he calls to them: "Come, join us, serve under my
banner."[28]

Contempt for the *gentilshommes* is never far below the surface. It is
expressed casually, unthinkingly, by wealthy magistrates who would
draw their swords if someone questioned their own nobility.[29] Such
people naturally despise the *gentilshommes des champs* for their poverty

and their ignorance. But the same contempt shows, barely below the surface, among the plainest bourgeois, even while he is trying to become a *gentilhomme*.

We can find a nice illustration of this in Molière, who has his character Georges Dandin speak out plainly on such matters. Dandin is meant to be ridiculous. He is a bourgeois who married the daughter of a *gentilhomme* and now pays the price of his social ambition: his noble wife, assisted by her parents and by her noble lover, makes a fool of him. The court audience laughed at Dandin. But Dandin is an honest man whose only mistake was to marry Mademoiselle de Sotenville; the Sotenvilles, on the other hand (the name means "dumb-in-town"), have not a shred of honesty. They gave their daughter to Dandin for one reason only: his money. As Dandin says, he has become an expert on *le style des nobles* and he paid dearly for his expertise: "It is our money they are marrying."[30] The bourgeois Georges Dandin—or, for that matter, the *noble homme* Charles Loyseau—does not see the *gentilshommes* as eternal oppressors against whose exactions there is no remedy except bloody revolt. No, for Dandin-Loyseau the nobility is a paper monster, ridiculously poor, ignorant, and inept, living out the last phase of its historic existence, clinging to empty honors and ridiculous titles, and really quite weak, ready to be pushed out of the way. The nobility in this perspective is good for one thing only: its elegant fleeces will serve to disguise the wolf-like rapacity of the gentry as it takes over the land, the church, and the government, all the while protesting that nothing is happening, and that things are what they always were.

5

Land and Lordship: "Ex Labore Honor"

The bourgeois *conquérant* dreams of living a life of leisure, surrounded by his lands and acting out the part of the seigneur.[2] More surely than any parchment letters patent, the ownership of seigneuries is said to lead away from the bourgeois *condition.* Under no circumstances does the purchase of a fief modify the new lord's status instantly. But, sooner or later, the fief will serve to back up the claim that one has "lived nobly."

When Thomas Bohier conceived the desire, some time before 1494, to possess the seigneurie of Chenonceaux in the Loire Valley, he did not require it to add the luster of landed property to his name. Bohier had given up *marchandise* long ago, had never, to tell the truth, soiled his hands with it.[3] Nor did Bohier think he was going to make a profitable investment in this land, which was partly planted in inferior vineyards and still lacked the château he was eventually to build there. No, Bohier wanted Chenonceaux: that was that. And he was going to proceed cautiously, deviously, with great patience, in this matter that involved a few thousand livres—giving it his full attention, letting his passion punish him as if Chenonceaux were his mistress.

His first move: in 1494 he makes an offer to the seigneur of Chenonceaux, Pierre Marques, for the adjacent seigneurie of Houdes.[4] A foot in the door. Bohier does not show his hand. The offer is made through a third party, Jacques de Beaune, who, at the time, can still masquerade as a simple bourgeois.[5] Marques, obviously on the verge of bankruptcy, needs cash badly. Through his relative, Beaune, Bohier generously offers to help Marques: he offers to buy a *rente* from him. That is to say, he offers him a sum of money in exchange for an annual, and perpetual, payment of 352 livres. The principal would have been somewhere between 3,000 and 4,000 livres (since a *rente* was usually about 10 percent), and the land would have served as collateral.[6]

Once we see a *gentilhomme* or a *laboureur* hooked in this way, we know the inevitable outcome. To be sure, there is always a clause in the contract which seems to give the victim a chance—the chance, namely, to buy the contract back, if he can get together the original amount of the loan. It is a loan, but with the peculiarity that the borrower, instead of paying off the principal plus interest, keeps paying the interest indefinitely without ever reducing the principal. On a 4,000-livre loan, for example, instead of paying back 8,000 over a ten-year period and being done with it, the poor man will have paid back only 4,000 livres in ten years, and fifty years later he will have paid another 20,000; and these *rentes* are inherited, like a curse, from father to son ad infinitum.[7]

Marques of Chenonceaux put up a good fight. One has the uneasy feeling, as one follows Bohier's moves, that his victim's struggle gives him a sportsman's satisfaction. He has him hooked, and he gives him a little free play, from time to time, just for fun. Having sold Bohier the right to receive 352 livres per year, Marques struggles to keep up the payments. Since the total income of his seigneurie is estimated at only 450 livres a year, there is not much margin left, especially if Bohier is manipulating Marques's creditors—something we can only guess at here, but so normal a procedure that a champion like Bohier would seem, somehow, to be letting us down if he missed that trick. Predictably, two years later Marques gives in: he sells Chenonceaux outright to Bohier for 7,374 livres.

Our master-*rentier* is in no hurry, however. He spins out a generous amount of line: Marques is allowed to stay on the estate, as a tenant, for an annual lease of 450 livres. Naturally the time comes soon enough when Marques cannot pay the rent. Bohier moves in for the kill. At the last moment, someone comes to the rescue. Marques's niece Catherine, having been clever enough to marry money—good, solid *bourgeois-parlementaire* money—offers to buy Chenonceaux back from Bohier. (It is a right a relative may exercise at will, according to such contracts, within a certain period of time after the sale.)

Bohier takes this very well for someone whose prize catch has been taken away from him. He even goes so far as to lend Catherine a large portion of the sum needed to buy the property back from him! Frankly, Bohier seems to enjoy playing this game. He bides his time. From his neighboring estate of Houdes, he watches events at Chenonceaux. Catherine's husband, François Fumée, is a worthy opponent. He makes the first move by attacking Bohier's rights to Houdes in court. A nine-year-long vendetta follows, expressed mostly in suits and countersuits. In the end, inevitably, total victory for Bohier, who outclasses Fumée completely when it comes to financial resources and political connections. On 8 February 1513, the Fumées are expropriated, Chenonceaux is put up for auction, and Bohier buys it for 15,641 livres, that is, something like double its original price. Even allowing for twenty years of inflation and improvements, it seems to me that Bohier's kind of sport is costly. But he can afford the expense. On 10 February he takes possession. A week later, busy elsewhere, I imagine, he gives homage for his new fief by proxy—his old ally, Poncher, ex-financier and currently bishop of Paris, acting in his stead.

Now that the prize is his, Bohier delegates much of the responsibility for the completion of this little masterpiece to his trusted lieutenant on the home front, his wife Catherine, *née* Briçonnet. More land is bought to give the Chenonceaux property breathing space. Permission is obtained from his suzerain to raise the status of the fief from seigneurie to *châtellenie*. At last all is ready to build the magnificent château we can admire today. It was completed, under Catherine's supervision, in 1517. The event was celebrated with the solemn consecration of the castle's chapel by Thomas's brother Antoine, now cardinal-archbishop of Bourges.

Thomas Bohier is a prize example of the *bourgeois conquérant* of the turn of the century. Of his sons, one is a baron and governor of Touraine, two others are bishops, a fourth one is a *bailli*. Thomas himself, however, when he is laid to rest in the family's sumptuous marble tomb in Saint Saturnin Cathedral in Tours, in 1524, is still remembered there as the city's mayor. The Bohier family's sprint toward the highest honors is short enough so that they can be remembered as bourgeois financiers. Their career is on a grand scale, like that of the other *généraux des finances*. But we will find their complicated and almost gratuitous passion for ruining lords and peasants and collecting their lands repeated at all levels of the gentry. No sooner has he left *marchandise* than we find our *Sire* and *maistre* armed with a *license ès loix*—a veritable license for hunting the financially vulnerable—and making sorties from behind his law office, his notary's study, his little office in the *présidial*, scouring the countryside for likely victims. For every Bohier, we shall find thousands of small-time operators like maistre François Micheau, a lawyer in the small town of Civray, in Poitou.

We catch Micheau in the act of swallowing up a *laboureur*'s farm in a contract of 24 April 1603. The *laboureur*, Bertrand Serpoux, is selling his family farm, his *héritage*, for 720 livres—but the poor man is not getting a single sou out of the transaction. He is at the mercy of the lawyer, Micheau, who deprives him of his livelihood and generously allows the ruined peasant to live out his life in "one half of a small cottage located at the end of the village." The lawyer did not ruin the peasant overnight. The contract of 1603 is merely the culmination of years of patient scheming. The lawyer Micheau—and his father before him—had spent years lending money and grain at usurious rates of interest to poor Serpoux. By the time of his final ruin, Serpoux had incurred seven signed obligations going back to the year 1587 to the value of 431 livres and 11 sols. Some of these debts were owed to Micheau's father directly. (Micheau *père* appears in the contract as Loys Micheau, Seigneur de l'Ecu. The Ecu of which he was seigneur was a shop. It was common practice, in Poitou, for a successful merchant to take the name of his shop and call himself "seigneur de l'Ecu," which is like an innkeeper, for example, calling himself "Lord of the Coach and Four.") Some of the obligations were incurred toward other lenders whose contracts had been quietly bought up by the Micheaus. In addition to these seven fateful obligations, Serpoux owed the Micheaus 288 livres 9 sols in cash and grain—no doubt the result of fifteen years of failure to pay interest charges, of loan-contracts shrewdly rewritten each year, in apparent generosity, but whose eventual purpose is disclosed on that fateful day in April, the cruelest month, when all the reserves of grain have vanished, when the poor begin to starve, and the parish registers fill with the names of dead children.[8]

Whether the land is worth 700 or 15,000 livres, the method is the same. The unlucky landowner—*gentilhommme* or peasant—who needs cash for one reason or another, falls gently into the moneylender's spider-like web. Sooner or later the victim is swallowed up. Deep, secret rhythms govern this process. There are happy times for the working farmer, when the blandishments of the smooth-talking city men are more easily resisted. At other times the need is desperate and the peasantry of an entire region is dislodged by the unforgiving, Malthusian equation which represents the relationship between population, land, and productivity.[9]

Not that the luckier *laboureurs* do not also climb upward to wealth and a bourgeois way of life at the very time when the Micheaus acquire law degrees, royal offices, and, eventually, gentry status. We shall see that Raveau's summing up of the situation in Poitou is valid for most regions: "This sixteenth century was an age of extraordinary social transformation and emancipation for the peasant classes and for the Third Estate of the towns as well, which acquired nobility then with a facility no one suspects; a facility which, it must be added, came to an end rather suddenly, for the moderately wealthy bourgeois of the seventeenth century."[10]

In the early years of the sixteenth century, at least, one sees so much openness, so many fortunes quickly made, that it would be hardly an exaggeration to speak simply of the rise of some families and the fall of others. Alerted to the surprising successes of *laboureurs* as land buyers in Normandy at that time, we find, in Poitou, for instance, families that are like armies on the march, one wing in the *laboureur* camp, another in the bourgeoisie, with plenty of generalship from uncles and cousins entrenched in ecclesiastical benefices or municipal office.[11]

In describing this rush to wrest lands from unlucky peasants and *gentilshommes*, seasoned observers like Paul Raveau, Lucien Febvre, or Yvonne Bézard resist the temptation to impose a blueprint-like vision of "class" pitched against "class." At the same time, they all note that in this big free-for-all, in which *laboureurs* and merchants participate side by side with *officiers*, there are big winners. Everywhere, always, the *officiers*, the *bonnetz carrés*, are the big winners.[12] This is true in the Paris region, where Bézard observes the striking "number and frequency of property transfers," where, in the fifteenth century, there are absolutely no old noble families left in possession (with one exception), and where the majority of the nonclerical seigneuries belong to "the world of the robe, this class which is still ill-defined."[13] This "ill-defined class" swallowed up both peasant and noble lands in the countryside surrounding Paris—and everywhere else where local monographs allow us to make at least a rough estimate of what is going on.[14]

Armed with money and with the law in their hands, the *familles* that had long ago achieved economic control in their own city and in the *plat pays* surrounding it are now bidding for possession of the kingdom. The rich merchants of Lyon, who had been buying noble lands on a small scale as long as anyone could remember, set their ambitions much higher now. The Gondi, *honorables hommes*, *bourgeois de Lyon*, in 1520 will no longer content themselves with buying local estates and building castles on them. They are destined for the highest honors in church and state.[15] The Paffi, spice and drug merchants, rich and notable enough to achieve municipal office in Lyon by 1540, buy a barony in the Mâcon area in 1564, take the title in 1571, and are *baillis* of Mâcon soon after. The Gadagnes, bankers of proverbial wealth ("riche comme Gadagne"), in the Lyon city council by 1536, lend money to the crown and soon produce a *seneschal* of Lyon, a lieutenant general of the Lyonnais. And on the way they are picking up seigneuries and pretty genealogies. In 1588, barely fifty years after their achievement of municipal notability, we find them sitting in the Estates-General as representatives of the nobility.[16]

The fortunes of these financial families of Lyon produced quick success stories which were remarked upon by contemporaries who viewed them as exceptional cases. A man like L'Estoile, who writes from the point of view of a *parlementaire* whose own family's rise had followed the conventional path from *marchandise* through education to office, senses the Gondis' rise as alien, not so much because of their Italian origins and connections as because they went from finance straight to military nobility.[17] We are reminded of an elementary fact: money alone, especially money achieved in commerce or commercial banking, elicits no respect from the gentry—at least not openly. The gentry affects to despise money: as they see it, only crude bourgeois, shifty Italians, and penniless noblemen are after money. The gentry has higher things on its mind.

What we are pursuing here is a clue which may force us to modify our judgment. We see bourgeois buying noble estates, we see them changing their names, and we jump, too quickly, to the conclusion that they wish to be *gentilshommes*. It is certainly true that we shall have no difficulty in finding such men, only a generation or two removed from clear bourgeois status, lusting for the accoutrements of old rank, swaggering in the streets with swords and elegant ribbons, buying commissions in the army, cutting a figure at court, marrying the daughters of *gentilshommes*, and generally wishing to become members of the *noblesse* of the sword. Nor are they always ridiculous.[18]

One must not suppose, however, that it takes the exceptional circumstance of the wealth of the Gondis, Paffis, or Gadagnes to open a military career for men of *roturier* origins. Whether this is still true fifty years later or not, it is quite clear that in the late sixteenth century, at least, the profession of arms was open to the gentry. In these families it happens on occasion that a son (often the *enfant terrible*) takes up arms, seized by snobbism or rebellion. When that happens, there are no real social obstacles in his way. His father may be tearing his hair; but if he is an indulgent father, he will finance and help the black sheep on his way. The son who chooses the profession of arms is not necessarily the pride of the family. On the contrary, he may be the one who was too stupid or too rebellious to succeed in the *cursus honorum* of the gentry. We can find a good example of this in the Pasquier family.

The father, maistre Estienne Pasquier, is a moderately wealthy *advocat general* at the *chambre des comptes* of Paris, someone whose portfolio of *rentes* and seigneuries may have been in the range of that assembled by his colleague Loyseau. Although maistre Pasquier had inherited a respectable little seigneurie in the Brie country, not far from Melun, he never seemed tempted to drop his own name in favor of the *nom de seigneurie*. Tact? Discretion? Self-consciousness? Lack of ambition? I think I have a better answer. Pasquier probably belonged to an old Parisian family;[19] I say "probably," because he himself, so voluble in all other respects, maintains the most remarkable silence concerning his parents.[20] I think it may well be because the Pasquiers are Parisians of old date that they do not change their name. This apparent modesty, this reluctance to shed old bourgeois names, runs true to pattern. We find it, in the fifteenth and sixteenth centuries, among most of the prominent families which have for several generations been members of the more notable Parisian bourgeoisie, particularly among the families which handed down municipal offices from father to son. Were they afraid of being laughed at by their peers, who knew them for what they were? Or did they take special pride in maintaining the old names and thus distinguishing themselves from the hordes of provincial parvenus who, like Grudé–La Croix du Maine, changed their names once they were in Paris and free of skeptical neighbors? I am not sure, of course. They were not sure either, I imagine. But the pattern is there for us to observe.

In Pasquier, who may indeed have wished a decent obscurity onto his parents and relatives, I am reasonably certain that we are seeing a kind of pride at work. He is proud of being an old Parisian—and fond of Paris folklore, fond of its old buildings, prepared to defend the language of Parisians as a model for France; and he is proud, above all other things, of his profession. Or, to be more precise: it is not the practice of law per se which commands his respect and admiration. It is, more particularly, the way of life of the higher magistrature which enlists his total, joyous approval. He can think of nothing better on earth.

A man like Pasquier has been trained to become an intellectual from early childhood on. Before he had reached the age of twenty, he was formed for life: his world would be, henceforth, the world of books. The horizons of his imagination, essentially limited to the ancient Mediterranean world, were filled with noble Romans, whose virtue he was enjoined to emulate. His heroes, however, were more likely to be lawyers and professors than generals: Socrates and Cicero—and, his own masters, the professors of law and of classics who were to serve as models—*hommes illustres*—for the French gentry. The aspiration to "live nobly" expressed itself, not in the pursuit of knightly ideals, but in the less mystical, if equally fervent, joys of "good letters." The country was inundated, almost overnight, with amateur scholarship and amateur poetry. Weighty correspondences, some meant for eventual publication, sped across the kingdom in couriers' pouches, hastily sealed in some country house, unobtrusively composed during the long sessions of provincial tribunals.[21]

The great festive occasions in the lives of men like Pasquier, the public events they liked to recall, were not battles or religious ceremonies but tournaments of words: outstanding public lectures, fierce courtroom harangues, and poetry competitions, improvised and rather silly. The dress, the manners, the recreations of Pasquier's circles had very little in common with the pleasures of *gentilshommes*. They may have met at the Jeu de Paume, they passed each other on horseback on the dusty roads leading to their country estates, but the two worlds stayed separate in most respects. On horseback on a summer afternoon, or on the bowling green after dinner, Pasquier and others like him were always engaged in learned conversation.[22] These serious pleasures were extolled with such evident satisfaction that one would be very far off the mark imagining a Pasquier dreaming of a different life, wishing to be a *gentilhomme*. And yet, maistre Estienne seems to have quietly obtained *lettres de noblesse* in 1574.[23]

Of his sons, only the eldest, Théodore, born in 1558, followed wholeheartedly in his father's footsteps. He kept the family name, although he could have called himself after his seigneurie of Espinay. He studied law and eventually took over his father's expensive and important royal office of *advocat general* in the *chambre des comptes*. He married, very properly, a Mangot woman—who belonged to an old and distinguished Parisian *parlementaire* family—and, in a second marriage, the widow of a wine merchant.

The second son, Nicolas, had everything done for him by his father's money and good offices. Provided with the office of lieutenant general in the *sénéchaussée* of Angoumois, he settled down on the family estate of Mainxe, near Cognac, started calling himself Monsieur de Mainxe, and married a noblewoman. The third son, Pierre, was the black sheep of the family. While still in his teens, he ran off to Italy instead of pursuing his studies and eventually, under the name Monsieur de la Ferlandiere, commanded a company and fought under Henri IV. The fourth son, Guy, also opted for a military career at first and called himself Monsieur de Bussy. Wounded in battle, he prudently changed his mind, became an *auditeur* in the *chambre des comptes*, and sat in the Paris city council. The youngest, Jean, alas, was not so lucky. As Monsieur de la Miraudiere, he died heroically at the siege of Mehun-sur-Loire in 1589, holding out, alone, against the attacking force commanded by Georges Babou de la Bourdaisiere; it is worth noting that for the Babous, as for the Pasquiers, this was the first generation to perform on the battlefield.[24]

Military careers were open to the sons of lawyers and judges in the sixteenth century. If only some chose the sword, it may be because it was not attractive enough. This cannot surprise us. With Loyseau's diatribes against the *traisneurs d'espée* still ringing in our ears, we know that there is a profound class prejudice against war and violence embedded in the minds of the gentry. They abhor duelling, and wars of conquest, in their view, are sheer folly. Yes, but are there no honorable wars? Is not the defense of the fatherland a citizen's highest duty? Was not Socrates himself ready to take up arms when duty called? And has not the profession of arms always been held in high esteem?

These contradictions will remain unsolved. The question we must ask is this: Is the profession of arms sought as a means of social advancement? We have watched bourgeois *honorables hommes*—in Poitou, in Burgundy, in Provence, and elsewhere—become lawyers, landowners, and officeholders, turn into *nobles hommes*, change their names and their life style—all without ever resorting to a military career. Perhaps at this lower level, on the threshold of "living nobly," the option of taking up arms is rarely available. In the higher reaches of the gentry, we do occasionally encounter honorable mention on the battlefield: we have just seen a Pasquier and a Babou at war. These are not exceptional occurrences.

Could the occasional choice of a military career have been a form of
social emigration, a way of taking care of younger sons for whom one
could not provide? My impression is that the spacious country houses
of the gentry filled up with large numbers of children. "The plurality
and company of children is useful to the household, each is a new
tool and instrument for getting richer," says Montaigne, rather out of
character here. (*Essais,* p. 369.) Bachelors are unheard of, daughters
are married off at a tender age, and, when a spouse dies an untimely
death, a replacement is soon found. In these circumstances there are
always so many sons and daughters whose futures must be assured
that it is not surprising to find—once the family offices have been
filled and the chief, and costly, alliances contracted—a younger son
opting for the religious or military life, sometimes against the father's
most violent opposition. It seems to me that military careers held little
promise of social advancement. Unless, like a Zamet or a Gondi, one
had such overpowering wealth and influence at court that one could
aspire to the highest commands at once, it was fruitless to buy a
commission. To be a captain or an ensign gave one no more *qualité*
than one already possessed as *noble homme*, Monsieur de la Ferlandiere;
and promotion to the highest ranks was very unlikely.

Nicolas Pasquier did not need a military background to pursue his
social climbing. He was quite acceptable by virtue of his wealth and
political power, his seigneuries, and his alliances. When he married,
on 28 April 1592, the daughter of François de Bremond (*haut et puis-
sant* seigneur, *chevalier,* baron of Balanzac, etc.), he allied himself with
one of the oldest and most powerful noble families of the region. They
were his neighbors at Mainxe, and they gave him their daughter in
full knowledge of his social status. As a royal magistrate in nearby
Cognac and the son of a famous attorney and man of letters, Nicolas
was well known. He was known to have connections in high gentry
circles. The Pasquiers were quite good enough as Pasquiers. The ease
and openness with which they marry in and out of *noblesse* would be
surprising at any other time. Nicolas and Suzanne had four children
in five years—Suzanne died in childbirth in the summer of 1597. Of
those children, one, quite noble, married a Bremond cousin, another
married a military man, a third married a baron. Meanwhile Nicolas,
within a year of his wife's death, married Louise Mangot, whose
sister was already his brother Théodore's wife. By that time, he appears as *escuyer* in the contracts and is a *maistre des requestes.*

Usury knowing no bounds, Nicolas had been lending money to his
own relatives, the Bremonds, who owned the seigneurie of Balanzac. Bremond owed him over 23,000 livres when Nicolas finally

seized the property. In 1617, two years after his father's death, Nicolas paid off other creditors to a total of 26,236l. 16s. 4d.—and slowly sank toward genteel poverty, installed in the château of Balanzac and beset by lawsuits.[25]

Is this a case history in the "treason of the bourgeoisie"? The bourgeoisie was "betrayed" long ago, when the Pasquiers left *marchandise*—and the Mangots, Du Tillets, and Phelypeaux before them. But Nicolas Pasquier, Monsieur de Mainxe—who is before us now, baronially encastled—does he belong to a new wave of "social treason"? Appearances are against him, to be sure. But in spite of the crenellations of his castle, against all the evidence of his baronial sons-in-law and his declining income—Nicolas can be convicted only of foolishness. He is no traitor to his class. We can affirm this with some degree of assurance, because he wrote a book on the subject, under the title *Le Gentilhomme* (Paris, 1611).

In this work, the author—Nicolas Pasquier to his readers, and not Monsieur de Mainxe—sets out to draw an ideal portrait of the *gentilhomme*. The question is, What does he mean by *gentilhomme*? He appropriates the word without ever defining it and molds it to fit his own ideal. The result is a clumsy and humorless but most revealing sketch of the virtues desired by the gentry.

This *gentilhomme* of his must not "laugh indiscreetly and uncontrollably." He is not to speak "fiercely and audaciously." He should train his face so as to appear—not exactly disapproving—but somehow knowing and sure of himself. This inspires confidence. In his dress he must stay away from unusual fashions and strike a note of *honnesté* and modesty, avoiding glamorous and attention-getting clothes. He must eschew both gambling and drinking. He must not swear. He must work hard; he must be provident and wise; he should plan and foresee those things which may be profitable to him. He must love his *patrie* with unexampled ardor. Let him think, often, of the hazards and afflictions which might befall him, lest he be surprised when they come.[26] He must not be prodigal with his words: a word lightly spoken cannot be taken back any more than an arrow which has left its bow. Soberness, then, is recommended, in word and deed. It is best to present a cold appearance on first meeting and to be quite humble in greeting a person; and all the time one must consider everything said and done from every angle: consider where things are being said, for what reason, what the speaker's secret motives may be, and where all this may lead eventually.[27] Voluptuousness and anger are condemned. Prudence is recommended above all other qualities: the *gentilhomme* is advised to "measure the end result of all actions." Good sense and discretion are counted as "the greatest riches in the world."[28]

As for idleness, it is compared to stagnant water which "spoils and putrefies": it is the nurse of all vices. To counter this evil, the model *gentilhomme* must be "trained to work" when still young: *dressé au travail*. On the subject of "travail," Nicolas waxes lyrical. He recommends a laborious regime of exercises, to which the young man is to be harnessed, body and soul: "Let him pass on from one exercise to the next, let one task succeed the other in precise rotation, work coming after work," until this work without respite kindles in him "a very vehement activity, a pressing need, an unceasing diligence." Thus fortified, a *gentilhomme* will resist the attractions of leisure, which lead to vain and delicious pleasures and a lazy idleness which induces nothing but shame. Properly trained, he will find that work leads to glory, honor, and freedom.[29]

How could a *gentilhomme de race* find worthy precepts in such counsel?—good only for "making flies laugh," as a vicious critic put it.[30] Nicolas's *gentilhomme* is a cold, calculating fanatic in whom the virtues of the bourgeois are elevated into a moral science. Is there anything noble in this *gentilhomme* who finds honor and glory in hard work and not on the battlefield? What would Nicolas's *gentilhomme* be doing in combat? What profit is to be had there? This is certainly a ticklish question for Nicolas. He does, as a matter of fact, feel obliged to commend the profession of arms, in an aside: 2 pages in a book which runs to 359! War, naturally, ought to be the *gentilhomme*'s "principal profession," we are told with no conviction at all. It would indeed be quite impossible to reconcile this profession with the life of the *gentilhomme* as pictured in the other 357 pages of his book. The author, quite at a loss here, advises the *gentilhomme*, if it should come to battle, "to consider carefully before throwing himself into danger"—and goes on to more important matters.[31]

Monsieur de Mainxe's lack of clarity can be as instructive as maistre Loyseau's dialectical malice. It does not seem to occur to Nicolas that he is describing his own kind and that this portrait would make the *traisneurs d'espée* laugh like flies.

Maistre Estienne had obtained letters of ennoblement, and his son titled himself *escuyer*. Granted. This brought—or prepared— exemption from certain taxes. A son may go off to battle, failing "to consider carefully before throwing himself into danger." But the son's military career in no way adds to the family's social status. Monsieur de Mainxe's closeness to barons, barons' daughters, and baronies gives a certain *cachet* to his children, but no more than they received from the Mangot connection and no more than Théodore's children inherited. Théodore remained plain Pasquier and a lawyer and married a bourgeoise after having married a Mangot. His children encountered no difficulty in being recognized as technically noble, even though they continued the family's tradition of law and royal office. The Pasquiers may have been "traitors to the bourgeoisie" a long time ago, but they did not betray the gentry. They helped form this class, they proclaimed its virtues, and, despite marginal alliances with barons and bourgeoises, they stayed in it, they burrowed, they reveled in it.

There is a point in time, roughly situated between the wars of the League and the wars of the Fronde, when the gentry, Narcissus-like, can be surprised contemplating its own image with supreme satisfaction. "It had a life, it had *moeurs*, yes, I would go so far as to say that it had virtues which were its own, somehow outside the three orders of the country," explains the Count de Molé, speaking of the magistrature of that period and himself a loyal descendant, despite the jarring particule, of the distinguished Molé family.[32]

Monsieur de Montaigne was more specific in defining this "Fourth Estate," which he knew as a "body separate from the nobility." The qualities he ascribes to this estate are those we found in Pasquier's *Le Gentilhomme*: "justice, peace, profit, scholarship, words, reason," in contrast to the nobility's "honor, warfare, virtue, action, courage, strength."[33]

In defining the mentality of a class, we cannot pretend to describe anything more than a dominant trend which is particularly noticeable at a particular time. Even this task is beyond our means: it would be hopeless to try to measure just how dominant it was or to specify the precise years when it became and ceased being so. That way lies pedantry and fantasy. What we can do, without aiming at the theoretical certainties of neighboring disciplines, is to accumulate case histories, even at the risk of tedium; to interrogate every kind of document—lawyer's brief, marriage contract, testament, household account, love letter, poem, play, philosophical tract, schoolbook, traveler's memoir—until we are ready to cross-examine, confident of being able to trip up a lying witness through sheer familiarity. We shall have to climb into their skins.

6

The Demigods of Our Age

The ironic phrase "demigods of our age" was often used in the six-teenth century to describe the most powerful gentry clans. Pierre de Saint-Julien, writing in 1589 from the point of view of the *noblesse de race*, admits that a tidal wave of usurpation had engulfed the fiefs of Burgundy. This is now a *fait accompli*. Saint-Julien seems to seek ac-commodation with the *demy dieux du temps present*.[1] Perhaps an al-liance can be formed with the greatest gentry families at the expense of newer candidates for usurpation? Saint-Julien cannot "ignore the fact that the noble families of Burgundy are no more eternal than those of other regions." Through purchase, alienation, and other ac-cidents, the ownership of fiefs has changed so frequently "that even the neighbors would be astonished" if they knew. In the county of Mâcon, he admits, "most of the noble houses are in the hands of new seigneurs who have entered through marriage, inheritance, or pur-chase in the last sixty years or so." Should one undertake to tell the truth about all these changes? Such revelations might be welcomed by some but would certainly be "most displeasing" to others. Saint-Julien on the whole wisely opts for discretion.[2]

If it is a fact that most noble names serve as a disguise for new men, then who are they? Where do they come from? How do they usurp?

They are men of the law, *gens de justice,* of course, who may be allowed a status superior to that of bourgeois. They may claim nobility of a kind, which Saint-Julien calls *Noblesse Civile.* But as for being *gentilshommes,* no. "*Gentilhominité* is a matter of blood." Tolerant though he is, Saint-Julien objects to seeing these men show up at the musters of the *bans* whose rolls are "stuffed with their names."[3] Royal letters of *anoblissement* make no difference: "Among those who know how to judge gold," such an *anobli* "will be easily recognized as counterfeit and worthless metal."[4]

Saint-Julien knows, however, when to make concessions to reality. "When it happens that some wealthy man of the Third Estate, virtuous in the exercise of his functions, has his children initiated into the world of arms with the intention of converting his civil nobility (with the prince's permission) into the kind of nobility which is acquired through arms; and should it then happen that this first man of the family to enter the road which leads to true nobility should ally himself in marriage with a gentlewoman of good family; and then, should his children, raised by this true gentlewoman—and their children and children's children—all, through four generations, marry noblewomen, truly daughters of *gentilshommes* of name and arms: then one can no longer doubt that these descendants are true *gentilshommes.*"[5]

This prudent and balanced definition is a concession. It is a retreat from myth. It is justified by Saint-Julien on the historically unassailable ground that "all nobility had a beginning." The fact is, Saint-Julien reminds his readers, that "if the Noble Estate had not been able to replenish itself from among the most advanced of the Third Estate," the old nobility of blood would have become extinguished a long time ago.[6]

This is all very true, even if it had been left unsaid in the past. The "demigods" are installed on their new lands; their power is indisputable. Will their loyalties remain tied to their clients among the notable bourgeoisie? Or will they make overtures toward the *gentilshommes* in the country and at court? Are they free to make such a choice? Their solidarity with middling and lesser gentry families is held together by an array of common interests so vast that one suspects that the choice hardly exists for them. Their ways of management, their education, their way of life make social treason very difficult.

From the splendors of Chenonceaux to the modest manors of small-town notables, the gentry's châteaux aspire to new levels of elegance and comfort, transplanted directly from the city.[7] The best talent and the newest style are put to work for Olympian patrons,[8] like Bohier or Villeroy. Lesser families leave their imprint on half-ruined feudal castles by remodeling them at least in part to suit their taste.[9] Instead of having thick, high walls, crenellations, and bastions, the new country house is all windows, all grace and symmetry, with wide entrances thrown open onto tree-shaded alleys and the vineyards and fields beyond. There is always room for house guests and relatives, and there are always a library, an office, and a music room.

Here the magistrate comes to spend his long holidays between court sessions. This is his private summer paradise. Here, bringing in the grape and wheat crops, at the head of his farmers, he returns to the rhythms of country life. "I am staying in this delightful place, where I have wished a thousand times you would join me," writes Cardinal Granvelle in the summer of 1564 from his native Burgundian lands.

> There are mountains, many and beautiful, reaching up to the sky, fertile on all sides, filled with very fine vineyards and all sorts of good fruit; the rivers and valleys are wide and beautiful, the water is clear as crystal, there is an infinity of springs, there are trout and other fish, innumerable and the best in the world; the fields below are fertile and the meadows rich; and while the heat is great on one hillside, right across, no matter how hot the day, you will find a delectable cool shade; and there is no lack of good company among the local people, relatives and friends. And the wines, as you know, are the best in the world.[10]

This is paradise as seen by the undisputed chief of the demigods of the Franche-Comté.

The new landowners are likely to be far tougher masters than the insouciant seigneurs of old, who lost their estates to shrewd *laboureurs* and bourgeois.[11] No one cheats these hard-eyed taskmasters, straight out of the pages of Nicolas Pasquier's *Le Gentilhomme* and Olivier de Serres's *Théâtre d'Agriculture*.[12] "Labor omnia vincit" is their philosophy,[13] profit their theology, and usury their relentless art. The satirists liken these men to "the crocodile who presents his newborn with something to snap at as soon as they come out of their eggs"—to test their rapacity; if the baby crocodile refuses to snap, "the mother tears him to pieces. Thus are the children instructed in the arts of finance and rapine before they reach puberty."[14] These "vultures disguised in long gowns"[15] hold their sharecroppers and farmers on a short leash. The attentions they lavish on their country houses and their gardens seldom get out of hand. They know their budgets, and other demands must be met. There is the house in town, at least as comfortable and well equipped as the country house. There are the dowries to be provided for, the sons' educations and offices to be assured—and, always, the expense, considerable for the less wealthy gentry, of books. "When it comes to books and learning there is no such thing as sufficiency," we are told by Du Verdier,[16] and modest fortunes like those of La Croix du Maine or La Popelinière really do seem to collapse under the strain of buying rare books and manuscripts. Here at last we find the weakness of our "crocodiles": they will sacrifice everything to letters.

And this is understandable. For what are they, without letters? Let us examine the foundations of the noble house of d'Ormesson. We shall see that, without letters, success is almost beyond the reach of even the most rapacious financiers—success, that is, by gentry standards. They can accumulate money, offices, lands, change their names, build splendid country houses, and yet be forlorn, defeated, and pathetic among the visible signs of wealth. Such is the fate of the nouveau riche who comes up too quickly. He can never join the ranks of the demigods, no matter how rich he is. He will barely be accepted by the middling gentry, in spite of his wealth.

An example is Olivier Lefevre,[17] who was born in Paris in November 1525, his father a clerk at the *greffe civil* of the *parlement*, his mother the daughter of a *procureur*. Small fry, *praticiens*. Olivier's son André, whose confidences allow us to follow Olivier's progress, is quite candid in setting down these *mémoires*. "I know very well," he asserts, with a show of righteousness, "that there are plenty of imprudent men who follow the vulgar error of preferring nobility to virtue and therefore hide the true origins of their fathers in order to appear of higher birth." But he, André, will tell the truth: his father was "the oldest son of a family mediocre in extraction and property." Furthermore, Olivier's father died when the child was only five years old. His widowed mother made a second marriage. This at least made it possible for Olivier to attend a good school, the Collège de Navarre, for three years. But the means were lacking for continuing his studies, and, as we shall see, this was a fateful turn of events, destined to cast its shadow over Olivier's later life. Olivier was withdrawn from school and apprenticed to a *procureur* "to learn to write and earn a living," that is, to learn to write contracts and other legal documents and in general learn the ways of "*phynance*." Olivier did well for himself without further schooling. His master recommended him, once his apprenticeship terminated, as a clerk to a fine specimen of the long-gowned vulture species, a future demigod, maistre André

Blondel, sieur de Roquancour, treasurer to the dauphin Henri. This
was the beginning of Olivier's fortune, for "he became known to M.
the dauphin Henri." In the client-patron relationships which hold
this world together, to become known to the prince, or to some other
distinguished patron, is the beginning of one's fortunes. Luckily for
Olivier, Henri—who came to the throne in 1547 as Henri II—was a
narrow-minded bigot without a proper education. Perhaps kings like
François I or Henri III, cultivated men, would not have wanted to
bother with knowing Olivier. But Henri II not only knew Olivier—he
loved him well! And is there anything in the world, anything at all, to
be compared with the bliss of being known and well loved by a king?
Sincerely, and with tears in his eyes, Olivier used to tell his son, quite
frequently after his king's death, "that he had suffered the loss of
wife, children, and friends, but that no loss could be compared to the
loss of a king who knows you and loves you well."

With Henri's elevation to the throne, his household *officiers*, naturally enough, were brought closer to power. Roquancour became *trésorier de l'épargne*, and Olivier, as his first clerk, drew an annual salary
of about one thousand écus. In 1553, at the age of 28, Olivier was
ready to strike out on his own: he bought an office. It was his brother
Nicolas's death that year which made Olivier independent. Nicolas,
who had followed a parallel career in the service of Preudome, *receveur général des finances*, had more sensational opportunities for increasing his wealth. He had struck out on his own three years earlier.
After borrowing money from his brother—and no doubt benefiting
from his brother's share of the royal knowledge and love—he had
purchased the office of *trésorier de l'extraordinaire des guerres*. He got his
investment back within the course of a single year "through the taxes
levied for the embarkation of the army which sailed from Brest to
Scotland in 1551." Two years later, when Nicolas died, Olivier became the chief heir to an estate of twenty-five thousand écus and to
the office of *trésorier de l'extraordinaire des guerres* for the Piedmont
region. Inheriting an office was no easy maneuver. Olivier had to pull
all the strings at his disposal at court to achieve this aim. The cardinal
of Lorraine was especially helpful to him. The inheritance was disputed by his half-brother (out of the Lefevre widow's second marriage), but Olivier won the case in court, and when the unfortunate
half-brother died suddenly, childless, his estate, too, fell into Olivier's
hands. Was Olivier known and loved by the Fates themselves?

Now his future was clear. In 1554 he bought the land of Ormesson,
and from that time onward he had himself called Monsieur d'Ormesson, a name he "retained permanently, never after that time being

known under any other name; for the name of Lefevre was too common, as my father used to say himself." Such is the irony of fate, alas, that no sooner had Lefevre become a seigneur than he was accused of embezzling public funds and forced to give up his office—for which, however, he was reimbursed, according to the standard procedure even in blatant cases. Olivier simply turned around and bought another profitable *trésorier* office, but the experience had shaken him. Recognizing "how difficult it was to subsist at court for any length of time without support and assistance, he resolved to marry and thus to ally himself with some family well chosen to support and defend him." The son's candid—and private—memoir seems to echo the sententious words of the old man himself, who no doubt spent much time in his later years giving lectures on "le moyen de parvenir" to his sons.

There is no sentimentality in the old crocodile's ways. He does not even know that he lacks gentility when he admits his true love for finance and business. One can see that he did not finish his *collège* education. His marriage to Anne d'Alesso is really an alliance, in his mind, to Monsieur de Morvillier, bishop of Orléans and *conseiller d'estat*, a very powerful man at court, an excellent ally: Anne was related to Morvillier through her mother, who was the bishop's niece.

To ally himself with Jean de Morvillier, however distantly, was a masterly move. Morvillier was truly a demigod. About fifty years old by then, he had been lieutenant general in the *bailliage* of Bourges, dean of Bourges cathedral, *conseiller du roy*, ambassador to Venice, *maistre des requestes* and, since 1552, bishop of Orléans—in name and income only, to be sure, since he was far too busy to leave the court.[18] He had the affairs of the diocese managed in absentia by three carefully chosen vicars-general—more or less like vice-presidents in a modern corporation. The really delicate and important vicariate-general, the one for temporal affairs, is safe in the hands of Morvillier's nephew. Morvillier's power does not depend on his offices and benefices alone. His is old power and old wealth. The family, originally notable bourgeois of Blois, had achieved the highest offices of state in the previous century. Jean, the last male descendant of the Morvillier family, was related to *secrétaires d'état* and *parlementaires* of the highest rank: he counted Bochetel, Bourdin, Séguier, Molé, Villeroy, and L'Aubespine among his nephews. Bishoprics and embassies were traded back and forth among these men as casually as Christmas presents. Nothing short of a catastrophic change of reign could present the slightest obstacle to their ambition. The Orléans

bishopric, however profitable, was taken entirely for granted. Morvillier felt no more need to visit his diocese in the seven years following
his nomination than his Bochetel nephew felt the need to take time
out to have himself consecrated as bishop of Rennes, although he held
the benefice, nominally, for ten years. Morvillier would not even
shave off his beard—which scandalized the Orléans cathedral chapter, or so they pretended—a beard being among the worldly signs of
princes, courtiers, and men of the sword, law, or finance, but unsuitable for ecclesiastical positions. No cathedral chapter could stand in
the way of a Morvillier, to be sure, who was known and loved by the
king, by the Guise, and, at least ostensibly and for the moment, by all
the demigods in the realm, including his old friend Babou de la Bourdaisiere, currently wearing a cardinal's hat in Rome.

Such, briefly, were the powers of Morvillier—well worth contracting
for, even if Anne's dowry, at 10,000 livres, seemed on the small
side.[19] It was a very good investment and just in time, for in the year
of Olivier's alliance to the Morvillier family occurred the greatest
catastrophe imaginable to him and his fellow financiers: the death of
the king, through a stupid accident which Olivier could never describe afterward without bursting into tears. In the confused and
tumultuous years that followed, painful inquiries were conducted that
included a general "recherche contre les financiers" and a wholesale
dispossession of all the king's household officers. These blackmail
tactics, conducted under Catherine de Medici's general supervision,
resulted in a compromise settlement which forced the *officiers* to pay
the crown half a million livres to regain their offices.

In the midst of these stormy dealings, Olivier survived splendidly,
with Morvillier's backing. He climbed steadily until he acquired the
very profitable office of *général des finances* for Picardie. By 1573 he was
intendant des finances and *conseiller d'état*. But the inevitable happened:
Morvillier died in 1577. Olivier instantly began to beat a strategic
retreat. He sold his intendancy and managed to get permission to
retire from the court, which was no easy matter, since he was neither
known nor loved by Henri III and had to use the good—and no doubt
costly—offices of a man whom he had advanced "dans les finances"
to intercede with the king. When Olivier was ready to sell his favorite
office, the jewel of his collection, he became a trifle sentimental. He
went out of his way to find a good home for his beloved Picardie
office and sold it to a Monsieur Picart, for "one thousand écus less
than he had been offered elsewhere" because he was convinced Picart
would handle it well. Whether this means that Olivier's professional

pride required someone who would squeeze "his" taxpayers according-
ing to all the rules of the art or whether he wished to find someone
who would go easy on them must be left to the reader's imagination.

When Olivier, Monsieur d'Ormesson, had divested himself, albeit
reluctantly, of his financial offices and of his political concerns, he
retired to his country estate to try, for the first time, to be "a private
man." But as his son informs us, he found he could not stand the life,
because he was *non lettré*—without culture. At last, in his fifties, Monsieur d'Ormesson, who had survived so many calamities, faced the
absolute limit, beyond which money would not carry him. Deprived
of an education in classical culture at an early age, he was not able to
live the life of the gentry in the full sense. In the circles in which
Morvillier had moved, Olivier remained an outcast, a mere
financier—a *bonhomme*, as Henri IV was to call him, with some affection, perhaps, but with a definite and clearly understood condescen-
sion such as would never have been the lot of an *homme lettré*, even
were he penniless.

Olivier no doubt understood this very well. He gave up on the
country life; but intent on giving his children, at least, the chance of
full membership in the world of the gentry, he deployed every reserve of connection and power at his disposal to obtain, for the first
time in his life, a respectable judicial office rather than a financial one.
This was not easy. He was not sure that he would be accepted. Fortunately, after some delicate sounding-out of *messieurs de la chambre des
comptes*, he was given permission to buy the office he coveted, a
presidency in that distinguished assembly, for which he paid forty
thousand livres in 1579. The days of open wheeling and dealing were
over. He had now become Monsieur le Président d'Ormesson. His
dress, his manner of living, his investments must now all be of a
conservative kind, appropriate to his new station in life. The nouveau
riche financier had joined the ranks of the old families, if not quite
fully and really in person, at least potentially, through his children's
prospects. To insure his children's entrance into the highest ranks of
the gentry—this was the task Olivier settled down to for the last
twenty years of his life.

Of the seven boys and eight girls his wife had borne him, only three
sons were to survive the old man. It was their future he was working
for. They were sent to the best schools; seigneuries were settled on
them, and one of the boys, at least, made a formidable marriage: to an
Hennequin! But even so, it was a very close thing altogether, as
André is candid enough to admit.

The old man had to navigate through the treacherous years of the League without becoming compromised. In 1588, during the violent commotions of the Guise bid for power, when the Paris mobs were murdering magistrates thought to have royalist sympathies, while many of the *parlementaires* left town to stay at the king's side, Olivier played a cool game by letting it be known that he was too ill to leave his bed. He was not too deeply compromised with the League in this way, since he participated in none of its affairs; nor did he declare his loyalty to the crown openly by leaving Paris in the wake of his colleagues, whose houses, servants, relatives, and precious libraries were endangered by their departures.

Olivier paid one thousand écus of protection money, "to avoid worse and avoid being labeled a *politique*" in 1589. But by 1593, when the wind was shifting, he was frequenting "those who were called *politiques*." During the entire period of troubles, from 1589 to 1594, Olivier stayed in Paris but managed to fix it so that the warring bands of thugs and soldiery left his estate at Ormesson unharmed: "for he had good friends on the king's side and others on the side of the League."

Having survived the worst years, the family prospects, with the return to normality, had to be cultivated in new ways. Olivier spared neither effort nor money. Until his dying day he never lost sight of the essential: his offices must be transmitted to his sons, and this could be secured only with the highest kind of backing. Money alone could not achieve this aim. Each time the Treasury blackmailed him into paying special fees to insure the "survivance" of his offices, he complied. But he knew perfectly well that the crown's promises were not worth the paper they were written on—even when the paper had cost him ten thousand livres. At his death, the only question would be whether his sons were well enough connected to resist the crown's rapacity. With this end in view, and having already married off one son to an Hennequin girl, Olivier shored up his defenses by offering lavish entertainments at his house on the rue Beaubourg. Even the king came sometimes, ready to say the good word so eagerly awaited from his lips. "Without le président d'Ormesson, there would be no fun in Paris. He is the father of youth." This nice compliment is said to have been made by Henri IV on the occasion of one of the many parties—*compaignies*—given at the Ormesson house during the last winters of Olivier's life. One can imagine the old man hearing of the king's gracious jest with tears in his eyes. That is what he was working for. He no longer had the strength to participate in the revels he had paid for. He probably did not enjoy that sort of thing anyway. We see him, as his son remembers it, retiring to his bedroom as soon as the last guests have been greeted. But how he must have cherished the king's words. He must have gone to sleep, wrapped in his furs, repeating to himself, gratefully: "Sans le président d'Ormesson, on ne se resjouirait pas à Paris!" Was Olivier, at last, once again "known and loved"?

Just barely enough known and loved. On 26 May 1600, riding back from Ormesson, the old man fell from his mule. He was hurt. After being brought back to his house, he died in his bed. The funeral cost six thousand livres. Le président d'Ormesson died on Saturday. Monday morning his son took his seat in the *chambre des comptes*. To those in the King's Council who tried to prevent the inheritance of the office—to declare it vacant and sell it, once again, to the highest bidder—Henri is said to have replied, simply, "I was fond of *le bonhomme*." The *bonhomme* had won after all. His son André is candid about it:

> It was a great grace God showed us in the conservation of this office. Had we lost it, my brother d'Eaubonne would have been all right, in view of his very advantageous marriage [to Mademoiselle Hennequin]; but my brother Lezeau and I would have had only lawsuits and claims as our inheritance. We would never have had the means to acquire offices and to push ahead and advance ourselves in the world as we have done since.

The lesson to be drawn from the anxiety of the Lefevre d'Ormessons is that even a very large estate is insecure if the family is not fully accepted by and bound to the gentry. Old Olivier Lefevre, according to his own estimate, was worth over three hundred thousand livres. He owned three seigneuries, a house in Paris, and five expensive offices: those of *président* in the *chambre des comptes* (for which he had paid forty thousand livres some twenty years earlier), *secrétaire des finances, maistre des requestes, conseiller,* and *commissaire aux requestes du palais.* While much of his estate was tied up in lands and offices, the remainder, some ninety thousand livres, was in the form of *rentes,* debts due, furniture, and cash. André, in 1615, guesses that the value of his father's estate would by then have doubled because of inflation, especially in the value of offices. This was a very considerable fortune indeed. To be rich, in Lefevre's day, meant being worth about one hundred thousand livres.[20] Le Président d'Ormesson was very rich. But he had more trouble getting his sons established than might some

présidial judge worth one-fourth of his estate—but lettered. The inescapable conclusion is that it takes enormous wealth to overcome the
handicap of lacking letters. We shall find ourselves moving, I suspect,
toward a definition of social class in which income plays a secondary
part.

It is often the wealth of the gentry which most offends its opponents.
Naturally enough—because money is usually the first, the easiest,
means of usurpation. But, more important, it is because "money is
considered vile."[21] Vile, that is, in contrast to noble. As such, money
presents the choicest target for the polemics against the bourgeois
gentilshommes. From the fact that they are rich it is easy to jump to the
conclusion that they are nothing but rich, that they have nothing else
to recommend them—no grace, no savoir-faire, no culture. And further, is it not unchristian to be rich? To the nobility, the simple merchant is surely vile, but at worst he can be accused only of being a
parasite, of buying cheap and selling dear. It is the man who rises
above *marchandise*, to become the moneylender, the *rentier*, the financier, who is the worst public enemy. He is a thief on a grand scale:
"While ordinary thieves, who content themselves with robbing individuals, are hanged, those who rob the king and the public live at
ease, reveling among all the delights" their stolen money can buy.
They exact "usury and presents" and "make free with His Majesty's
funds, having become full partners in sovereignty."[22] For how does
one become wealthy except at the expense of the public? Usury and
corrupt practices are the source of the new wealth of the "vultures,"
of the "crocodiles" who graze and devour the fruits of the land like a
plague of locusts. Quickly made fortunes inspire reservations even
among the most devout adherents of the gentry's own canons.
Typical in this respect are the obituary notices privately recorded in
the *livre de raison* of maistre Nicole Versoris, a Parisian lawyer. From
his vantage point on the lower rungs of the gentry world, maistre
Versoris is awed by the death of each of the demigods. A hush seems
to settle around him as he records the death of a Budé. The execution
of Semblançay—formerly Jacques de Beaune, the perfect type of the
financier—fills Versoris with sympathetic sorrow. "In my time," he
comments, "I have seen him respected almost like a king of France."
But even Versoris cannot conceal a slight uneasiness at the profits
accumulated by *trésoriers* and their ilk. He is a religious man. On the
death of a *trésorier* who was said to hold nine or ten thousand livres in
ecclesiastical income, Versoris emits the pious wish: "May God allow

that this is not too much!" And he waxes philosophical on the occasion of another rich *trésorier*'s death: great wealth—and now, overnight, nothing.[23]

It is money which allows the bourgeois to rise above his station. But
he does not join the gentry until he is able to claim at last that his
status does not depend on his wealth. That is the secret of the new
class. Office and land do have their intrinsic charms. But they are
desired so passionately because they will justify the family's new
status as wealth alone cannot. Wealth that is unconnected with inherited lands and titles must be buried in haste.

The gentry had not always been so anxious to cut its ties to *marchandise*. There is something new about the pressure felt in the sixteenth century by wealthy merchants who wished to live nobly.
These merchants and bourgeois had been mayors and aldermen since
the fourteenth century. Many had even been technically ennobled a
long time ago. Some had been ennobled, automatically, as aldermen or
mayors—perhaps not a very serious kind of nobility, but it could have
been a *commencement de noblesse* had they begun to live nobly. Others
had actually been ennobled by letters patent as early as the fourteenth
century, when living nobly was not a requirement and when class
lines were so flexible that one could cross them, back and forth, with
impunity. But since they did not follow up their advantage, nobility
must not have meant much to them. They went on buying and selling. It is only in the sixteenth century that these very same families
suddenly take nobility seriously and embrace the familiar *cursus honorum*.[24] Until that time there had been no national opportunities to
tempt the municipal oligarchs. It was only when the crown began to
raise taxes in earnest that their horizons rose slowly beyond the walls
of their good towns. The *familles* of Rouen, Lyon, Bordeaux, Tours,
the *ricots* of Issoire and Saint-Flour, the *sires* and *sages maistres* of
Poitou, the *maistres des forges* of the Rouergue and of Burgundy, prepared to exploit the kingdom.

7

Schools

To serve the king, for honor and for profit, one needed talents and resources which were not fundamentally different from those perfected in the city halls: capital, of course, and family alliances, but also the ability to *write*. "He who knows how to write can go far," we are told. "Long live the magnificent pen"—and its honorable adjuncts, paper and parchment.[1] To write, in this sense, means to write contracts and other business and administrative papers. It was the kind of writing young Olivier Lefevre learned in a *procureur's* office and went on to perfect in the service of a treasurer. Such skills had been indispensable for a long time among the leading families of every town in the kingdom. Perhaps more was required now, when ambitions rose beyond the *consulat* and the *échevinage*. To move on to the *bailliage* and *présidial* courts, to look beyond to the dizzying attractions of *parlements* and *chambres des comptes*, to consider the vertiginous profits to be realized in the royal financial bureaus, in the treasurers' offices, at court, at war—all this was possible, but it required something more than the notary's skill and the savoir-faire of the local bourgeoisie.

Beyond the walls of the cities where they reigned supreme—secure in the possession of real estate, assured of their precedence in banquets and processions, owning the land as far as the eye could see, basking in the rich smells of dried fish, wine, and wool gloriously filling their houses—beyond this small world where they were known and feared, these men, alas, were mere bourgeois, tongue-tied in the presence of Latinizing prelates, awkward in the sight of arrogant noblemen. To overcome these debilities, the notable bourgeoisies of the good towns devised the "means of arriving" (le moyen de parvenir) chronicled in this book. The process was set in motion on a small scale in earlier times, where we can perceive it only dimly, through occasional scraps of evidence. In the sixteenth century, it becomes a well-publicized campaign of very large dimensions. Its motor, constructed almost from scratch and with great ingenuity, was the scientia, the formal learning of the humanist schools which were founded, endowed, administered, and staffed by the notable bourgeoisie. Fueled by an enthusiasm of almost obsessive quality, these schools were to accomplish what wealth alone could not: they were to teach the bourgeois to live nobly.

Rich merchants had always had the opportunity to rise in the world, but they did so only at the cost of immolating their most cherished beliefs, their virtues, and their possessions on the altar of their ambitions.[2] But all this was "when the times were still dark." Now light was to come, with the advent of "good letters."

The celebration of letters must be understood not merely as an intellectual fashion but also as a profound cultural revolution. The king, as "Protector of Letters," was also protector of the status of the high bourgeoisie. The Renaissance in France was the creation of this class and its passport to honors.

We are surprised by the intensity of the feeling concerning letters. The praise given to books and writing is like the blind love of a father for his favorite son: "We could not live without letters," explains the principal of Amiens Collège, with pedantic passion. "It would be easier to count the grains of sand in the deserts of Arabia and the waves of the Ionic Sea than to explain the advantages which proceed from writing."[3] Rabelais's Gargantuan appetite for books is by no means exceptional: it is just one joyous echo of the general hunger for learning, the indulgent craving for books, which manifests itself wherever the bourgeoisie is turning into a gentry in sixteenth-century France. We can hear the same tone in the pleasant Discours published in Poitiers in 1557: "I love nothing so much as books, a great many books, and I read all of them within my power ... and I beg everyone to write more of them." The author addresses himself to various kinds of people and exhorts them, in turn, to write books:

"The merchant who does not write down everything he observes in the way of importance in his profession, the price of goods according to the season, the fair, the region—let him be excommunicated if he fails to write it all down." Parish priests are invited not only to keep registers of births and deaths but also to write down everything which concerns the families, the households, the condition of their parishioners, and the size and wealth of their parish. If he had his way, the author of this *Discours* would see to it that there was "no region, no town, no village, no hamlet, no church, no castle, no house, no family, no mountain or hill, no land, no spring, no meadow, woods, or vineyard lacking its own book—or at least its own chapter in a larger book." "Go to it, my friends," he exhorts all around him, "go to it and write books, many books . . . . If they are not all printed, . . . they will be written down at least, and kept in chests in public places."[4]

Such good-natured exhortations were not mere rhetoric. Wherever the gentry met, in learned *rencontres,* the talk was of books and good letters in general. From the early hours of the morning to the end of the day, they had pen in hand and were scribbling verses, correcting them, going over their children's and grandchildren's lessons. They were never far away from their cherished books, those serried ranks of splendidly bound volumes, lovingly cared for, kept in sumptuous bookcases, under lock and key, in the inner sanctum of the household, the private study that had replaced the private chapel in the *hôtels* of the gentry. Books were their lares and penates, reading- and writing-stands their altars. In the privacy of these comfortable chambers, they could revere their ancestors, the Ancients, and take comfort in the writings of their masters, the great jurists of their youth. They had earned these joys, earned them largely. Was there a town in the kingdom which did not owe its schools to the diligence and the generosity of these men? They founded schools instead of chapels, they endowed professorial chairs instead of perpetual masses.

Despite the scarcity of documents, we see a new kind of school being founded at an astounding rate, according to a definite pattern. Often, at first, the visible decadence of the medieval cathedral schools is accompanied by open hostility or sabotage against these archaic establishments which could at best be inefficient vocational schools for would-be parish priests. Then, the municipal authorities (led by a few rich and notable citizens) take control of schooling. Money is offered by leading citizens and by the city council, and buildings are found or built. The city council publishes detailed regulations for the governance of the new schools; specifies the curriculum, the tuition fees, if any, and the salaries of the masters; allows expenses for the hiring of new teachers, seeks candidates out as far as necessary, and judges their merits in open competition. All this in the sacred name of learning and good letters, and no expense spared.

The examples abound. The Rouen pattern is classic: decay of the cathedral schools, vigorous intentions of *messieurs de la ville*, who talk of creating four grammar schools in 1518; an endowment of six thousand livres by a *conseiller* in the *parlement*; the *parlement*'s trustee-ship of the new schools, in cooperation with the Hôtel de Ville. One of the leaders of the Rouen *parlement*, le président Feu, explains the policy: "The children who will attend these schools will have the opportunity of great achievements. Let us remember Bartholus [a famous jurist] and other great personages who reached great perfection from a small beginning." The schools, it is clear, will allow the cultivation of talents hidden among the humblest boys, and all this cannot but be "to the great profit of the Christian republic."[5] The Rouen *parlement*'s vigilance for good learning extended to the remaining schools of the diocese. Dissatisfied with the education dispensed at the diocesan Collège des Bons Enfants, it ordered the principal fired and set out to recruit a new man who would be capable of "instructing the children in virtue [*bonnes moeurs*], letters, and erudition." Such a man was found in Jean Aubery, *advocat* at the *parlement*, a man "deeply versed in Greek and Latin letters."[6] The utility of learning is such that even the children of the poor—including orphans and waifs, both boys and girls, from the age of five up—are ordered, by municipal regulation, to be assembled in a place "where they shall be instructed in morality [*bonne vie*] and taught to read and write."[7] This social legislation of 1543 already had a long ancestry in the Rouen city council. As early as 1405 it had granted tax exemption to Perrette Alorge, who belonged to one of the city's notable families, for her activities as a teacher.[8] This same city council had, on occasion, pushed its respect for learning so far as to provide grants-in-aid to scholars in need: to maistre Escombart in 1454 and to Dimitrius Bichardus and Thomas Partos of Constantinople in 1456.[9]

The situation is similar in Bordeaux. Here the city council creates a new *collège* in 1533, provides twelve hundred livres a year for its operation, and buys a house with sufficient room in it to allow a considerable number of students to live in with the teaching staff. The motives of such generosity are said to be the desire "to augment the welfare, the profit, the honor, and the convenience of the city." It is for this reason, say the aldermen, that they have reached the decision "to found and endow a *collège* similar in form and manner to the *collèges* of Paris."[10] In Bordeaux, as in Rouen, the *collège* is guided from the start by the initiative of a *parlementaire*.[11]

In Lyon, the city council, hoping at first to satisfy the new educational needs at moderate expense, contracts with a religious *confrérie*, which already has a school for the children of its members, to provide schooling to all inhabitants who desire it. For this the city grants 400 livres a year. But this turned out to be a poor solution, and so, by 1527, the city council took on the running of the *collège*, spent 580 livres on building costs, and hired a well-known scholar, Guillaume Durand, as principal. He was followed by a learned physician from Paris at 100 livres a year in salary.[12]

The feverish foundation of *collèges* was not limited to great commercial centers, but can be observed in towns of almost any size. In Albi a municipal grammar school of some kind had existed, at least in fits and starts, since 1403. It had been installed in 1411 in a house rented from a rich notary at 4 livres 10 sols yearly and staffed by at least one master at 20 livres. Here, as in Rouen, the city council had occasionally provided grants for study in Paris, presumably in recognition of the insufficience of local schools. Here, too, schooling was provided essentially free of tuition for the inhabitants, although at the secondary level modest fees were levied. In 1543 the city council at last resolved to found a full-scale *collège*, to be operated according to its detailed regulations. Sufficient funds were made available to pay several instructors, to seek out a professor of Greek in Paris, and to make all classes freely available to the inhabitants.[13]

In Aurillac the conflict between the city council and the abbé over the right of appointment of teachers comes to a head in 1503 and is settled, by compromise, in 1530 in the usual manner—a kind of small-scale concordat on the model of the crown's treaty with the papacy. That is, the city presents the candidates, the abbé approves them. Together with the members of the city council, the royal *officiers* in the *présidial* court take a very direct interest in the running of the schools. And, as often happens, the actual impulse for the foundation of the new *collège* comes from a large endowment provided by one of the city's *familles*. In this city the widow of Ferrando de Villeneuve endows the future *collège* with one-half of her earthly goods in her will of 1548. The capital, mostly in the form of *rentes*, requires capable trusteeship. The executors are relatives who are also notable municipal or royal *officiers* and, at the same time, bourgeois or former bourgeois and lawyers. Jean de Veyre, seigneur de Claux, was qualified as bourgeois in a contract of 1565, but he was also given the status of prior of Ginoilhac and was provided with *lettres de noblesse* in 1581. The other executor, Pierre de Combes, was a tax collector who belonged to a consular family. The staffing of the Aurillac *collège* reflects the intellectual and social tastes of the notable councillors and *officiers:* in a contract dated 1601, the principal, maistre Hervo, *licensié ès droits*, of Paris, promises to teach "the fear of God, morality, and other humane letters."[14]

In Auxerre we find, once again, the familiar decline of the cathedral school and a great endowment in 1535 by one of the *familles*, the Charmoys. Here the enthusiasm was so infectious that another *famille*, the Delaportes, *conseillers* at the *bailliage*, proposed to found a second and perhaps rival *collège*. In Sens it was the Hodoart family (*advocats, procureurs du roy, conseillers du roy*) which founded the *collège* in 1537 by contract with the city council. They provide a house, 57 livres in yearly *rentes*, and grain and wine in addition. The contract provides that there shall be four masters; that a business manager chosen by two canons, the lieutenant general of the *bailliage*, the *advocat*, the *procureur du roy*, and the mayor shall be responsible for the financial affairs of the *collège;* and that the city council shall act as full trustees of the institution, responsible for hiring, firing, discipline, curriculum, and so on.[15] The same story, with minor variations, can be told for neighboring cities and small towns like Avallon, Joigny, Tonnerre, Chablis, and Villeneuve-le-Roi.[16]

There is no region of the kingdom exempt from the pattern. The municipal deliberations of the sixteenth century can be used to chart the spread of the *collèges*. Even where, on the surface, there appears a variation—the preponderant role of a zealous and cultivated bishop, for example—it turns out, on closer examination, that despite all the honors due to the influential prelate, it is still, in reality, the city council and the *familles* it represents which are truly responsible. One example is Auch, a small fortified hill town in the southwest, containing about two thousand residents, six hundred houses within the walls, and a surfeit of priests.[17] The seat of an archdiocesan administration whose income is estimated at seventy-five thousand livres in 1594, the town is dominated by the imposing structures of the archbishop's palace and the canons' cloister. The leadership for the establishment of the *collège*, naturally enough, appears to come from the archbishop, the cardinal de Tournon—and the initial endowment from the will of his predecessor and relative. But the money and the leadership provided by the cardinal archbishop turn out to be rather theoretical: by 1550, an endowment totaling perhaps at most three thousand livres in capital, part of which had to be borrowed from a banker. (Thirty years after its foundation, the annual income of the *collège* was to approach two thousand livres.) Needless to say, the archbishop's donation did not go far. It was the city council which purchased a house and proudly had the city's coat of arms engraved over the entrance; the archbishop sued to have it replaced by his own, but he lost his cause. The choice of principal and instructors was also in the hands of the city councillors. It was a burdensome duty. Again and again we find the council occupied, in its deliberations, with the urgent needs of the *collège.* On 27 September 1558 "the chief business of the council concerns the *collège:* we are on the eve of Saint Rémy," the secretary notes sadly, and there is no principal. The council wishes to hire a Monsieur Chemin, the absentee bishop's agent refuses to approve the appointment, and the council goes ahead and offers the contract to Chemin anyway, for four years.[18] These principals, in Auch as elsewhere, despite the objections of the church, are frequently lawyers, almost always secular men, and often married.[19]

As one follows the birthpangs of the municipal *collèges,* one is struck by the ubiquitous conflict between the clerical administrations and the city councils. Everywhere the diocesan authority, usually represented by the cathedral chapter, opposes the creation of secular schools. It is, first, a question of old corporate privileges and monopolies which the canons wish to protect. But it is also a question of money. The city, as it takes over the onerous burden of providing free public education, finds it natural to ask for the cathedral chapter's material contribution—especially since the canons' incomes, the fat prebends, the rent rolls of abbeys and priories, the endowments and buildings of old hospitals, poorhouses, and lepers' shelters fill the coffers of the clerical hierarchies and often support the extravagances of high-living courtiers, of absentee clerical lords, who are abbots or bishops in name only. The cities' complaints, by mid-century, have become almost ritual. They do, in fact, lead to one specific reform, that ordered by royal edict in 1560: an endowment equivalent to one canon's living is to be applied, in each diocese, to the needs of the schools.[20] Everywhere, however, the canons resist the application of the edict, everywhere they are taken to court at great expense, and often many years go by before the funds are actually forthcoming.

In the town of Saintes, for instance, the clergy recognizes the need for public education in 1560 and agrees that funds must be provided for this purpose, "so that the youth shall be better instructed in letters and so that employers should have access to more capable workers." The money should come, say the clergy's representatives, from the secular taxes, but the church should control the choice of masters.[21] The city council says, on the contrary, that the city should have control of public education and that the canons should comply with the edict and provide at least part of the necessary funds. Usually the city fathers are carried along by their enthusiasm for learning and start taking charge while the canons procrastinate and refuse payment. In Saintes the *collège* is started in inadequate buildings and the masters are hired by the city but paid inadequately. They threaten to quit.[22] At last, in 1583, twenty-three years after the royal edict, the city obtains a judgment against the chapter from the Bordeaux *parlement.* Things begin to look up: two new masters are hired. But the city is still unable to provide the two hundred livres promised as salary and is forced to solicit funds door-to-door and to beg the citizens for discarded furniture to set up the teachers' households. In November 1583, the city at last is able to buy a decent house, from the apothecary Vivet, for four hundred écus, and the old schoolhouse is sold at auction.[23] But there the school's troubles do not end. The new principal is constantly under attack by the chapter: he is sued, he is subjected to libel, he is physically threatened by the priests.[24]

This struggle for control of the schools between the municipal and the clerical authorities accompanies the creation of the *collèges* everywhere, and more than money is involved. When the financial problems are solved by a generous grant from one or more of the local notables (in Saintes it is the Guitard family, of the *présidial,* which makes the chief contribution),[25] the struggle continues, probably because of ideological differences. While the city councils look forward to "great achievements" which will "profit the Christian republic," the church is suspicious in the extreme of the "profit" to be found in the new *collèges.* While city councils proudly proclaim the foundation of schools "in favor of the public good and so that everyone will be free to acquire learning,"[26] the church fears the spread of heresy and libertinism as the inevitable outcome of schools over which it has no control and which are in the hands of wandering professional instructors who not only teach the Roman authors, in unexpurgated editions, but also teach Greek—and are notoriously vice-laden besides.

There is no denying that these fears were justified. As we shall see, the instructors favored by the municipal elites were, typically, classicists in the Erasmian mold and even, quite often, men with Protestant leanings. But let us not fall into the trap of seeing the conflict as one opposing Catholic to Protestant. The issue was both deeper and more complex. The time would come, at the turn of the century, when *collège* after *collège* was taken over by the Jesuits. The gentry of *bailliage* and *présidial*, the *familles* of the *consulat* and *échevinage*, and the wealthy and learned magistrates whose endowments had created the *collèges* were none of them favorably disposed to the Jesuits. They nevertheless handed over the direction of the schools to the Jesuits, often with great reluctance but satisfied that the curriculum was to remain the same, as we shall see.[27] That was the essential matter: not the regrettable emphasis on one shade of Christian doctrine or another, but the continuance of the great enterprise of teaching "good letters."

In this sense it may be wrong to speak of serious opposition to the aims of the gentry. The canons who refused funds and challenged the cities' right to appoint principals and instructors were mostly defending their income and their privileges rather than opposing the new education. After all, these clerics were often the brothers, uncles, and cousins of *messieurs de la ville* and *messieurs du présidial*.[28] As long as the new learning did not lead to outright heresy, there was no serious opposition to it from any quarter; at worst there was only indifference or lack of understanding. That the nobility on the whole had little interest in the *collèges* is quite likely. We do not usually encounter noblemen in the role of benefactors. Nor do we usually find the children of noble families sitting on the benches of the *collèges*. We do, as a matter of fact, find evidence here and there of an outspoken fear of Latin learning among the nobility. Occasionally, however, we hear the bitter voice of the *gentilhomme* bemoaning the lack of education among his own kind.

Obviously, the new *collèges* of the sixteenth century are the creation of a particular class of people. But does this necessarily imply a class bias in the running of these schools? Were they meant, as Imbart de la Tour once suggested, to exclude the lower bourgeoisie, the artisans, the *laboureurs*? Were these schools designed as factories for turning out *officiers*, as vocational training schools whose chief aim was to perpetuate the gentry monopoly over justice, finance, and government in general—to say nothing of the gentry's imposing share of clerical benefices?[29]

It is true that everywhere one has the impression that all the money and energy is channeled, as Imbart de la Tour points out, toward the secondary schools, the *collèges*, the *grandes écoles*, or grammar schools, "which represented classical culture."[30] It is true that these *collèges* were meant chiefly as a preparation for higher learning, for the study of law or medicine at the universities. It is true that much Latin was spoken in these schools. But is it true that the common people did not frequent these schools, that the *familles* meant to exclude the lesser sort from those schools which were so largely their own?[31]

What we should like to understand is the spirit in which the gentry celebrated the benefits of "good letters." Did the gentry sincerely believe that education is good for everybody? Or was the praise of letters a grandiose pose masking the selfish and purely practical needs of a social class? I doubt that the question can be resolved, especially in the absence of a more systematic treatment of the history of education in France.[32] An investigation into such matters as primary schooling might modify Imbart de la Tour's generalizations. If there had been a total absence or a noticeable neglect of primary schooling, then one might see the *collèges* as forbidding institutions completely out of the reach of the average baker's or tanner's child. But there were primary schools available to all classes. Wherever probes have been made in the archives of the smallest towns and villages, the results have been surprising. In Provence the archivist of the department of the Var, Mireur, read through the municipal records of some thirty rural communes, taken at random. He found very few to have been absolutely without schools. He found schools in the sixteenth century administered and paid for by local elected officials almost everywhere, including such insignificant *bourgs* as Aups, Besse, Bormes, Callas, Châteaudouble, Claviers, Correns, La Garde-Freinet, Le Luc, Mons, Montmeyan, Rougiers, Saint-Zacharie, Seillans, Nans, and Pierrefeu—to say nothing of very small towns such as Draguignan or Saint-Tropez. These schools taught reading and writing to boys—more rarely to girls as well. They were most often tuition-free ("les enffans non pagaren ren" in Saint-Tropez in 1585). There are indications that many did teach Latin and did prepare students for entrance to higher schooling in the *collèges*. Evidence can be deduced, for example, from a competition between two teachers in the village of Claviers, near Draguignan. Broc and Babellon wanted the same teaching post. The children's parents petitioned the city council for arbitration. As a result, an inspector or consultant was brought in from the neighboring village of Bargueron, and this man, maistre Guiche, a physician, pronounced Babellon fit after examining him on his competence in Latin. The fact that it was customary in these small towns to hire the instructors by competition, as was done for the staffing of the *collèges* in the larger towns, also suggests that more than reading and writing was demanded. The city brought in candidates for these positions from out of town, paid their expenses while they demonstrated their ability, paid their salaries, and administered the schools. Occasionally we discover that the instructor is a lawyer by profession, hence has an advanced degree.[33]

In an entirely different part of the kingdom, in the small town of Tonnerre, Quantin found that formal schooling was a normal pursuit for boys, and even girls, and that the surrounding villages had schools too.[34] The same kind of evidence can be found in Normandy and elsewhere. No matter how small the town is, in the sixteenth century the desire for education is so powerful, and the initiative of the leading citizens is so effective, that schools are founded.

Certainly these schools were not all equally effective. Consider the moving ceremony we can witness in the year 1574 in the small town of Montmarand: in front of us is *honneste dame* Catherine Auvergnat, widow of *honorable homme* Simon Malley. She is meeting with the city councillors, in front of a notary, for the purpose of founding a *collège*. For this purpose she gives the city full property rights over her house—"the house of the Three Kings—together with its dependances, high and low rooms, attic, walls, garden." In addition she endows the future *collège* with *rentes* representing a capital of four hundred livres for the salary of a principal to be chosen by the councillors. Among the conditions she specifies is that the poor children of the town will pay no tuition and that the children of the Auvergnat family will be perpetually exempt from tuition fees. As for the children who can afford to pay, they shall pay twenty deniers monthly—a modest sum. The councillors accept the gift and the conditions. The notary observes, as he must, that "the said [*dame*] Auvergnat declares *she is not capable of signing her name*"—and two of the four councillors are illiterate as well.[35] Most likely this school will not be up to the standards of a larger town, if only because the salary of thirty livres a year is not enough to attract first-rate masters and also because of the absence of a cultured group of notables who could guide the school's destiny and help it out with gifts when necessary.[36] But it was almost certainly sufficient to provide the elements of an education as a prerequisite to attending a full-fledged classical school in some other town.

Naturally, sending a son away to school is not within the means of the poor. But the sons of the richer artisans and *laboureurs* as well as the sons of small-town merchants can go off to school: we find provisions made for their education in the archives of every province.[37] Even those parents who cannot themselves bear the burden of paying for their childrens' schooling have the option of sending them as apprentices to a master artisan or merchant who will contract not only to care for the child and teach him his craft but also to have him instructed in reading and writing. Such contracts, *baux d'apprentissage* or *baux à nourriture,* fill the archives of every town. These contracts include detailed stipulations that the children "be sent to school and taught their faith, to read, to write, during five years." The length of studies stipulated varies from one to six years among artisan or shop-keeper families. It can be longer, as it was for Catherine, daughter of a tax collector, who was placed with a small-town lawyer's family for eight years to attend school.[38]

A third line of defense against illiteracy was provided by free-lance writing masters and all sorts of teachers who set up shop in their homes without license. We usually know about them only through the fulminations of the authorities. Repeatedly the official schoolmas-ter or principal asks the city council to enjoin his private competitors from practicing their profession. This undercover teaching is clearly a permanent feature of French society. Sometimes the free-lance writ-ing master opens up shop with official permission, as did le sieur Duprat, of Bordeaux, who arrives in Saintes in March 1584, "having learned that there was in Saintes no master for showing the youth how to write all sorts of letters and to teach them to count and to add up figures in writing, to read in the French language," and so on. For this reason, he explains, "he has the desire to stop here" and wishes "to set up a shop and hold school" and desires a license from the city granting him exclusive rights.[39] The spread of free public schools in the course of the sixteenth century must have made life difficult for the free-lance writing masters. We find one of them, Voullayre, in a Provençal village in 1614, so badly in debt to a local merchant that he finds himself faced with one of those usurious contracts usually de-signed to ruin peasants: Voullayre, the *maistre-escrivain,* acknowl-edges that he owes the equivalent of twenty-five livres to the mer-chant Goyran, "which he declares having received both in the form of cloth and in money lent." To pay off his obligation, the writing-master undertakes to teach the merchant's son to write and figure.[40]

More dangerous competitors can be found at all levels of education. In Saintes the principal of the city schools complains to the council: "There are several schools which entirely spoil the *grande escholle* [that is, the municipal grammar school]. The children who attend these other schools, such as the one run by maistre Jehan Le Chantre, ordi-narily walk to the château and throw stones and other things against the house of the *grande escholle.*" The council duly prohibits maistre Jehan "and all others from holding any exercises for the indoctrina-tion of children; and there shall be only the *grande escholle.*"[41] In the small Norman town of Eu there are similar complaints from the principal of the *collège* against Christophe de la Fosse, who runs some sort of free school, "it being certain that the schoolboys left the *collège* on the slightest pretext to go to the said sieur de la Fosse, where they had more freedom."[42] Such competition from free, or underground, or free-lance schoolmasters continued to accompany the *collèges* in France even under the firm and systematic administration of the Jesuits, whose complaints can be heard throughout the seventeenth century: "A number of persons without proper titles or degrees receive at their houses schoolboys of all classes and seem to want to tell our teachers their business."[43]

In sum, then, there were several ways of acquiring an elementary education in the sixteenth century, not only in the major cities, not only in towns, but even in small villages, as long as they were not too remote.[44] No class of the population, especially within the walls of the towns, was denied access to elementary schooling. For this reason, the Latin grammar schools, the *collèges,* which were the pride of the gentry, were not really closed to the lower classes. Bright and industrious boys, given a few years of schooling, could easily find their place in the *collèges.* What is more, most of the *collèges* I know about made special provisions for beginners, small children who could not read—*abécédaires,* as they were called. A special master would be assigned to them to teach them their ABC's.

Still, there is no denying that the children of the gentry had enormous advantages. Even if not every one of them was equipped with a private Latin tutor and all the other advantages described by Montaigne, they were, of course, prodded constantly, surrounded by books and learning, and every day helped by relatives with their homework. They knew that their studies would be rewarded with desirable positions purchased for them by their families. On the other hand, one should not forget that the *conseillers* and *présidents,* the *advocats* and *trésoriers,* who found it so easy to "push their sons in the world," were themselves the sons and grandsons of merchants and sometimes artisans and *laboureurs*—and they, after all, had "arrived"! It may well be that poverty itself is not negligible as a spur to greater efforts. This is the amusing thesis of a play called *The Schoolboys,* written by a *collège* principal, in which the poor boy gets the better of a rich bourgeois boy. Whereas the rich boy already has his father's promise of a priory and sees no need to work hard, the poor boy is pushed along by "the love of letters and the love of time, which, once lost, cannot be recuperated." He much prefers "to follow his studies, which, in the midst of a thousand evils, will make our labors easier to endure." He wishes "to escape from the filth in which the sordid

populace and the ignorant lie defeated." While the rich boy finds time
for all sorts of amusements, the tough hero is able to postpone his
pleasures: "Adieu chanson, adieu sornette," he says to himself—
goodbye to all that. "Adieu Babille, adieu Grassette"—he does not
even have time for girls. Instead, he wants "of learning to have entire
knowledge" and invests all his efforts in "reading, the support of
future life."[45]

Granted that tuition at the *collèges* was almost universally free or
nominal, especially for those who could not afford to pay,[46] and
granted that elementary schooling was freely available, it remains
true that the Latin schools benefited primarily the sons of the well-
to-do. Beginning with the sons of the *familles* who ran the town and
for whom the *collège* was as natural a place as the tanner's workshop
was for his son, we can easily imagine a succession of less and less
wealthy families who have to make greater and greater efforts in
order to send a son to the *collège:* the merchant-bourgeois and the
master artisans may still have found it relatively easy. For the less
prosperous, a Latin education was not so easy to acquire. There was
the expense of books and materials, and, for those who lived too far
from town, the need to place the boy with a relative or even to pay for
his room and board. This last expense could be the most serious
obstacle of all.

The cost of maintaining a boy in school, if he did not live at home,
was beyond the means of simple workingmen or peasants. As an
example, we have the accounts of a student at the Collège d'Auch,
the son of a physician, who boarded with an apothecary, a friend of
the family. The cost of his room and board ran to 9 livres monthly.
Because the apothecary's accounts are very complete, we can see that
Denis, who was ten years old when he started at the *collège*, spent
four years and five months at the apothecary's house and paid total
boarding fees of 477 livres. In addition he spent 123 livres on his
clothing. Schoolbooks and materials seem comparatively inexpensive:
The Works of Cicero, 4 livres, 10 sols (but good forever, unlike modern
textbooks); a *Caesar,* 16 sols; an *Iliad,* 1 livre; a *Seneca,* 12 sols; add 3–6
sols for a sturdy binding and small amounts for paper and ink (a pot
of ink at 1 sol). Bénétrix works all this out to a total cost of 12 to 13
livres a month.[47]

The *collèges* were primarily designed as day schools whose pupils
typically lived at home or, if they came from out of town, lived in a
private boarding house or en famille with a relative or business acquaintance. At most, they ate lunch in the school. Sons of notables,
sons of merchants, lawyers, physicians, master artisans, even the

occasional son of a *laboureur* or vintner could all enter the *collège* as young as seven or even five; or they could join the classes at a later stage, since the progression from class to class was purely a matter of competence.

Once inserted into the gears of this educational factory, they were processed into a fairly standardized product. The question that now concerns us is, To what extent, and how effectively, did the *collèges* inculcate the values of the gentry? We know from exceptional cases of prodigious feats of assimilation—of artisans' sons becoming cardinals and *présidents* through their *collège* experience (d'Ossat or Jeannin). Exceptional cases apart, can it be said that the *collèges* acted not only as social escalators but as agents of a cultural revolution which taught the values of one class to society at large? It is difficult to escape the impression, as one follows the fiscal heroism of one small town after another, that the *collèges* performed an indispensable social function in addition to teaching Latin letters.

The one basic social function performed by the schools was to keep the children off the streets. This is clearly spelled out in some municipal deliberations. A random example comes from the small town of Gray in the Franche-Comté: "The duty of a good and diligent master is not confined to the walls of his room. He must inform himself about the behavior of all the children in his charge, he must arrange for someone to inform him loyally of all the insolences the children perform in the streets, and even at home."[48] From the small town of Lectoure, in Gascony, where the city council in June 1595 agonizes over paying a record salary to maistre Gilles du Quemeneur, *parizien,* who held out for one hundred écus yearly and showed "great contempt for the city's offer": in desperation the city gives in, after consulting *Messieurs* of the *sénéchaussée,* the *"conseillers, avocatz,* and other lettered persons." When Quemeneur promised to teach Greek in addition to Latin, the city could not resist, "it being a great hope for the profit and advantage of the youth which might otherwise fall prey to debauchery."[49]

The children in question are principally the children of bourgeois who are living nobly, but they are also the children of merchants and others who are being prepared to live without working in a workshop or countinghouse, to live off their *rentes,* to become, if they are not already, *nobles hommes.*[50] In the *collège,* the boys are taught to despise not only manual labor and commerce but the idle life of the *gentilshommes* as well. At the same time, a number of new virtues are inculcated in them, and an entire life-style founded on books and learning is revealed to them.[51]

The creation of *collèges* in almost every town of any size gave formal, institutional shape to a social process: the nurturing of a new class in society.[52] Everywhere, the children of the *rentiers* and would-be *rentiers* found themselves separated from the other youth for a period of about ten years. They were separated from work in the usual sense as well as from the normal pleasures and even the normal language of the streets.[53] Above all, their childhood, their dependent status, was painfully prolonged beyond the customary age. As Ariès has suggested, a child was normally considered to have joined the adult world and often had begun to enjoy the privileges of adulthood quite early, somewhere between his seventh and his fourteenth year. He wore adult clothes, and no aspect of adult life, including sexuality, was hidden from him. He could become a husband, a bishop, a king. While all this continued to be true of the popular classes and of the nobility as well, the bourgeoisie *rentière* deliberately withdrew its sons from these traditional maturing processes and sequestered them in the *collèges* up to the age of seventeen or so, only to have them go on, if possible, to the law faculties for several more years. A boy educated for living nobly ceased to be a dependent only around the age of twenty, and, even then, it was only after he had been invested with an office and provided with a suitable bride that he became a complete adult. It was his marriage contract, quite often, that announced his coming-of-age. Such a radical reorientation of habits and goals was not accomplished easily. At every step of the long road to maturity we can find rebellion. But on the whole the system was amazingly successful; it is, after all, still with us, in all its essentials, four centuries later.

It is precisely because we are so accustomed to compulsory and systematic formal education in our day that we have difficulty in appreciating its novelty in the sixteenth century. We tend to take it for granted that children between the ages of approximately six and sixteen will attend school, full time, in a building established for this purpose, where they will be segregated from adult society every day, to be seen and heard only in the evening. But this widespread system of day-long schooling for children caused a striking change in the life of French cities and a profound change, first of all, for the child himself. Instead of being integrated into the adult world as an apprentice, as a clerk, as the master's son, and instead of being surrounded by adults and by children both younger and older than himself, he was suddenly led away to a building he had never entered before and put into a classroom with a large number of other children roughly his own age. From then on, and for years to come—until

adulthood, if his career worked out as it should—he would remain a
member of this group and have little association with any adults
except the single, dreaded, and distant master at the head of the class.
We must imagine the young *abécédaire,* seven years old perhaps, star-
ing for the first time at the forbidding doors of the *collège* some September morning at six o'clock, in time for mass or assembly. The
doors are very much like prison gates: an outer door of oak, with
three large iron locks, and an inner door of pine, with one lock.[54]
Once past the doors, under the watchful eye of the doorman, who
sometimes doubled as the *abécédaires'* master and was, no doubt, an
important personage, the child enters a small lobby. A spiral stone
staircase leads to the principal's apartment and to the classrooms. The
first room at the top of the stairs is a large hall, the *salle de philosophie,*
in which the most advanced students gather but which also doubles
as an assembly hall. It is clean, spacious, and well lit, with four big
windows, two of which look out onto the garden in back; for furniture, a long oak table with benches and a pulpit for the professor.
Further down the hall are the other, smaller classrooms, each
equipped with benches and a pulpit. The first room beyond the
lobby, at street level, is the business manager's room and office; he
lives in, with his wife and children. Next, in the dining room, are five
long tables and benches, buffets that hold dishes, the inevitable pulpit, and a chair in a corner to hold up the pot full of wine. Adjacent to
the dining room are the kitchen and larder (with a large stock of lard,
some salted geese, a ham, five cheeses, candlesticks, a broken-down
harquebus, and two old hats). There is a laundry room further down,
and a storage room, with beds where servants sleep. A cellar below
contains thirty barrels of wine and the supply of grain needed by the
kitchen, which bakes its own bread. In the courtyard are stables and
horses. Altogether, then, a world of its own, in the image of the
richest *hôtels* of the gentry, a house—a household—such as the mayor
or the *procureur du roy* might own. That resemblance is not surprising,
since the *collège* building, in many towns, is just such an imposing
house, willed by one of the city's richest citizens.

Literally, the schoolboys are invited to join the world of the gentry
the moment they cross the threshold of the *collège.* In contrast to the
easygoing life they were used to, they now find themselves propelled
into a universe where order reigns. If they have the misfortune of
being boarders, they are roused at five o'clock sharp, herded into
assembly hall for mass at six, and rushed through breakfast. Then
classes start: two hours, followed by an hour of study hall. Lunch, at
eleven, provides no real break from the discipline, for during the hour

allotted to them in the refectory they remain under the vigilant supervision of the masters, whose duty it is to watch out for *"incivilitez"*
and enforce decorum and propriety both in the conversation and in
the deportment of the children.[55] Often the lunch hour is the occasion
for some serious reading from the pulpit. Promptly at noon they are
marched off to class again. An hour's work is followed by recess, then
reading and homework. At three o'clock another two-hour class begins. Most of the children are allowed to go home at five, after an
eleven-hour day *intra muros,* only to face homework. Meanwhile, the
boarders, who have been up since five, retire to their rooms, where
they recite their lessons with the masters' help. They have dinner at
seven, study hall again at eight, and, at last, bedtime at nine. Fortunately there were Sundays and many holidays: one or two free after-
noons a week were common.[56]

In the sixteenth century everyone worked long hours, but the order, the punctuality, and the regimentation must have struck the
boys as alien and shocking, irreconcilable with their "outside" lives.

This order was perfected further inside the classroom. Let us in-
spect the Bordeaux *collège* in 1583.[57] The beginner, aged seven or less,
is led to the *abécédaire* class, which is the Tenth Form. Clutching his
two textbooks, one an alphabet, the other a small Latin grammar, he
takes his seat in the last rank of benches. When the master enters, he
and his classmates stand up and the lesson begins right away. Taking
a Latin sentence such as *Miserere mei Deus,* the master pronounces
each word, spells it, and pronounces each letter, then each syllable.
He shouts, "m, i: mi"—the pupils repeat it after him. "S, e: se;
mise"—and so on. The pupils take turns repeating after the master the
pronunciations and spellings. Everyone in the first rank—the front-
benchers or most advanced—takes a turn. The pupils in the second
rank follow, hesitantly, aided by the front-benchers, who turn around
and point to troublesome letters with straws as the master pronounces the words. And so it goes, rank after rank. The newcomers,
back in the fifth row, must learn first to recognize the letters of the
alphabet, then to write them down on paper. Their work is handed in
for correction each time. Naturally, the seven-year-old cannot concen-
trate all the time: he is likely to draw pictures in the margins of his
sheet of work paper. Let him be, says the principal, he must not be
punished. Such drawing can be a useful preparation for art. In time
the new *abécédaire* moves up one bench and then another, until he
finds himself in the front rank. When the front-benchers master the
content of their two books and have been examined by the master,
they are ready to graduate and move on to the next class, the Ninth

Form. These small graduation ceremonies, involving one or several students at a time, take place three or four times a year. The principal is called, he comes, approves the promotion, and solemnly conducts the child to the next class, where he introduces him to his new master.

The Ninth Form is, at the Bordeaux *collège*, the largest. It is held in an amphitheater, with six ranks of benches. The newcomer takes his seat in front, on the bottom rank, and moves up gradually, as his competence improves. The advantage of the amphitheater is not only that it can hold more students but also that the master can clearly see every one of his numerous charges. In this class the children must learn to read and write Latin and French fluently. Their textbook is a bilingual edition of Cato. They read aloud both the Latin and the French, they translate, they practice writing by copying out a different passage each day, and they have their work corrected by the master.

This process goes on for ten years, as the students move from rank to rank and from one class and master to the next, reading more and more difficult texts: some letters of Cicero, some dialogues of Cordier's in the Eighth, more and more of Cicero as the years go by, also Terence, Virgil, Ovid, and all the other classical texts that became standard fare in the sixteenth century and are only now beginning to fade out of the secondary school curriculum.

Roman literature and classical Latin were not the only subjects taught in the *collège*. They were the core of the curriculum; but as soon as a reasonable competence was assured in these subjects, the student was invited to enter the arcane world of Greek. At Bordeaux there was one professor of Greek who lectured daily, beginning on 1 October, in a separate classroom. All students were welcome to attend his course. Starting in the fifth class, all students spent an hour each day, beginning at one o'clock, in the Greek lecture hall. The public lecture in mathematics followed at two o'clock. History—ancient history—was also taught regularly as part of the program in the second and first classes. Further, and of inestimable value, there was the teaching of French. This part of the curriculum may have been the most important of all. It is difficult to say just what was taught and how it was done, because there were no standard textbooks of French literature officially connected with the curriculum. One can judge this part of the program only by its results: the *collèges* turned out young men who could write letters, essays, poems, plays, and speeches in elegant French. It is in a *collège* that the poets of the Pléiade were formed, it was in the *collèges* that entire generations

of men of letters learned their craft. French was not taught as a separate discipline: it was an inextricable part of the teaching in each class.
Far from banishing French from the schools, the masters commonly
used French in their teaching. Throughout the classes of the Bordeaux
collège, for instance, the masters interrogated the students in French,
explained the Latin texts in French, and required from the students
that they translate Cicero into French, both orally and in writing.[58]

The teaching of grammar and rhetoric was not confined to Latin
and Greek.[59] The elegance of ancient literature served as the model
for the teaching of a more precise and elegant written French. The
amount of time devoted in any given classroom to the practice of
French no doubt depended on the master's inclination,[60] but, starting
with the very first class, an effort was made to teach every child "to
pronounce and write French well, as much as Latin."[61] We do know
for certain that the children entered school illiterate and emerged ten
years later able to express themselves in elegant French, capable of
writing both French and Latin verse with facility, and with some
knowledge of Greek and mathematics, always a great deal of history
and philosophy, and sometimes even natural science and law.[62] An
occasional graduate knew some Hebrew, and it was common for a
graduate to have acquired a good knowledge of some modern language as well, perhaps as a result of informal tutoring and reading
under the supervision of an Italian, Spanish, German, or English
instructor, of whom there were many in the French *collèges*.[63]

Beyond the dry outline of the curriculum, such as Vinet's Bordeaux
program, we must imagine things as they really were. Not all the
boys participated fully in the intellectual life of the school. No doubt
the true "intellectuals" were always a small minority. However small
their number, they formed a vigorous coterie, together with the more
learned masters and the more learned among their parents and relatives. One cannot escape the conclusion that in many small French
cities intellectual life was more active in the sixteenth century than it
has been at any time since.[64] It is the extracurricular life—the production of plays, the unending stream of verse written and often published, the *salons* and *rencontres*, the local publishing houses, the
bookstores—which must be understood to complement our understanding of the *collèges* and their functions. The *collèges* were lively
institutions and very controversial ones. That is why they were so
keenly desired by some, so feared by others. Keeping the *rentier*
youth off the streets was their minimal achievement. But they also
ensured that the children did not "waste their time," and when the
masters did not perform to the students' satisfaction there were loud

complaints.[65] The schools were not taken for granted in the sixteenth century. They were new and their survival was precarious, always threatened by lack of funds, by epidemics, by civil war, riots, disturbances, and heresies. They were costly, they were precious, they were necessary. The conquest of good letters was costly not only to the city fathers and to the families; it was costly most of all to the students themselves, who had to set aside, with great force of character, most of the normal joys of childhood and adolescence in order to transform themselves into scholars, often against their natural inclinations.

We can follow the history of these various sacrifices, these violences done to the traditional ways of living, in many of the memoirs of the time, but nowhere better, perhaps, than in the private correspondence of the Milsonneau family of Saumur.[66] Maistre Milsonneau was a prosperous lawyer who undertook full responsibility for the education of the children of his second marriage over a period of some twenty years. He led the boys from the *collèges* in Saumur and nearby Loudun to the celebrated Bordeaux *collège* and then on to advanced studies in Toulouse and in Paris. The family kept not only full records of the expenditures incurred throughout but also progress reports from the masters and principals and, what is more—and very rare indeed—letters from the boys at school and university. The financial sacrifices were considerable because there were three boys to educate, and each of them was out of town most of the time. Room and board seems to have run to twenty-five livres for each boy each quarter, or one hundred livres a year, and in addition there were other expenses, such as travel, clothes, books, and little extravagances. Even the well-to-do Milsonneaus seem to have had some trouble at times keeping up with the incessant demands of the principals and of the boys themselves, whose most accomplished epistolary genre is the elegant begging letter. "Monsieur," writes young François to his stepfather, from Bordeaux in 1595, "I would have written sooner, had a suitable occasion presented itself before now, both to reply to your three letters and to thank you most humbly for the fifty écus which you were good enough to send me in addition to the ten brought by Louis." What we learn from the Milsonneau archives is that scrupulously detailed accounts were kept of the expenses and that the pleas from the boys were seen and noted for what they were. No matter how casual the request for money, hidden somewhere in the chatty letters, a stern black pen in the father's hand always went straight to the point by underlining the amount requested and making a note in the margin. But it was not only Monsieur and Madame who had to do violence to their best instincts and reach deeper each

time into their purses to bail out the boys from one situation after
another. The boys too—and perhaps they most of all—had to pit
themselves with all their power against their natural inclination to
"debauchery" and idleness. We read of one or the other of the
brothers straying from the serious pursuit of his studies and being
brought back by firm reprimands from an older brother or relative. All
the time the boys are profoundly aware of the need to make sacrifices:
"I assure you," writes François,

> that such liberal courtesies [namely the sending of more écus] will
> raise my courage for studying so much that you will never have
> occasion to regret all these expenses. After all, they [the expen-
> ditures] are, if you consider the matter carefully, small things when
> compared to the value of the acquisitions I expect to make in the
> liberal sciences.

Setting out for Toulouse, he writes:

> I hope to do even greater things there, things which the incompe-
> tence and the ignorant laziness of our professors here have not
> permitted me to aspire to thus far. I will be so diligent in my
> attendance at public lectures, I will listen with such care to the
> best professors and will be so vigilant in noting down their
> courses, and then in studying the notes and committing them to
> memory, that I shall at last be capable of taking my place next to
> you, so that after some practice of law I shall in the end, through
> my merit and your patronage, arrive higher still. The glory of my
> ancestors inflames my heart, but the venerable affection I have for
> literature in itself pushes me to great things. I do not know what
> destiny intends for me, but my high courage, together with vir-
> tue, entertains such hopes in me that I must someday be some-
> thing great or nothing at all. Mediocre things will never do for
> me. I am happy to hear of the progress of my cousin Abel. This
> will serve as a spur to me, to equal or surpass his prowess I
> will never endure the shame of seeing relatives of mine becoming
> more worthy than I myself of sitting in the chairs [magistrates'
> benches] of my ancestors. This honest competition will hold me
> so tightly to my studies that I will not have an opportunity for
> debauchery.[67]

The tone of these letters is sometimes heroic, even though the glory
and honors have nothing chivalrous about them. Nor would anyone
guess, from the virtuous posturing of this noble scholar, that he is a
prodigal son, often in the past distracted from his studies by wine,
women, gambling, and other costly *débauches* which landed him and
so many of his contemporaries in deep trouble.

There was certainly nothing new about troublesome students in Toulouse or Paris. What was new, rather, was that the old tolerance vanished, that parents, officials, and principals bore down with unprecedented vigor on the schoolboys. There was no tolerance for the wayward scholar, because good letters were seen as an absolute good. One could laugh, with Rabelais, at the idiocies of the old "Gothic" learning, the senseless, grotesque habits of clerics. But the new learning was something else altogether. There was nothing useless or otherworldly about good letters.

When maistre Milsonneau sent his sons off to school, he was not entrusting them to monks, to perform rituals beyond his competence. He expected the instructors to turn his sons into copies—if possible, improved ones—of himself. Nothing about their education was foreign to him. He might have been seen mentally following the boys' progress while looking out of his second-story study at the world beyond, at the Loire that flows under the bridge, carrying barges loaded with wine casks. Behind him, his own acquisitions in the liberal sciences are neatly arranged on the bookshelves. Valla, Bembo, Erasmus, Cicero, Caesar, Juvenal, Alciato, Zasius, Hotman, Rabelais, Cujas, Horace, Herodotus, Quintilian, Ronsard, Latin prose, French poetry, the histories of Vignier, Du Haillan, Paolo Emilio, Bodin's *Republic,* Greek dictionaries, legal treatises by Du Moulin and Papon, Plutarch, of course, Pliny's *Natural History,* the collected *Coutumes* of Anjou, of Paris, of Burgundy, the *Institutes* in six volumes, Tiraqueau's legal works—all these volumes are there, sturdily bound in calfskin or parchment.[68] Milsonneau believes in the absolute and supreme worth of a classical education. He knows exactly how costly it is to acquire, he marks down year after year the hundreds of livres that are swallowed up in the process; he knows also of the pleasures foregone, the efforts of the will. But he knows finally that the investment is an excellent one, in every way.

Rising in the world, for maistre Milsonneau, is not a matter of "escaping from the filth in which the sordid populace and the ignorant lie defeated," as it was for the poor schoolboy of Perrin's comedy. This escape had been accomplished already in the Milsonneau family. There is no lack of comfort, no lack of money or of culture in this household. The cellar of Milsonneau's house is well stocked with barrels of white wine and claret. The main rooms on the ground floor are spacious and filled with heavy carved furniture: tables and chairs made of matching woods, buffets filled with enormous quantities of linens, great ornamented chests containing sheets and pillow cases, matching stools with seats covered in tapestry work. The law office, downstairs, is simple and businesslike: a big table, a chair, two stools, a wooden cabinet, shelves, supplies of stationery, a small Coustumier d'Anjou. But upstairs, next to the master bedroom filled with clothes (including twenty-four mens' shirts) there is the pride of the house, the private study. Here, in the midst of the books—the more precious ones locked in wooden cabinets—there is a book stand, a writing desk in the shape of a pulpit, and a large table. When he climbs up the stairs to his *haulte estude,* maistre Milsonneau sheds the business life of his lawyer's office. He is Monsieur de la Baraudière. He forgets the trivial concerns of a bourgeois of Saumur; he leaves accounts and contracts behind him. It is an altogether different man who enters the room where Cicero and Erasmus reign: Monsieur de la Baraudière has joined the company of noble minds.

Monsieur de la Baraudière, or des Baraudières—no one is quite sure of the spelling, since the name of the country estate had only recently been appropriated and will soon supplant the Milsonneau name entirely—will remain *advocat* at Saumur to the end of his life. But because he is related, through his second marriage, to M. du Maurier, formerly Aubéry, who is *secrétaire de la chambre du roy* and ambassador in Holland, the sons of his second marriage can look forward, after all these years of study, to high office in the magistracy.[69]

Social climbing and more lucrative positions in the magistracy are not, however, the sole benefits to be looked forward to. Madame des Baraudière's son François reflects his family's views faithfully when he writes, not only of the career he looks forward to, but also of the "venerable affection" he claims to have for literature. What is taught in the *collèges* is above all a way of life. "A young mind must understand the Arts so that he can make his way in the world," affirms one of Des Caurres's pupils; and although the young man expresses at the same time his hope of some day becoming a "senator,"[70] there is no clear connection between the curriculum of the *collèges* and the skills required of royal magistrates in the *bailliages* or even in the *parlements*. In the seventeenth and eighteenth centuries this lack of connection will become obvious when more and more of the *conseillers* and *maistres des requestes* take up their functions at a very early age, after receiving permission—as a matter of course and, no doubt, at some cost—to dispense with the required standards of maturity and education.[71] Officeholding will become a purely financial and political arrangement. But the coming decline of the *collèges* and the near extinction of the famous law schools will not seriously affect the professional training of the *officiers*: they had very little of it at any time. If the *collèges* and the law schools were indispensable *pour voguer* in the sixteenth century, it was not for the professional preparation they dispensed but rather for the general culture they had to offer and for the habits and manners they inculcated. That sense of order, already observed in the daily schedule of the schools and in the arrangement by classes, was merely the most visible sign of a new mentality which consciously set itself apart from the traditional habits of medieval society.

This is the mentality of the new man celebrated by Rabelais. In contrast to the caricature of the old monkish pedant—who wastes his days in sloth, remote from the world, a worthless parasite, whose so-called learning is a pitiful pretext for idleness—the new man subjects himself to a fruitful, if drastic, regime of rising before dawn, conquering science after science, not pausing during his meals, making use even of the time spent in the toilet to have edifying pages read to him by his tutor, and studying the stars on his way back from the outhouse. This new man is to become a "veritable abyss of learning," not so that he may rise in the world—he is already Prince of Utopia—but so that he may live a more virtuous and pious life. The end of education, as understood by Rabelais, by Calvin, by Montaigne—who write, after all, for an audience composed of others who resemble them—the goal of all study, is moral philosophy: to reach wisdom in this world, to learn right action, to become reconciled to life's vicissitudes, to become, in a word, a philosopher.

8 Living Nobly

Mon mestier et mon art, c'est vivre.
Montaigne, *Essais*

Was wisdom to be learned in the schools? This would be expecting too much. The holy fervor which moved the gentry to found *collèges* was to lose something of its Gargantuan frenzy before the end of the century. A classical education was indispensable, perhaps, as the instrument which made wisdom possible. But it was far from certain that learning, in itself, had the power to make a man virtuous.

It was not technical expertise in philology, grammar, or law that the gentry looked for in classical literature but rather a harvest of exemplary lives and *sententiae* to help them "live happily and justly in human society."[1] In contemporary handbooks of wisdom culled from the classics, the gentry could peruse the moral philosophy of the ancients to devise models for "living nobly." In such works they found praise, "not for those who invented arms to make war upon their neighbors and kill them, but rather for those who advanced the progress of learning and peace." "What a world of difference there is," exlaims Guevara, "between those who wet their pens in ink and those who cover their spears in the blood of their fellow human beings: the first are surrounded by books, the others are covered with murderous weapons; the first study how man should live, the others are concerned with looting and robbery." The ideal put forward in

Guevara's compilation is that of a man "learned in Latin, eloquent in his own vernacular language, well-founded in histories, with some experience of the Greek language, and, above all, very diligent and curious when it comes to seeking out and perusing books."[2] The same respectable views are to be found in another early and popular French compilation from Roman sources, the *Lucan, Suetoine & Saluste en Françoys* (1500): "Learning is the most precious treasure man can acquire." All these moralists condemn idleness in the name of the ancients: "One must not be idle. Idleness was unknown to the ancient clerks and wise men, who studied, some of them philosophy, others geometry or other sciences, and still others compiled chronicles and books concerning ancient history."[3] This literature, of which Montaigne's *Essays* and Charron's *Sagesse* were to be among the most prominent examples by the end of the century, made classical precepts available to an audience which had not had the good fortune to be educated in a *collège*. But whether in translation or in the original, these moral precepts, as Montaigne saw it, could not really be learned. It was never enough to be exposed to them. One had to be, in the first place, as Rabelais put it, "nobly born." Or, as Montaigne more delicately put it, the study of letters could be truly fruitful only to "those whom Nature brought into the world with aptitudes more suited for generous rather than lucrative activities."[4]

Formal schooling, as dispensed in the new *collèges*, if we are to believe Montaigne, had failed to "augment human nature." The schools, founded everywhere with high hopes, had become diploma mills. Instead of making better men, they had created a generation of pedants and opportunists. At least, that is the way it looks to Montaigne, who claims to find the cause of this perverse malfunction: "Is it not because study, in France, has hardly any object other than profit?"[5]

In his view, the trouble is that while the *gentilshommes* scorn learning—or are exposed to it too briefly, before plunging into a profession which has nothing in common with books—there remain usually only people of low condition for whom learning is a means of arriving, a way to make a better living.

How Montaigne would have disapproved of the motives of the Bourneau boys, how he would have scorned the Milsonneaus' clearheaded view of education as an investment! No matter that the Eyquems, now Montaignes, had achieved wealth and position in a way comparable to the Milsonneaus' progress. Montaigne could persuade himself that he lived more nobly than maistre Milsonneau.

How does one live nobly? Here we enter a domain far more

intangible than the comparatively simple discrimination between *no-bles hommes* and *honorables hommes*. This is no mere matter of law or even of custom. Wealth, power, tax exemption, marriage, and sei-gneuries could raise a family's status technically. As this was happen-ing on a very large scale and at an ever increasing pace, the tidal wave of *arrivistes* threatened to engulf those who, like the Eyquems, had emerged from the crowd at an earlier moment.

What protection was there against such confusion? To be distin-guished from a *bonhomme* like le président d'Ormesson was easy enough: in spite of his greater wealth and greater office, he remained a *bonhomme* because he had "no letters." The king would never refer to Montaigne as his *bonhomme*. But letters, it was becoming clear, could be acquired these days, through hard work and modest in-vestment, by a seemingly infinite number of persons of low condi-tion. What then was left to distinguish someone like Montaigne from the newest graduate, inheritor of *rentes*, offices, and lands? Was not this question the secret motive of the writing of Montaigne's essays, the hidden spring of the literature of the time, barely understood by the moralists and poets who felt its pressure?

The great debate over the true nature of nobility, in all its varieties, dominated the thoughts of Montaigne's contemporaries. On a practi-cal level, we have seen the efforts made by jurists to reconcile the fact of social mobility with the theory of a nobility of birth. On this level, what matters is the acquisition of privilege.

But there could be no question of deciding, on the basis of a certifi-cate, whether a man lived nobly. When "living nobly" is no longer confused with the desire to pass for a *gentilhomme de race*, when the gentry devises a separate ideal of nobility, then the relation between living nobly and living the life of a *gentilhomme* must be clarified. *Collège* teachers will rail against the *gentilshommes*, whom they de-scribe as "filled with vain ambition." This is not true nobility, accord-ing to the principal of the *collège* of Amiens, for these "so-called *gentils-hommes* found their nobility not on their own merits but on the death of their ancestors: covering themselves with glory and honors which do not belong to them, they never do anything honorable; they are the shame of their lineage and deserve only scorn." "Any man of virtue is noble and, conversely, all the wicked are ignoble, principally these *gentilshommes,*" allows the Socrates of Picardy. What is a *gen-tilhomme* nowadays? "We recognize him from his pompous and ar-rogant way of walking; we hear him bragging about the nobility and antiquity of his house and race; he knows nothing of the liberal arts and gives himself up, instead, to the tragic exercise of the hunt; his body's prowess is dedicated to the service of Bacchus and Venus; in the manner of monkeys, he copies the ways of princes," and he "dresses in a bizarre fashion"; gambling, thievery, and murder are his habitual pastimes. He serves as a fence for brigands, he swears and blasphemes constantly, he does violence to his people, forcing illegal payments out of them; "he shows contempt for the magistrates, *of-ficiers*, bourgeois, and inhabitants of the town, whom such 'noble-men' consider as their natural enemies [*leurs contraires*] and speak of, contemptuously, as *roturiers* and *vilains*, although most of them live more nobly than they do."[6]

The problem is a familiar one. Did those who lived nobly mean to live as the *gentilshommes* lived? Did they mean to "abandon the liberal arts," to take up "the tragic exercise of the hunt," to give themselves up to a wild debauch of violence, drink, sexuality, and gambling? Did they mean to associate with and imitate those who showed contempt for magistrates and townsmen?

The position of the privileged notables, whose chief desire was to be safe from arbitrary exactions and humiliations, was never entirely clear. They "were and were not noble."[7] The title of *noble homme*, the landed estates, the royal office, the precedent of previous exemp-tions, none of these represented ironclad guarantees. The foremost families of any town always remained in danger. Their position rested on a precarious balance of power established in normal times between two worlds in chronic conflict: the fat world of the *familles*, richly ensconced in their comfortable stone *hôtels*, and the lean world of the common people, barely kept in check by the laws and agents of their natural enemies. The armed militia of the bourgeoisie, the bewilder-ing threat of half a dozen overlapping law courts, the preaching in the churches, bread distribution, sanitation and medical measures, hospitals and poorhouses endowed by the charitable rich—these well-worn dikes erected against the pressure from below could cave in at the smallest provocation: a bad harvest, war in the vicinity, epidemics.

A regiment of royal troops stopping in town for a few days was enough to upset the social equilibrium. The officers in command of the visiting regiment, especially if they were *gentilshommes* of high rank, felt free to disparage local notables. The presence of armed men introduced a third party, momentarily, into the rough, seesaw power politics of the town. Artisans, laborers, *mauvais garnemens* of all kinds, the unemployed, and beggars were likely to be caught up in the tension of this new situation, in which the bourgeois guard and the magistrates' agents no longer controlled the town. The exactions of the soldiery exasperated the small bourgeoisie of shopkeepers, masters, and employers, who, in normal times, could be counted on to support *messieurs* of the *présidial* and of the *maison de ville*. In moments like these, it was prudent not to insist too loudly on one's privileges, even if one had full rights to being *noble homme*. The gentry at such critical junctures found itself under fire from two sides: bullied by armed and petulant *gentilshommes,* on the one hand, and, on the other hand, threatened with violence by the common people.

The insults of the *gentilshommes* were small calamities, whose costs could be borne. One can imagine the state of mind of Guillaume Ruzé, bishop of Angers, as he stood in his episcopal palace, surrounded by the most notable officials of the city, presiding over a banquet in honor of the visiting duke of Anjou. The tables were loaded with exquisite wines, everything was prepared and ready. But the tension in the hall was almost unbearable. The host came from a family whose power and influence at court, in the *parlement,* and in the world of the financiers were well established. He was used to the first place in all official ceremonies; his status was unquestioned at processions and meetings (at Blois, in 1576, he had represented the clergy of his province). He was Monsieur d'Angers. But in the eyes of the duke's *gentilshommes,* he was merely a parvenu. To these courtiers, the local gentry, rich, privileged, responsible leaders, and noble in their own eyes, appeared as pretentious bourgeois. Hence the tension at the banquet, as described in Jehan Louvet's diary. At a given moment the *gentilshommes* "pretended to quarrel with one another" and, under that pretext, began to throw things at one another, "first napkins, then dishes, silver, and glass, breaking windows and furniture." The motive of this puerile demonstration, explained some of the courtiers, was that "it was unsuitable for a bishop, who was a man of low condition, to have the audacity to wish to give dinner to a duke of Anjou."[8]

Such slights and outrages were suffered with dignity. Far more threatening was the thought of the mob below, which might receive encouragement by witnessing the humiliations of the notables. In Saint-Maixent, a middling city not far from Poitiers, we can gauge the fluctuations of this delicate social machinery by studying the detailed diary of Michel Le Riche, Monsieur du Claveau, one of the town's two or three most prominent citizens.

Le Riche's father had been mayor of Saint-Maixent and *advocat du roy*. As early as 1536 he had "declared in the register that he held his land nobly" on the advice of "the lieutenant general and several others." Michel inherited his father's office and seigneurie. Even so, in a moment of crisis, when the established but fuzzy outlines of the town's social hierarchy suddenly come under brutal illumination with the visit of a prince and his soldiers—a disaster more to be feared than war itself—then even Monsieur du Claveau's pretensions, well established at least forty years earlier, must be discreetly set aside.

The duke of Alençon is the city's guest in 1575, and Monsieur du Claveau—"noble," exempt, privileged—goes out of his way to lodge men of the duke's suite in his house, for it had been prudently decided in council meetings that "the exempt as well as the nonexempt would have soldiers lodged in their houses . . . because the common people screamed and complained of being made to bear too heavy a burden." Le Riche's lodger turned out to be a *"gentilhomme* from the Limousin, called the sieur de Pompadour, who had promised to compensate me and pay for the food he and his men would consume in my house." Predictably, the *gentilhomme* left "without saying adieu and without paying," on top of which his men took away with them a number of valuable things which struck their fancy—"linen, dishes, a green rug, some books," and more.[9]

Nobility, in sixteenth-century France, was only in part a legal condition. It was, above all, a social condition that rested on a person's style and his state of mind. And, further, there was not one, but several kinds of noble styles and mentalities, each of which could be perceived, by observers with conflicting interests, as the only real way of living nobly. In its crudest version, living nobly could mean that a bourgeois had retired from commerce and that he played at being a *gentilhomme* on Sundays, in his country house, impressing, at most, the local villagers. His claim was strengthened if he managed to have himself struck off some tax rolls. This kind of nobility was strictly local: it wore off outside his village. No one took it seriously, except the interested party; and even for him his *qualité* was an act of faith for the sake of posterity. We can almost hear his plea: let him believe in his imaginary nobility, and his son after him, so that his grandson may have a chance to become really noble.

At the other extreme was the real *gentilhomme,* who came close to acting out the caricature of the rapacious and ignorant *traisneur d'espée* castigated by Descaurres, Loyseau, and many others. No one doubted his genealogical and legal right to nobility. It was his moral right to a privileged social position that was being challenged by gentry and bourgeois critics. If to be noble meant to be ignorant, poor, violent, and vicious, then how could an upright citizen aspire to nobility? From the perspective of the gentry, this was false nobility, the accidental remains, the wreckage of what may once have been, generations earlier, true nobility.[10] The problem, then, was to invent an ideal of the noble life that was distinct from bourgeois life and yet not to be confused with the terrible image of the purely genealogical nobility—abhorred and, besides, inaccessible.

The task was not an easy one. Models for this new kind of nobility had to be found outside feudal society. The noble Greek or Roman who was the gentry's model was not necessarily thought of as an actual historical personage.[11]

In seeking an ideal of the noble life, the gentry intellectuals took from the ancients only what suited them. The triumphal success of Montaigne's *Essays* was certainly due in large part to its subliminal message, which contemporaries deciphered without effort: hiding just below the philosopher's analysis of the human condition, there was to be found, in a most agreeable form, an encyclopedic repertory of the gentry's condition. More than any other book, the *Essays* painted in a "simple, natural, ordinary fashion" the aspirations of the gentry. Better than any collection of ancient precepts—which always missed the mark here or there—here was a candid portrait of a man who lived nobly, presented almost "tout entier, et tout nud."[12] And most important, his "nobility" was exactly the kind one could aspire to if one had an education. This man was neither a ruffian too proud of his lineage nor a disguised bourgeois too proud of his money. He was neither *gentilhomme* really, nor bourgeois, but a member of a new species whose distinguishing marks set it clearly apart from both Second and Third Estate.

The first and deepest mark of the man who lives nobly is that he is disinterested. He does not care for money: in this way he is superior to the bourgeois. "My father," writes Estienne Pasquier, giving himself up recklessly to fantasy, "my father, who put all his hopes in me, heaped up gold, goods, money, and estates. But I, born for my country [*patrie*], wished none of this. On the contrary, I wished to hand over most of my fortune to the people."[13] Montaigne, citing Cicero and Pythagoras, finds a neat way of distinguishing himself and his kind from merchants and *gentilshommes*. Life, he suggests, is like the Olympic games: "Some come to use their bodies in competition for glory; others bring merchandise to sell for profit; but there is also a third kind of people—and they are not the worst—who come seeking no other advantage than to observe and discover how and why everything is done and to be spectators viewing the lives of other men, in order to draw judgment and rules for their own lives from this experience."[14]

To the practical ancient who proposed illustrious birth, wealth, and virtue—in that order—as the three principal pleasures to be had in this world, the modern aspirant to the noble life is likely to reply obliquely, citing Plato in passing, that there is no durable wealth which can be left to one's children save those treasures "which fear neither the hailstones of the sky, nor the raging winds and waves of the sea, nor the hardships of the earth: that is, the liberal arts."[15] Material possessions are only too vulnerable to the ravages of Fate, "which knows how to open a hundred breaches to the assaults of poverty in the midst of our riches ... and send our defenses and fortifications flying *cul sur pointe*."[16] Indeed, "to a well-born man, making money is unpleasant,"[17] we are told by Jacques Peletier, Montaigne's and Pasquier's and Bèze's friend—lawyer, poet, *collège* principal, physician—and the delirious enthusiast of letters who probably wrote the *Discours non plus melancoliques* and whose motto seems to have been "Non valet qui sine studiis vivit." The note struck everywhere is contempt, not so much for wealth itself[18] as for the undignified—perhaps even dishonorable—occupation of the merchant.

The gentry's objection to commerce is, at least ostensibly, different from the nobility's stereotyped scorn. The merchant is nowhere blamed by the gentry for his lack of martial virtues or for his deficiencies as a courtier—Montaigne would never recommend adopting stylish dress or taking up either fencing or music lessons. The merchant is not blamed because he works hard; no one challenges the usefulness or intrinsic honesty of his work. And only the most hypocritical would use the old moral argument against usurious moneylending to stigmatize him. The merchant's genealogy is also not in question. The gentry reserves its hatred for the nobility and for the *canaille*. The bourgeois is merely reprimanded for being a philistine: too busy chasing after profit, he is likely to lead the unexamined life—and from this proceed all his other faults.

To live nobly, it is understood that one must have leisure.[19] But leisure is emphatically not to be confused with idleness. There is hardly a worse crime in the gentry's book than idleness (*oisiveté*). Work is noble—nothing is nobler than work. "For what is the purpose of our presence in this world, if not the conservation of this human society?"[20] "Labor omnia vincit" is one of the favorite mottoes of the gentry.[21] The *gentilhomme* is led to all the worst vices because he is *oiseux*,[22] but the man who truly knows how to live nobly transforms his leisure into noble work. He may give the appearance of being idle, as Montaigne manages so well to do, but it is a very special kind of idleness, like that of old Bourdin, *procureur général* at the *parlement*. He was famous for sleeping through all the proceedings. "He slept," explains Pasquier, "but it was a sleep full of lively activity." This inveterate sleeper "learned the treasures and secrets of the Hebrews, the Latins, the Chaldeans, the Greeks, and all other things conducive to virtue in this world" while he slept, and in this same sleep he managed "to acquire great possessions, lands, and seigneuries."[23]

The possession of property is to be desired, but its acquisition is a dubious activity, not easily reconcilable with living nobly. Wealth is admired—but it had best be old wealth, not "riches quickly gathered" but "goods justly acquired, little by little," as the *collège* principal Talpin makes clear.[24]

The ideal is to inherit a sufficient fortune and to live within one's means. Nicolas Pasquier advises in this sense: "Weigh in great detail just what your income amounts to and of what kind it is; whether seigneuries, fields, vineyards, meadows, woods, ponds—or *rentes constituées*—or a mixture of all of these." And then, knowing the sum of the income, keep your expenses at or below that level. "Saving is praiseworthy and *honneste*," he exclaims. "The best kind of *rente* you can have is in fact to hold your expenses in check tightly. All savings made in the way of household expenses are of an incredible worth and much superior to any other kind of income."[25]

To show his open contempt for commerce, the man who would live nobly makes much of the country life, *la vie des champs*. "I have shut myself up in this country place," writes Nicolas Pasquier from his estate at Mainxe,

> from which I draw more contentment than I would from the court of the world's greatest prince. I have conquered this advantage here, namely, that nothing torments my mind. Neither ambition nor avarice, neither love nor vengeance, has any power here.

> Having lived and tried and tasted the commerce of this world for some thirty years, ... I have adjusted now to the country life as the most happy and innocent of all ... a seedbed of happiness ... a happy liberty. In the midst of this contentment I have kept to small things which suffice for my fulfillment.

> Here one doesn't work to put all one's effort into assembling riches proceeding from other men's blood and sweat; ... instead, one glories in sobriety, in simplicity and modesty; ... everyone remains within the boundaries of innocence. Here one lives without the swelling of pride ... free of unbridled ambition and the mad pursuit of honors.

In sum, "True happiness is to be found in retreating to the country."[26]

This longing for the innocence of country life is so ever-present in
the letters and other writings of the gentry that it assumes the proportions of a massive guilt complex. The praise of the country life and of
privacy, of retirement from the affairs of this world, is more than a
literary cliché, more than a way of posing as *gentilshommes des champs*.
Couched in Christian or Stoic phrases, this longing to be free of
negotium, to retire and to die in the middle of one's own cabbage patch
(rather than on the battlefield, for example), is perhaps the deepest
common desire of the gentry. Montaigne's celebrated retirement in
his library-tower is no unusual act: the gentry, as a body, aspired to
precisely this kind of retirement, and many achieved it.

Nicolas Pasquier, who likes to play at being Montaigne,[27] needs to
go no further than his father's example when he thinks about the
ideal of retirement to the country, a retirement that is not devoid of
noble purpose and intellectual stimulation, for "we have our books
which are our silent guests."[28] His father is more eloquent on the
subject. He too loves his country houses. At Mainxe, he imagines
himself to be in Paradise: surrounded by an abundance of fruit,

> pavies, auberges, muscats, pommes, poires, pesches ... the
> sweetest melons I have ever eaten ... The best possible meat,
> bread, and water, and—this being a second soul for us—good
> wines, white as well as claret; fat carp, trout, pike: this large un-
> known river which ran through the Garden of Eden has been
> changed into the Charente, which runs from Angoulesme to the
> sea [passing in front of his own estates], bordered by meadows
> and graced with affluents like the little Touvre, of which Thevet
> said that it was paved with trout, embroidered with swans, and
> bordered with crab.[29]

Even though the Mainxe estate inspires such outbursts in the elder
Pasquier, he entertains some reservations about the unmitigated
pleasures of country life. "I'll tell you frankly," he writes to an old
friend, "that when I first arrive here, the fields arouse my spirits. But
two or three days later I am back to normal. Trees don't talk.
Therefore I find myself taking refuge in my books." He gets restless:
"I come and go, I busy myself around the house, from one room to
another, I go upstairs and come down again." "I find myself prying
into everyone's affairs.... I become a nuisance to my family."[30] In a
mock debate with a friend and colleague who is staying in the country, Pasquier makes himself the advocate of city life and its rewards:
"As I walked about, alone and lost in thought in my study, I

imagined ... you walking about in your park of Ferrières ... pruning a tree here, straightening a path there." But, however pleasant the country, he argues, it should be no more than a temporary respite, "a parenthesis" in the midst of the active life of the city. As for such rustic pleasures as hunting, he claims to "do more hunting in a quarter of an hour inside my study than you in a whole day out in the fields." The kind of hunting he has in mind is done with *escritoires* and *papiers*. And he mentions, further, "the friendships, obligations, alliances of persons we acquire here daily, which cannot be done in the country."[31]

Families like the Pasquiers were in the fortunate position of being able to duplicate, in the center of town, the admired privacy of country houses. "I come back to you, my old home, house built by my labors, house on the edge of the river Seine, in Paris, where I hope to finish my days, ... house in which I find a haven at the water's edge," writes Pasquier.[32] The spacious *hôtels* of the gentry were imposed on the warren-like urban sprawl, the imperious gestures that marked the presence of the demigods. Surrounded by heaps of wood-and-plaster houses that leaned against each other for help, the stone-faced Renaissance manor houses rose up, in the midst of rotting and dangerous slums, giving a new look to the old *quartiers* as surely as do the high-rise buildings of the 1970s. This alien magnificence deposited the pale reddish brick and the cream-colored quarry-stone of the Loire châteaux onto the Cité and the Marais *quartiers*. Acres of tenements were swallowed up and replaced with palaces built around interior courts and galleries and walled off with thick stone from the noise of the urban world. And for every luxury residence along the rue des Francs-Bourgeois (formerly the rue du Paradis)—the Hôtel Carnavalet, or the Hôtel Guénégaud des Brosses, or the Hôtel d'Assy, built and rebuilt by generations of *présidents* and *trésoriers*—there were dozens of simpler *hôtels* whose design and proportions betrayed the clients' deepest wish: a haven of privacy, a "parenthesis" in the world, a self-sufficient manor house, with its courtyard and gardens, its stables, haylofts, and cellars, where inexhaustible supplies of grain, wine, and salted meat were periodically carted in by the master's farmers.[33]

With enough money, many of the pleasures of the country house could be reconstructed in the city. Even middling wealth, like Pasquier's or that of his colleague and friend Claude Fauchet, was enough to provide a solid haven. Fauchet's *hôtel* on the rue de Grenelle, inventoried in 1587 on the occasion of his wife's death, gives a picture of such solid comfort.[34]

Among the superrich were families like the Du Prats, who owned an *hôtel* with a view of the Seine and with costly furnishings that included thousands of livres' worth of silver dishes, precious collections of antiques, weapons, ivory chess sets, terra-cotta statues, marble, paintings, tapestries—and books: the expensive Froben and Estienne editions, Saint Augustine, Erasmus, Bibles, Saint Jerome, Lefèvre d'Étaples, Budé and all the classics of course, Cicero in Badius' four volumes, Quintilian, and Plutarch, but also the Italian moderns in sumptuous editions and, in the original, Dante and Machiavelli. In sum, a Renaissance mansion that is an art museum as much as a home.

But there was also, in the country, their château of Nantouillet, where they kept twenty-two horses and four mules in the stables, and cows, sheep, and pigs. And, in the château itself, a wealth of furniture and tapestries and another library, this one of a less forbidding character. It was stocked mostly with French books and was meant for amusement as much as edification. There were romances like *Perceforest*, the *Orlando Furioso* in French, Boccaccio, Machiavelli, Heliodorus, Virgil, Plato, Guevara, all in French translation; Belon's *Nature des Oyseaux*, Commynes, Rabelais, the *Roman de la Rose*, and Pasquier's *Monophile*[35]—amusing, delightful books for the most part, silent guests waiting for the master's return to his "paradise of good health, comfort, serenity, convenience, delight, and all honest pleasures of agriculture and the country life."[36] In châteaux or simple houses, the gentry celebrated the long summer holidays, the *vacances* of the law courts, by leaving the paper work of the city and giving themselves up to their true vocation: reading the poets and philosophers.[37]

Around Marseille and Aix there were said to be eight hundred country residences occupied by *officiers*. In these *bastides*, set "in the midst of olive, lemon, orange, pomegranate, palm, and fig trees" (like Du Vair's house, which he called *La Floride*) erudite or gallant conversations floated all summer long in the scented air, while children scurried underfoot and cicadas buzzed in the foliage. Hunting was not encouraged on these estates of the gentry. Instead, harmless games like the *jeu de paume* were popular, and music filled the air. The lute, zither, harp, and guitar were popular instruments at garden parties. Walking in the woods seems to have been a pleasure recommended almost as unreservedly as conversation itself, the *rencontres*, which were easily the high point of such parties.[38] In the coolness of summer evenings, the magistrates become poets, free to follow mysterious paths through the woods, "ma Marguerite et moi," with

Amour walking ahead of them. Free of worries, "unconcerned with kings, court, or town," they luxuriate in returning to their lands ("O Médoc, mon pays solitaire et sauvage!"), which have the advantage of being "at the ends of the earth," as far as possible from the "malheurs de notre âge."[39] This theme is continually and monotonously intoned by the poets: "To be rid of the *palais* and of its court sessions; far away from the court; the mind tranquil ... in a healthy body," "simplicity between men who are held together by friendship"—all this is possible to the man who is lucky enough "to have found an inheritance and has not had to work for it."[40]

In their desire for the simple country life and its independence, the poets of the gentry come dangerously close at times to admiring the *noblesse de race*, as does Rapin, an *advocat*, a graduate of Poitiers, and a successful administrator, whose idea of happiness lies in being "far away from business, like the men of earlier times," and in "ploughing the field inherited from his ancestors." Oh, thrice happy, the man "whose nobility is known and was never put in question," whose house is built "without great sumptuousness"—but with all comforts; whose lands, clearly marked, surround his house. This happy man has no great prince or seigneur in his neighborhood, "but commands alone in his village." He is not involved in moneylending, lives within his means, and, "harming no one, fears neither notary nor *sergent*." In the little republic of his family and domain "he commands like a little king." In his *salle* he has weapons for his own defense, which he knows how to use. Three horses in his stable, a dozen dogs, and fishing gear complete his equipment. His pleasures are simple. He inspects his vineyards and supervises the work of hired hands. He savors the joys of tranquil possession by watching his cows amble along the banks of the river or by looking fondly over his plantations and pulling a weed here and there. In his orchards he does his own pruning and grafting to improve the trees. In the winter, in spite of rain and ice, he goes hunting; sometimes he can be seen at dawn, taking potshots with his harquebus at waterfowl. At other times he is found all bundled up in warm clothes, reading some good book that shows the way to virtue.[41]

"Do you know ... how I should like to live in order to be happy?" asks Tabourot, *advocat* and *procureur du roy* in Burgundy. "A sufficient fortune, acquired easily, through the liberality of some patron," "fertile fields," "a good fire going in the fireplace, rare appearances in court," "a tranquil mind, no excesses, good health, agile body in good shape; wise simplicity, easygoing meals without artifice, friends neither greater nor lesser than I; joyous evenings, but without drunkenness."[42] This list of desiderata is universal among gentry poets. To live nobly, it was clearly necessary to praise the simple country life if not actually to live it. The country life is the symbol of a lost innocence, an uncomplicated and mostly fictional past, recaptured to offset the tension of politics and business. The real past of these gentry families was almost invariably to be found in the counting-houses of hard-working bourgeois and merchants, who were no strangers to financial risks and the tough politics of the *échevinage*. But when the family reached the point of having pretensions to living nobly, the newly acquired seigneuries became the stages for elaborate *mises-en-scène* in which the family's past was rearranged: one was meant to assume that *advocats*, *procureurs*, and *conseillers* performed their duties in town as civic obligations and that they yearned, meanwhile, to return to their ancestral estates.

It would be a mistake, however, to see in these country houses nothing but affectation. Quite aside from the genuine pleasures to be had from contemplating fields and flowers or from seeing a harvest through, there was among these *advocats* and *conseillers* quite often a perfectly natural nostalgia for the *pays* of their childhood. These farms, manors, and seigneuries had, after all, been in their families for a generation or two, and sometimes longer. While the claims of immemorial possession, going back to the time of the Crusades—if not to the time of the Trojan Wars—were absurd, it nevertheless remains true that the gentry of Montaigne's time was perfectly entitled to sentimental associations with their family lands. Often they had played there as children; always they spent their summers there. These family lands were like anchors in the minds of many; their *pays* was their point of reference, even while their *cursus honorum* called them from small towns to provincial capitals and, eventually, to Paris. With rare exceptions, these members of the *parlement*, these secretaries of state and treasurers, were immigrants of a sort who never forgot, in their Parisian town houses, the *pays* of their fathers' origins.

These ties went beyond mere sentiment. When a gentry family that had amassed a certain amount of capital, obligations, and offices eventually arrived also in Paris, it was with the help of allies already ensconced at court, in the *parlement*, at the Hôtel de Ville, or, at the very least, in the university. The branch of the family that had "arrived," in every sense of that word, in Paris remained obligated to uncountable *parentèles* (relations) left behind. This was not, however, a question of gratitude. It would be more to the point if we spoke of

the new Parisians as having opened branch offices with roots in
Tours, Bourges, or Troyes. A bridgehead was established at the national level by municipal capital from all the corners of the kingdom.

One of the most curious and revealing of the visible ties between
the two worlds—the municipal and national—is the *collège*. A boy
from Aurillac or Le Mans did not choose his *collège* at random when
he went up to Paris to finish his education. The terrain had been
prepared for him a long time ago. Aurillac's notables, for instance,
were represented in Paris as early as the fourteenth century by the
Collège de Fortet, where Aurillac boys even found instructors who
came from Aurillac.[43] Boys from Beauvais were likely to attend the
Collège de Dormans, which had been endowed by an *advocat* at
the *parlement*, of Beauvaisis origin.[44] Boys from Sens would attend the
collège founded by the Grassin family.[45] When Jacques Amyot, the
future translator of Plutarch, left his father's house in Melun—on
the Grande Rue, where the Amyots made and sold leather goods—he
headed, naturally, for the Collège du Cardinal Lemoine, where three
of the instructors were from Melun.[46]

Long-term ties with the *pays* of one's origins also governed the
pattern of real-estate acquisitions. When, toward the end of his brilliant career, Amyot bought the château and seigneurie of Courtempierre near Melun at a bargain price, he did not do it on a whim or to
parade his success among his neighbors, since he himself had no
intention of leaving Paris. The seigneurie, managed by one of his
brothers, was a natural investment in the *pays*, one of several marking
the Amyot's rise. It was owned by that family right into the
nineteenth century.[47] When the Pasquiers, both father and son, extol
the virtues of their seigneurie of Mainxe, near Cognac, we must not
take too seriously their notion that in this Garden of Eden all worldly
cares were left behind. Rather, the Mainxe property was a tool with
which the Pasquiers, through their alliances, inserted themselves into
the carefully woven and ancient network of power of the *pays*.[48]

The Pasquiers were Parisians catapulted into Cognac society. Much
more typical is the story of a family which rises within the bourgeoisie
of its own *pays*, and acquires education, offices, and alliances as far
away as Paris but never ceases cultivating its membership in the
provincial society where its real estate, marriages, and other interests
continue to flourish. A particularly well-documented case is that of
Robert Garnier, lawyer, *lieutenant criminel* at Le Mans, and well-
known poet and dramatist.[49]

All in all, the country life must be seen as something concrete and
tangible, a necessary and not unprofitable part of the everyday

strategy of the gentry. It gave noble luster to a lawyer's life. Living in this way, with long holidays, was something that a true bourgeois and merchant could not afford. In this sense, the running of country estates was a luxury for gentry families. But it was also a necessity: that is how one maintained the family's grip in the *pays*.

Despite the poets' frequent sighs, occasioned by the corruption and ignoble habits of the Palais de Justice, the gentry, on the whole, was perfectly at home in both worlds. The seigneur's life is kept from becoming noble in the bad sense. Not for Garnier or Pasquier is this caricature of the *gentilhomme* sketched by the *procureur* Tabourot: "Braquemard calls himself a *gentilhomme:* he is, in his fashion. He gambles, he lives off his villagers, he keeps hounds, he swears with skill, and he owes a great many debts. There isn't a thing of value in his house. A final test: his teeth smell of venison."[50]

To live nobly, as we can see, did not mean to adopt, indiscriminately, the vices of the *gentilshommes des champs*. Such rustics, with their gamey breath, may have been *gentilshommes* "in their fashion," but, it was understood, this was a despicable fashion—which led to moral and economic bankruptcy.

Ready to best the *gentilhomme* on every other terrain, easily outwitting and supplanting him in his manor, in government administration, in the church, in diplomatic missions, even at court and in the boudoir,[51] the gentry was still bedeviled by one last aspect of noble behavior: violence.

Not that there were necessarily more cowards among the gentry than among the nobility. Not that a man with a university education was a priori handicapped when it came to swordplay. Most of the men we have encountered in these pages knew how to handle themselves in battle, if it came to that. On occasion, one of them could be sorely provoked by taunts directed at his origins. This is what happened to the son of Beaune-Semblançay, who drew his sword and killed a *gentilhomme* who had accused him of not being noble.[52] It was necessary, to be sure, to use the sword to maintain law and order.[53] We have seen *conseillers, advocats,* and *échevins* ride off in pursuit of highwaymen, or noble brigands. To defend one's interests or one's life when necessary, sword in hand—this kind of courage the gentry admired. Estienne Pasquier's letters, which follow the "troubles" of the civil war in France from the beginning, provide a perfect commentary from the gentry's point of view. "Dulce bellum inexpertis," he reminds his friends.[54] The *gentilshommes* and the common people "talk only of arson, war, murder, and looting."[55] The men of the *robe* (lawyers) alone keep cool heads.[56] Civil war is "a tragedy which will be played in our midst and at our cost [that is, the *gentilshommes* and the *peuple* may profit from it, but not our kind]; God willing, there will be no more at stake than our purses."[57] What was a reasonable man to do in the face of inevitable and senseless violence? Pasquier wished he could retire "to a foreign country for the duration"—*en forme de parenthèse*. But being a mature man and an officeholder, he resolved, in the best Roman manner, that the proper course lay in "living and dying like good citizens, with our state."[58] And that is indeed what the gentry did, on the whole, and quite honorably, as Pasquier is quick to point out: when the mob ruled Paris, he contends, none of the nobility had the courage to resist its depredations. "A man *de robbe longue*, on the contrary, a certain Taverny, held off the mob in front of his own house for eight or nine hours and died fighting. An example surely worthy of being engraved on Posterity's mind, so that one should know that valor proceeds from our inner being and that *l'habit ne fait pas le moine*."[59]

If there were exceptional circumstances, then, which justified the use of the sword, these were occasions chosen to resemble the civic patriotism of the ancients rather than the romantic bravura identified with chivalry. That the gentry did not, value swordplay highly is demonstrated in this anecdote told by Tallemant, son of a financier, about the poet Malherbe, son of a *conseiller présidial*.

A nephew of his came to see Malherbe once, having just finished nine years of study in a *collège*. Malherbe asked him to construe a few verses of Ovid's, which the boy could not do. Malherbe let him go on in his confused way for a good quarter of an hour, and then he told him: my nephew, believe me, you had better choose valor: for you are not good for anything else.[60]

Nothing is more candid than the anonymous *Discours des querelles et de l'honneur* (Paris, 1594), which raises the thorniest of all the problems confronted by the gentry in their daily relations with the nobility: How is one to respond to the provocations and to the challenges which forced one to fight pointless duels to satisfy some ignorant rogue's "point of honor"? "Is there anything stranger than to kill each other daily without knowing what constitutes a sufficient cause for fighting"[61]—especially if one's feelings on the subject of violence conform to the usual gentry contempt for *traisneurs d'espée*? The author of the discourse claims to admire "furious souls" led by martial sentiments as much as "generous souls" who abhor violence; but he does not hide his true feelings very well, for he declares the "furious souls" to be proper to beasts, while the "generous souls" are specifically human.[62]

To prepare the ground for practical advice to "generous souls" challenged to do combat by beastly *gentilshommes*, the *Discours* offers a mythico-historical argument. In the beginning, we are told, men were savages and lived without laws. The time came, however, when those with the best minds among men began to seek out the secrets of Nature and were soon admired as demigods by the rest of mankind: these intellectuals were *gentils*, the rest were *vilains*. Among the *vilains*, eventually, some, envious of the demigods' influence, seized power by brute force and brought about a most horrible situation, which the author describes as "barbarism." In the nick of time, Hercules stepped into this situation to protect the weak and the just against the bullying "giants." And to make this protection lasting, he called into being a kind of militia of *gentils*, of whom the knights-errant were a later version. The *gentil* guardians are said to have entered into a social contract with the rest of the population: in exchange for their protection, they received honors and "some part of the public revenue."[63] "These men, then, whom we now call nobles or *gentilshommes*, are thus elected [to the function of] protecting the public ... and not to do violence and to extort money from people as they now for the most part are doing."[64]

The position is clear: true *gentillesse*, true nobility, was in the Golden Age the quality proper to the *meilleurs esprits*, who were admired as demigods. In view of the depravity of mankind, the public was forced for many centuries to maintain a kind of police force of armed men, who began to usurp the status (and the income) of the original demigods. But since these guardians were failing to perform their duties—and since, we are given to understand, the worst of the barbarous age is over—the time has perhaps come to liquidate the depraved guardians and restore the *meilleurs esprits* to their rightful role of leadership in the republic. This kind of ideological daydream, anonymously expressed in 1594, is not entirely utopian in character. The Dutch patriciate and the English gentry could be incomplete and, no doubt, idealized models for an enlightened commonwealth in which leadership rested on wealth and civilization rather than genealogy and force of arms. It is not necessary to wait until the eighteenth century for public expression of such views in France. There is nothing in the least anonymous, for instance, about the inscription, carved in great Roman letters, along the façade of the gallery connecting, in splendid Renaissance style, two houses that belonged to a bourgeois who lived rather nobly in Moret-sur-Loing, near Fontainebleau, in the early sixteenth century. Here, for all to see, and only a short ride from the king's château, we can read: "Qui scit linguam frenare sensumque domare fortior illo qui frangit viribus urbes"("He who keeps his tongue in check and knows how to control his feelings is stronger than the man who conquers cities by the force of arms").[65]

In time, the "fallen guardians," unable to control their feelings, may exterminate one another like rats and so make way for the true *gentils*. But meanwhile, what is one to do if provoked, sword in hand, by the last of this dying race, as is only too likely to happen daily in court? "I have seen many a good man at court," writes the author of the *Discours des querelles*, "who, having acquired much honor in the course of the long years when he was seeking his fortune, and enjoying a good reputation, which he was now more concerned with keeping than augmenting, in view of the hazards and labors our kind [*gens de nostre vacation*] are continually exposed to would suffer great pain and displeasure" in the face of some sword-dragging braggarts, "unknown men, but of race and valor, if only according to their own testimony. These desperadoes, envious of our tranquillity, and hoping to be talked about, come to seek quarrel with us—and there is, alas, never any lack of support and help for them at court."

What was one to do? Refuse the challenge? This would have been dishonorable. Accept it and fight a duel? This meant "to hazard in one day everything one had worked for all one's life." To put it bluntly, such an affair offered "very little advantage, with a high risk of loss" (*pour peu de gain, beaucoup de pertes*). The only way out of this dilemma was to forbid dueling, and this, in effect, would be one of the chief aims of gentry lobbying at court. Their goal was achieved with Henri IV in 1609 and was reaffirmed under Richelieu's administration.[66]

9

The distaste for fighting duels was not peculiar to gouty old financiers in Paris. That same feeling was present among men who were physically fit, men for whom dagger and gunshot were familiar hazards and whose lives were, on the surface, indistinguishable from those of true *gentilshommes*. The perfect example is that of Gilles de Gouberville, sieur du Mesnil, who is usually said to personify the *gentilhomme des champs* of the sixteenth century.[1]

Gouberville ought to be the best-known man of his time, for he kept the most obsessive diary of the age.[2] About him we know so much that we may be able to push our sketchy tracing of the frontiers of social categories toward greater precision. Gouberville lived a complicated life astride several worlds. It is not surprising that Vassière and others chose to describe him as a *gentilhomme*. He did have a foot in the world of the nobility—and in several other worlds as well. Without prejudging the case, let us become acquainted with him.

For our first meeting with Monsieur de Gouberville, let us catch him in what ought to be a revealing situation: he is being insulted in public. Unlike any real *gentilhomme* who has just been challenged, he looks at the assailant coldly and announces, "You are hereby fined 50 sols"—and goes on his way.[3]

Gouberville's real name is Gilles Picot. He is the first of his family to
abandon the Picot name. The change of name is no light matter.
Gouberville takes it very seriously indeed, and he achieves his end,
legally and officially, in 1570 only after many years of worry and, no
doubt, some considerable expense.[4]

Is Gouberville trying to pass as a *gentilhomme*? On the tax rolls he is
formally counted as exempt, the only worthwhile privilege he cannot
simply take for himself. When the family's right to tax exemption is
challenged, Gouberville and his relatives dig deep in the chests full of
family papers: "This afternoon I went to Breteville to see my cousin,
who is ill. We spent the afternoon looking for letters to show that he
was descended from a noble lineage." Having found some letters
"after dinner, I was up until midnight setting out the records of
various sorts mentioning the nobility of my predecessors and found
some going back to the year 1400."[5] To convince the competent authorities of the authenticity of his documents was another matter,
even for a man as well connected in the *pays* as Gouberville. We soon
find him in deep argument with the president of the court in Saint-Lô
over this matter.[6] It is not only that Gouberville fears the fate of
convicted usurpers, who are likely to be fined, as the Davy family was
to be in the following year, 1556.[7] Gouberville's ambitions are rather
complicated and contradictory: he wants to be noble for one tax purpose, bourgeois for another. Monsieur de Gouberville is also a
bourgeois of Cherbourg, where he owns an apartment house and
where he performs his guard service with the bourgeois militia.[8] As a
putative nobleman, he is obliged to show up at the muster of the
gentilshommes in Saint-Lô and pay a contribution in cash in lieu of
actual military service in the king's armies. It is precisely this expense
Gouberville, like all the other bourgeois of Cherbourg who own fiefs,
tries to avoid. Armed with a certificate of residence in Cherbourg—a
document that testifies to his status as a bourgeois of the town—
Gouberville rides into Saint-Lô, in November 1555, hoping to impress
the court. Alas, the Cherbourg claims to exemption from the *ban et
arrière-ban* contribution are turned down.[9] Gouberville starts out on a
round of conferences, caucuses, business lunches, and plain brib-
ery.[10] Despite all his efforts, and after mobilizing all the resources of
his alliances, Gouberville does not succeed in getting himself exempted from the *ban* contribution, and he is eventually billed for
twenty-two livres.[11]

M. de Gouberville's rightful social place is still unclear. Let us take a
closer look at his daily life, beginning with his work. If he were a true
gentilhomme, we should find him, as in Vaissière's idyllic description,

leading the sober and glorious life of the French nobility in its "golden age," "when it could favorably be compared to the English gentry,"[12] when *gentilshommes*, like Gouberville, felt at home only on their lands, when the city was "odious to the *gentilshommes*," who formed a privileged social class, essentially rural and warlike in character.[13]

But Gouberville does not seem to find city life at all odious. He collects his rents and performs his bourgeois guard duty in Cherbourg—where, most likely, the Picots came from. He thinks nothing of walking or riding to Cherbourg, accompanied by his cronies, Cantepye and Symmonet, on the pretext, for instance, of delivering a shipment of butter to be sent on to Rouen.[14] In the course of a typical week in August 1551, at the height of the harvesting season, Gouberville finds time on Monday to ride into Cherbourg, where the commandant of the garrison at the château asks him to lunch. On Wednesday he spends time in the fields, harvesting with a crew of twenty-eight hired hands. The very next morning he is back in Cherbourg, where, as soon as he enters town, he is asked to lunch again at the fort. Cherbourg is full of exciting things, and Gouberville is a notable and honored guest whenever he arrives in town. Gouberville has plenty of legitimate business in Cherbourg: butter and timber (for masts), among other things to sell, fish and rents to bring back, and, above all, politics.

Cherbourg attracts Gouberville as powerfully as his orchards attract honeybees. He never misses a chance to go into town. He does his Saturday shopping there, but always returns to Le Mesnil that night, because on Sunday, at the village church, important business is invariably transacted. This Sunday he manages to intercept one of his neighbors "between the mill and the church as he was going to Vespers" and gets 18s. from him for three years of arrears on a 6s. *rente*.[15] A friend drops in, inevitably, for Sunday dinner; and, as the reader with long experience of the eating and drinking habits at the manor house can predict, the party lasts into the night, the guest sleeps over, and on Monday morning Gouberville accompanies his guest back to Cherbourg. He does not get back to Le Mesnil till late in the afternoon, having had some business in court—and, also, having been unavoidably delayed at a wine-tasting.[16]

Gouberville keeps a clear head; Tuesday morning, he rides off to hold court in Valognes, as he does most Tuesdays. But he seems to have enjoyed the company of Guillaume Langloys, his Sunday guest, so much that we find him again in Langloys's company on Wednesday, riding off to Monstebourg to measure some land boundaries and sup with the lord of the manor.[17] On Sunday, Gouberville again

attends to the serious business of the weekly money collection, never
to be missed: 20s. collected from Vaultier, 11 from Jehan Paris, 7s. of
rente from Drouet, 22 from Mesnage. After Vespers, his neighbor
Guardin comes over to ask his advice on a contract. Gouberville is a
lawyer, a jurist of no mean talent. In his house he has the basic law
books necessary in his profession, and, when he needs something out
of the ordinary, he borrows it.[18] The tax collector in Valognes comes
to Gouberville for a formal law consultation on the question, "Should
a blind widow be taken off the taille rolls?"[19]

The courtroom in Valognes is the center of Gouberville's world. His
best friends are lawyers, judges, *procureurs, greffiers*. On a typical day
he rides off to Valognes early in the morning, spends the morning in
court, and has lunch with the *advocat du roy*, the *procureur du roy*, and
other *officiers*. The long business lunches, washed down with many a
pot de vin offered by clients, are usually uproarious occasions which
fill a third of the day and, as often as not, end up engendering equally
pleasant suppers which drag on into the night and oblige Gouberville
to sleep over in town. The restaurants, where all serious business
seems to be conducted, are usually run as a sideline by minor court
officials, like Denys, the "sergent qui tient hostellerie" in Valognes,
who has his counterparts in the other small towns nearby. The company in Valognes may not be as exalted as in Cherbourg, Rouen,
Caen, and Saint-Lô—all of which Gouberville frequents as a matter of
course—but it is by no means boring. Gouberville arrives for lunch at
Denys' establishment with Symmonet and maistre Cabart, the *greffier*,
to find a court clerk and others at table. He goes on to Verdier's for
supper with a neighboring estate owner, M. de Petiteville, the wife of
his tenant Jehan Paris, the wife of maistre Poulain, and the wife of the
élu Pynart. The meal extends into a party, with dancing till past ten
o'clock. Again, Gouberville sleeps over. The next day, at lunch, he
sits with three strangers and an acquaintance, maistre Colas; and
when he rides home, in the afternoon, at last, he is accompanied by a
procureur and his close friend maistre Cabart.[20]

Gouberville is always itching to go to town to meet both friends and
interesting strangers. The only thing which limits his traveling is the
expense. He always starts out with a great deal of zest, especially
when he is riding off "against" some opponent in a court case, almost
as if, according to his diary, he is riding off to some valiant feat of
arms: "Around three this afternoon I rode off with Symmonet to go to
Rouen against Gatteville."[21] His expeditions are spun out like Don
Quixote's campaigns. After starting off to Rouen, Gouberville makes
a leisurely night's stopover at the inn in Monstebourg, where he has

supper with maistre Le Gros (15s., all-inclusive). He rides off at five in the morning, through the dark and frost-covered fields, and makes another night's stop at Russy, at the estate of his uncle Jean (a curé and head of a large family), where he meets his assistant, Cantepye, just back from Rouen. The next day they arrive in Bayeux, have supper at maistre Cornet's house with a distinguished company, including Gouberville's most illustrious relative, his brother-in-law, the lieutenant général of the *bailliage*. The next day, the fourth day, Gouberville's party settles at an inn outside Caen. After another stop in Honfleur, they finally ride into Rouen on the fifth day, at dusk. There they stay at the Tableau inn, where they use their rooms for endless conferences with lawyers. This becomes so expensive that Gouberville runs out of cash: the hotel bill, in Rouen, is 7l. 10s. for a two-week stay. He has to leave three gold chains in lieu of ready cash.[22]

The social life at Rouen seems more exciting than the round of business, drinking, and gossiping in Valognes. It is during the dullest weeks in winter that Gouberville sets out for Rouen. He takes one such trip in December 1550: arriving in town, he hires a room at the Silver Eagle, takes off his boots, cleans up, and goes to visit maistre Le Prevost, who runs a kind of luxury resort for out-of-town gentry, who stay with him for weeks on end, ostensibly for their health but in fact, I suspect, to get away from their wives and to forget the dullness of small-town winters. Here he naturally finds congenial company and is invited to stay for supper. When he gets back to his inn, he finds an acquaintance there to talk to. The next day finds him dining at Monsieur Trexot's house, where he meets other visiting *officiers*.[23] He is closeted in deep conversation with the *bailli*, Jacques Davy du Perron—no doubt talking about *recherches de noblesse* of the *gentilshommes* in Coutances, tax exemption and debts, since this is the Davy who styled himself *chevalier*, held the office of *grand bailli* of the Cotentin (and as such led the court battle when his family was later declared usurpers and eventually fined).[24] In a more spiritual temper, Gouberville attends the midnight mass at a priory in company with two *conseillers* from the Rouen *parlement*.[25] But the holiday season leaves its marks on Gouberville and his friends: quite frequently his diary records his checking in at Le Prevost's for a cure—a *diete*, as he says. This time, he stays in this informal sanatorium from 28 December to 2 February in good company with a crowd of bourgeois, lawyers, *officiers* and ship captains; the bill runs to sixteen écus.[26]

Clearly, M. de Gouberville enjoys city life. He certainly cannot be confused with the threadbare adventurers who sally forth from ruined castles to provoke trouble in town: *traisneurs d'espée,* whom Vaissière tracks down through the royal pardons they obtain for the murders they commit among the bourgeois.[27] The *gentilshommes,* in Normandy as elsewhere, are faced with economic ruin and turn to banditry,[28] while their lands are being sold at auctions manipulated by men like Gouberville and his friends,[29] and while the Picots, Trexots, and Davys become the new seigneurs and *escuyers.*[30] The hopelessness of the *gentilshommes'* economic position and their violent reaction against their natural enemy, the *officiers,* can be witnessed everywhere.[31] What has not always been so clear is the degree of class solidarity found among the gentry: when one of theirs is attacked, they are quite capable of a quick riposte.

We will find striking confirmation of this solidarity in Tulle. On Thursday night, 29 November 1607, Monsieur maistre Pierre de Fenis, *conseiller du roy* and lieutenant général in Tulle, traveling on official business, stops over in a nearby village for the night. Around nine o'clock in the evening, a *gentilhomme* of the vicinity, accompanied by ten or twelve horsemen, arrives at the inn and forces his way up to the room occupied by maistre Pierre. Acting in dumb fury, the *gentilhomme,* no doubt the victim of countless pressures and spoliations at the hands of maistre Pierre and others of his ilk, finds himself acting out a surprising sort of charade. Opening the door to the judge's room, he finds maistre Pierre lying on his bed reading a book. The *gentilhomme,* pistols at the ready and sword in hand, carries out a series of strange aggresssions against his victim: he throws him off the bed, kicks him, tears off his shirt so that the judge remains naked down to his belt as he faces the pistol of his tormentor, who continues to beat him. But he inflicts no serious damage; instead, he proceeds to mark his victim by shaving off one side of his beard! Afraid, for some reason, to go any further, he runs down to the stable and hamstrings maistre Pierre's horse.

Meanwhile, one of maistre Pierre's assistants—he was accompanied by his brother-in-law, the *procureur* Lagarde, his *greffier,* and others—gets away and rides through the night at top speed to bring the news back to town. He arrives in Tulle around midnight and makes straight for the house of maistre Pierre's father. By three o'clock in the morning, the *officiers* and bourgeois of Tulle have formed themselves into a mighty raiding party of four to five hundred men, ready to go to the rescue of their endangered leader.[32]

We know enough about Gouberville by now to realize that, in a confrontation like this one, he would be the one lying up in his room

with a good book. Which is not to say that he does not know the uses
of pistol and sword. His official position places him in charge of the
forests, rivers, and beaches administered from Valognes. In a larger
sense, he represents the crown in all matters which affect royal or
public domains in the area. His responsibilities include the conservation and protection of these lands and their economic management:
the sale of timber, for instance, and the prosecution of unauthorized
logging. His authority extends to all acts committed on these public
domains: the hunting-down of outlaws who take refuge in the forest,
the defense of beaches threatened by pirate or enemy raids, the
chasing-down of poachers. We see him armed and on horseback,
riding through the forests, patrolling beaches, supervising country
auctions, catching criminals one day, and presiding in court over the
attribution of grazing rights the next day.[33] At times, he is asked to
hunt down a cattle thief.[34] When forest fires break out, it is Gouberville who is in charge of the fire fighting.[35] When English ships raid
the coast, it is Gouberville who assembles all the men of the parish
and marches them off to defend the beaches near Cherbourg.[36]

At home, in his large farm of Le Mesnil, Gouberville becomes a
simpler man and, at the same time, absolute master. He is completely
in charge of this large household with its many dependents: brutally,
easily the master who punishes, beats, whips if necessary, takes the
servant girls to his bed, or lends a hand, anywhere, with the farm
work. But Le Mesnil is in no way cut off from his other worlds: when
Gouberville does not go to town on business or for pleasure, the town
comes to him. The main room at Le Mesnil is always full of visitors.

We follow Gouberville out to his fields, where he harvests wheat,
peas, oats, flax, buckwheat, and hay.[37] Farther out, in the wet
meadows, he keeps his flocks of sheep. He supervises the shearing
and negotiates the sale of the wool himself.[38] When his farm work
requires his presence, he stays on to supervise the sowing of wheat.
Meanwhile, his assistant, Cantepye, represents him in court in Rouen
and keeps in touch by letter. The saddler arrives to repair the har-
nesses. A client drops in to negotiate a lease of crown land and stays for
lunch.[39] On another morning he gets Cantepye and another man
started on the transplanting of forty-six hundred young plants in his
tree nursery. We see him taking time out to head a posse of nine
hunting down a man for whom a warrant has been issued in Di-
goville, while an assistant goes to take his place at the court session.[40]
The next day Cantepye is sent to Valognes to take care of various
escritures, while maistre Cabart comes to lunch at Le Mesnil. Cantepye,
his trusted assistant—and the husband of his illegitimate sister,
Guillemette—is a jack-of-all-trades: he can represent Gouberville in

court, act as his legal secretary, work in the fields, take an ox to
market (9l. 10s.), or a heifer to the butcher (4l. 10s.), sell 30 livres'
worth of sheep, go to Barfleur on business, collect *rentes*. With all
that, Cantepye, whose family name is Langlois, styles himself *escuyer*,
sieur de Cantepye. This does not prevent Gouberville from sending
him on errands, on foot, to town; and, when Cantepye misbehaves,
Gouberville beats him.[41]

All the vague notions we inherited from thirteenth-century romances
and eighteenth-century polemics are quite useless in the face of the
real people who come to life in the Gouberville diary in a variety of
roles. What we perceive as contradictions were not perceived as such
by Gouberville, who wielded an accountant's pen with greater ease
than his sword, or by Cantepye, the *escuyer* who is beaten by his boss.

The Gouberville diary opens up the power structures of the Cotentin district for our scrutiny. From the country estates to the various
royal *bureaux*, from the clubby, small-town *élection* of Valognes to the
grandeur of the Rouen *parlement*, runs an invisible network of alliances, which is the map of power in the *pays*. This web of marriage
alliances and *rente* contracts is tough and dangerous: it swallows the
properties of improvident *gentilshommes*, debt-ridden peasants, and
absentee clerics. It is a trap for the crown's interests as well, and it can
resist the most powerful assaults. Crown and church can inflict severe
wounds, but the gentry recovers: the Davys, condemned as usurpers,
will rise to power anyway. One or two Picots, suspected of Protestant
leanings, will lose out, but M. de Gouberville goes on, on the best of
terms with his curé, thinking his private thoughts and making profitable deals for the collection of tithes.

Gouberville's friends are *greffiers*, *advocats*, *esleus*, *sergents*, but also
conseillers and lieutenants généraux, curés, and simple *laboureurs* and
farmhands. Gouberville appears so entirely at ease in exactly the
same way with each of them that it is impossible to suspect that these
men and women belong to a society which is said to be hierarchical.
When Gouberville comes down from his bedroom in the morning and
finds maistres Cabart and Anquetil waiting for him, he accompanies
them on their way just as if these bourgeois and *greffiers* were his
equals.[42] He eats lunch at home with the cloth merchant's nephew on
Sunday, and next day he dines at the table of Captain Poton in the
Cherbourg fort.[43] The courtesy he shows to court clerks, *procureurs*,
sergents, and *laboureurs* is in no way artificial. He takes the greatest
pleasure in the company of these men and their families; he counts

them among his closest friends.[44] He shows no more courtesy to someone like maistre Loys Davy, sieur du Perron, when he drops in to ask for a letter of introduction to his brother-in-law, the lieutenant général at Caen.[45] We find him making a special trip to borrow jewelry from a relative, to be used at the wedding of a tenant of his.[46] Schoolmasters drop in at Le Mesnil with a simple gift of pears.[47] The parish priest, Jehan Auvrey, offers him a white rose, freshly picked in his garden.

Among his guests are Parisian merchants,[49] barbers, saddlers, schoolteachers, monks and abbés, and students. But he is also at home among more notable company, and the tone of his comments does not change. We find him at a Sunday banquet held in honor of the daughter of the *élu* Borlande, to whom he is remotely related; here we find *procureurs du roy, chanoines,* various tax officials, and seigneurs with their wives and daughters.[50] The only thing which is the least bit striking in Gouberville's social habits is the absence, or near absence, of *gentilshommes* in his daily encounters. There is Monsieur de Saint-Nazer, one of the most powerful men around, but he is wearing a *nom de terre.* His real name is Du Moncel, he is lieutenant in the admiralty of Cherbourg—and Gouberville's brother-in-law.[51] The same is true of Baron de Cresnay (or Cresne, Cresnes), who is Nicolas du Parc and married to Gouberville's niece (or almost niece, not clear). It is true, however, that the Cresnays' style of living is more noble and certainly more expensive than Gouberville's. They own a château near Avranches and another at Montfarville.[52]

When it comes to *gentilshommes,* Gouberville seems to keep his distance. He fails to pay court when the governor of Normandy, Martin du Bellay, arrives in Valognes: Gouberville sends his apologies and explains that he is constipated.[53] He speaks warmly in his diary of his constant visitors—merchants, *drapiers,* bourgeois, *greffiers, cordeliers,* and others but finds nothing nice to say about "a little *gentilhomme* called Brealy ... who supped and slept here and told us a million lies."[54] These are perhaps small matters. What seems more conclusive is that in his relations with the more prestigious landed families—those who hunt with hounds and do not seem to hold office—he practices what looks like a quarantine policy. That is, he sees these people only on his secondary property at Gouberville. There he is likely to dine with his cousin de la Ferronnyere, with M. de Fermanville, or with his cousin La Vallette.[55] I have the impression that Gilles Picot behaves differently at Gouberville: more nobly, more idly. At Le Mesnil he is never idle; he is always fussing

with his bees, his pigs, his sheep, his horses, his hired men—and
with wenches. When it snows and he stays indoors, there is a heap of
escritures waiting for him—piles of contracts and accounts. Visitors
come on business even in the worst weather. At Gouberville, on the
other hand, he seems transformed into a man of leisure. We find him
walking along the beaches with friends. He eats lunches at the Cresnays' château. When he comes home to Le Mesnil, he seems to be in a
hurry to make up for lost time. There is no day of rest among the
lawyers and *officiers:* Gouberville thinks nothing of sending Cantepye
to Cherbourg on Sunday to get some legal work done.[56]

Among Gouberville's more "noble" acquaintances, there is Monsieur *l'escuyer* Poton, the commander of the Cherbourg garrison,
who often invites him to his table. Poton hunts in the grand manner
and presumably has other tastes to match. This may be why Gouberville emphasizes his nobility by referring to him as Monsieur *l'escuyer*
and defers to him—as he does not to such people as Davy, the *bailli,*
or the lieutenant général at Caen and other important *officiers.* There
are plenty of *escuyers* around M. de Gouberville, to begin with, Cantepye. But when Françoys Damours, archer of Poton's guard, comes
by to borrow a dog, it is an honor for Gouberville. Damours too is an
escuyer.[57]

All these are mere clues. But these clues, fragile though they are,
keep coming up. We see Gouberville, up to his elbows in harvesting
barley and oats at Le Mesnil in August, with a crew of twenty-two,
receiving the impromptu visit of M. de Cresnay and M. de
Bourgneuf, who come hunting, equipped with "falcon, many
spaniels and greyhounds." Gouberville does not join them.[58] On
another occasion, in the summer of 1555, when Gouberville is in a bad
temper almost constantly because of the *recherches de noblesse* and
because he is worried about losing his office, we find him in trouble
with the *vicomte* of Valognes,[59] who had asked him for some timber
from the public forests for his personal use. Righteously and cor-
rectly, Gouberville refuses. He insists that this is against the law.
They quarrel and come to blows. Gouberville records these events on
the next day: he is ashamed of himself and is so worried about the
consequences that he uses a Greek-letter code for the entry. In this
difficulty, Gouberville appeals to his two most noble-like relatives,
Monsieur de Saint-Nazer and Monsieur de Cresnay, who come to
Valognes to smooth things over.[60]

The political and religious storms which sweep over this corner of
the kingdom will raise tempers and sharpen old rivalries. But Gouberville and his friends manage to weather all these troubles. They control

the *pays,* no matter what; they need not worry about their position in the politics of the *élection* or of the *bailliage.* Nor need they worry about their social status—the rare occasions excepted, when powers from the outside world reach into theirs (when Paris decides to extort money from the tacit nobility, for instance). Otherwise it really does not matter whether one is noble like the baron de Cresnay or the sieur de Gouberville or the archer Damours or the foreman-secretary Cantepye. The baron with his greyhounds and the farmhand who takes butter to the marketplace are both *escuyers* and both usurpers: in the *pays* it does not matter.

It is when a man travels outside his *pays* that we see in him a different light. Let us follow Gouberville on his painful pilgrimage to the royal court in Blois, in January 1555.[61] Only the most dire need could force Gouberville to make such an unpleasant and expensive trip. This time, he needs confirmation of his office. He sets out, then makes a farewell stop in Caen, where he is still an important person. He will carry letters from his brother-in-law, the lieutenant général in Caen, to maistre Morin in Blois. This is an efficient and predictable move, since the lieutenant général is without question the most powerful relative at his disposal for "pushing himself in the world." And he will need plenty of push, because he cannot count on his ancient name (still Picot, then), nor is he rich enough to influence the financiers at court. He will, eventually, submit an unsuccessful bid of thirteen hundred écus for the office of *maistre des eaux et forests.* It is surprising that he thought he could raise this kind of money. He lost out to a richer man, but he did at least get his lieutenancy confirmed.

There is no clear answer to the question, How does Gouberville appear to others, once he has left his *pays?* Nobody can tell a *gentilhomme* by his appearance: "Il y a le nom et la chose," as Montaigne puts it. ("Is there anyone who can stop my stableboy from calling himself Pompey the Great?") M. de Gouberville rides into a world where his name means nothing and where people will certainly not judge him on his appearance. Every mile that brings him closer to Blois brings him closer to being stripped of the last vestiges of his local status. What influences can Gouberville bring to bear away from home? His relationship to the lieutenant général La Bigne would carry weight in some circles, especially when backed by money. But to be presented at court as M. de Gouberville, a *gentilhomme* of the Cotentin, brother-in-law of the lieutenant général La Bigne, is to reveal, at once, that this *gentilhomme*'s alliances are among the *messieurs maistres* of the *bailliage* and *présidial* courts. This would not be a good recommendation for a *gentilhomme de race*. (In the *bailliage* of which Châteaudun is the principal town, not a single *officier*, from the *bailli* on down, appeared in the catalogue of the noble families.)

One alternative is for Gilles to find refuge in anonymity, to hope that the *gentilshommes* at court (he would, no doubt, exaggerate their nobility in his mind) could not distinguish him from one of their own. That might be possible, in brief encounters. But even if nothing betrays him in his dress, in his equipment, in his manners, what if he should fall in with a troop of *gentilshommes* boasting of their military campaigns and of their gallantries? What battlefields and what boudoirs can Gilles speak knowledgeably of?—he who goes to court to avoid the *gentilhomme* obligation, the *ban et arrière-ban*, he who is satisfied to tumble servant girls, he whose gallantries are addressed to *greffiers'* and *procureurs'* wives? And what if he is challenged to a duel? No doubt, a resourceful man can get around many of these difficulties. But the more natural course to take is to associate with one's own kind, among whom one is appreciated for other virtues. And that is what Gouberville does.

In Falaise, not quite out of his territory yet, he stops at the inn of the Three Maries and shares the dinner table with a *"gentilhomme* who comes from somewhere near Caen" and an old *advocat* from Falaise. In Châteaudun, stopping at the sign of the Crescent, he is really away from home, but he finds congenial company in the person of a *conseiller* from the Dijon *parlement*, no doubt himself on the way to court. The two of them team up for the rest of the journey. In Blois, between courtesy calls and serious business, Gouberville kills time. He drinks with Labarre, the queen's wine steward; drops in at the performance of a comedy "in French prose" at the abbey of Saint-Gomer; and even forces himself, at least on one occasion on 17 February, to play the courtier's part, no doubt acting on good advice: in attendance at the royal supper, that night, he is given the honorable task of carrying the baby granddaughter of Monseigneur the Connestable. He does not enjoy this. Fortunately, the ball ends early: by eight o'clock that night, utterly exhausted no doubt, Gouberville is back in his lodgings, unable to swallow more than a couple of eggs for supper.

His business finished, Gouberville rides out of Blois, after some three weeks' stay, much relieved. On his way back, lighthearted, he has time for some serious touring. In Châteaudun he strikes up acquaintance with a man from Caen, and they walk through the city and visit the château. They make a detour to visit the cathedral in Chartres. It takes Gouberville two weeks to get home. On the fifth of

March, he is back home at last, among his roses and bees, ready to resume the normal round of his activities.

Watching M. de Gouberville away from his home grounds, we have confirmed our guesses: he is a *gentilhomme* in the manner of Nicolas Pasquier and no *gentilhomme des champs*, and this despite his agronomist's expertise. Despite? I think there is a misunderstanding here. When Vaissière offers up Olivier de Serres, Noël du Fail, and Gilles de Gouberville as representatives of the best sort of *gentilshommes campagnards*, he is deluding himself. It is no accident that he chose three men of such dubious nobility as his star witnesses. The true *gentilshommes des champs* knew very little about agriculture, and they were not likely to invest time, science, energy, and capital in their failing properties.[62] They preferred to collect rents and feudal dues, of small value, and generally left the management of their own lands to *laboureurs, fermiers, bailes,* and other entrepreneurs, who made themselves rich at the seigneur's expense. Far from being the "golden age" of the French nobility, as Vaissière allows himself to believe, the sixteenth century in France was the "golden age of profits" for the entrepreneur who ran his own domains.[63]

Montaigne senses these distinctions: being genteel himself, he claims to have no interest in farming.[64] If Gouberville had met someone like Montaigne, he would have bored him stiff talking about his pigs. But if a *gentilhomme* with experience of military camps and court life had listened indulgently to this rustic barnyard talk, he would gradually have discovered that this man Gouberville, far from being simpleminded, was, on the contrary, a technician who ran a large agricultural enterprise for the sake of profit, thus mixing a farmer's work with a bourgeois's resources. In a word, he was the enemy.

Whether Gouberville's enterprises are profitable is hard to say. The diary rarely, if ever, shows him borrowing money, while, on the other hand, money from various sources comes in almost daily—from rents, *rentes,* other arrears brought up, and from small-scale commercial banking. It is hard to say whether the sale of the produce of his estates alone shows a profit when balanced against his expenses in wages paid and in materials bought, but the Gouberville business is a large affair, and there is good reason to think that his over-all operation is profitable. The fields and orchards at Le Mesnil are only the most immediately visible aspects of Gouberville's enterprises. He raises wheat, for which he gets as much as 12s. a bushel in 1556.[65] He runs a dairy operation and ships his butter to Rouen, as we have seen. He raises cattle, pigs, sheep, and horses on a respectable scale. His apple orchards benefit from the most advanced pruning and cross-breeding experiments,[66] and he distills an *eau de vie*—a kind of applejack, no doubt—probably for commercial purposes.[67] The size of his operation can be guessed at from the large crews who work for him in season, in addition to the dozen or so farmhands regularly employed at Le Mesnil, to say nothing of the troop of women this confirmed bachelor keeps around the house—mostly young servant girls hired on yearly contracts at the annual labor market.[68]

The servants, inevitably, get advances of one kind or another, fall into debt to their master, and receive little or no money on payday; some at times even find themselves in the position of owing money to Gouberville. My impression is that M. de Gouberville deals fairly with his people. They are not entirely at his mercy. For instance, when he pays off his servant girl, Guionnne, he counts out her money in the presence of her brother. The chances of being victimized, it seems to me, were small, since the hiring of servants was open and regulated. This was done at annual "hiring fairs" (*loueries*), at which wage-earners and employers came together in village squares on specified days, under the watchful eye of local authorities. It would have been difficult to pay less than the going price for given services to men and women of proven competence. At Valognes and Montfarville this fair was held on Saint Magdalen's day, 22 July; in Teville, on the twenty-sixth, Saint Anne's day; and in Negreville, on the eighteenth. These fairs were held in an atmosphere of music and dancing and were presided over by the local seigneurs and curés. When a servant is dissatisfied at Le Mesnil—it is usually a teenage girl in her first months of service—she simply walks out and goes home to her parents. And if the master is dissatisfied with a servant's work, he either feels free to beat him—a privilege acquired through seniority—or he will call the young man's father, ask him to punish his son, and, upon refusal, pay the servant his due and fire him.[69]

Excluding Gouberville's half-brother, Symmonet, his half-sister, Guillemette, and her husband, Cantepye, who were the executives of the Le Mesnil enterprise, the permanent staff of ten to fifteen men and women was easily doubled in August and September by seasonal hiring. This large labor force was needed to keep the astonishingly varied branches of the estate in good order. There were separate stables and barns for horses, mares, oxen, cows, sheep, and pigs. There was also a large herd of goats. By far the largest number of his cattle and horses ranged freely in the grazing lands and forests around, in the manner of the ranches of the American West. We can get only brief impressions of the size of these herds on the occasion of round-ups, such as the one conducted in June 1562, when a crew of twenty cowboys set out to castrate one-year-old calves.[70] The sheep at Le Mesnil were shorn in May, and the wool was sold in large quantities to a Parisian merchant, who came to seal the bargain.[71] The horses were rounded up in log corrals (*parcs*), which, wherever possible, were built along a stream.[72] These roundups took as many as thirty men at a time, volunteer crews who were paid off at the day's end with rounds of wine at the inn.[73] Dissatisfied with the inefficient traditional roundup technique—hordes of men stampeding the wild horses into nets and eventually corrals—Gouberville experimented with new methods; he directed three cowboys to follow the herd and push it toward the corral.[74] Once caught, the horses were hobbled and branded.[75] Pigs were raised at Le Mesnil in large numbers. They were sold in Cherbourg: twenty-three pigs at three livres or more apiece in November 1559; a lot of fourteen for sixty-seven livres in 1561; another lot at about the same price the year after. Other lots were sent by sea to Paris and to Rouen.[76]

Nothing is small enough to escape Gouberville's idiosyncratic but firm accounting of his large operation. A man who owes him 14 sols but cannot pay is hired to do ten days of work, from which he gains 2 sols.[77] A bushel of wheat owed to him by his tenant, Berger, and whose value probably did not exceed 12s., produces an "arrears" fine of 12s., which, two years later, is solemnly received after mass in front of the village church.[78] At the other extreme of the Gouberville banking business we catch sight of "the sieur Digny, *presidial*" (that is, *conseiller* at the *présidial* court) who comes to see Gouberville at home in December 1560 to ask for a delay in the payment of his debts until Easter, "which we agreed to."[79] (This sieur Digny is almost surely the father of the poet Malherbe.) Another sizable business operation is the leasing of the right to collect tithes due to the cathedral chapter at Coutances. This kind of tax-farming is usually negotiated by competitive bidding, with the tax farmer offering to produce a fixed sum for the chapter and counting on collecting far more. M. de Gouberville has enough political power, and his relations with the canons, abbés, and curés are close enough, that his bid—no doubt a very low one—is unopposed.[80]

There is no limit to Gouberville's energy. With the help of Cantepye and Symmonet, and in partnership with various other investors—beginning with his Uncle Jean—Gouberville does not let any opportunity pass him by: wherever there is a profit to be made, we find him trying his hand at it. Why then does he bother with his office of lieutenant, which brings in only 23 livres in annual salary—often in arrears—and takes up a great deal of his time in court work in the *élection* at Valognes and elsewhere?

There is no way of overstating the importance of this office for Gouberville, for his father before him, and for the Picot family as a whole and its alliances and *parentèles*. The office, in the family since 1522, is the indispensable instrument of the family's fortune and successes. Clearly, it is not the salary which makes the position attractive. Through the lieutenancy, Gouberville belongs to the political leadership of the *pays*. He must retain the office at all costs: with it, he prospers.

The court sessions, the auctions, the sales of timber and grazing rights, all these no doubt carry luscious profits with them, perquisites of office, opportunities for fiscal fraud. His office puts Gouberville in the position, always, of being helpful to some and refusing to deal with others. More directly, we must remember that Gouberville is above all a livestock farmer. Some of his horses, his cattle, his pigs and sheep and goats graze on public lands. The clear impression is that Gouberville is able to obtain royal grazing rights for his own herds because of his office. (These grazing rights are very valuable, sold by lease at high cash prices.) I have no doubt that the loss of his office would have had immediate and disastrous effect on the Gouberville farm.[81]

We can see that the various and apparently disparate sides of Gouberville's life do, in fact, hold together. The lawyer-judge-sheriff is indispensable to the landowner. The businessman who notes his smallest expenses with such care is also the farmer who tends to his fruit trees personally. The holding of office would be pointless for the man who did not have commercial or agricultural interests to forward in this manner. The seigneurie prospers in the hands of the gentry *officier* and experienced businessman as it does not in the hands of a *gentilhomme*. Not only because Gouberville keeps track of his expenses, watches over the farmhands, experiments with twenty-nine different kinds of apple trees: for even so, it would be hard to show that the farm turns a profit.[82] And yet we know that Gouberville is not getting poorer.

The seigneuries, in the hands of the gentry, are modest building blocks for growing fortunes: land engendering more land, grain more grain, in the course of a patient game whose master moves are often, of necessity, secret. What happens to Gouberville's wheat? Why does not more of it come to market? Does he eat it all?[83] Well, here and there, we can see what happens: he invests it. Why sell a bushel for 12s. today if you can lend it and get 6s. a year in interest for it? The seigneurie becomes, in the right hands, a fairy-tale implement for perpetual plenty, like those magic tablecloths which keep sprouting lavish banquets on command. Is it not magical, this seigneurie, which, according to modern calculations, should be going bankrupt but whose seigneur is clearly a wealthy man?[84]

10

Wealth

*Le marchand acquére, l'officier conserve,
le noble dissippe.*
   A bourgeois of Lyon

I own 30,000 livres in rentes—*and I'm
dying!*
   Joke attributed to the poet Desportes on his deathbed

*I hope God does not find the amount ex-
cessive.*
   Pious reserve expressed by the
   lawyer Versoris in a similar connection

Can Gouberville be described as a wealthy man? I would not presume to say just how much he is worth. He can bid thirteen hundred écus for an office, that is, more than three thousand livres.[1] He eats well and allows himself all sorts of little luxuries, common among his kind: oranges, pomegranates, good wines.[2] Not for him, though, such regal presents as Negro slaves, received, on occasion, by his more exalted friends and colleagues.[3] Gouberville's fortune is a modest one. He has less than two thousand livres tied up in his office, a few thousand in real estate and *rentes*. His annual income, from all sources, may be less than one thousand livres. This is certainly suffi- cient for a comfortable living, especially since there are no sons to establish in the world and no daughters' dowries to scrape together. The properties are well managed, the buildings in good repair; there is plenty of meat and cider to go around, and the servants wear new clothes and shoes. This is a middling, largely self-sufficient little em- pire, such as the gentry dreams about in its more bucolic moods; but it is a world removed from the great Parisian fortunes.

If wealth is a "means of acceding," as the jurists say, to *noblesse politique*,[4] does it necessarily follow that a gentry family's wealth plays a significant part in determining its status? Is there an economic threshold, an entrance requirement? Can one be poor and belong to the gentry—as one can be poor and noble?

Certainly, the gentry is a social class in which poverty must be anomalous, almost by definition. The beginnings of gentry status, after all, are to be found, almost always, among the *familles*, which are the richest of their city and *pays*.[5] Poor men are hard to find among these messieurs of the city council, of the *échevinage* or the *siège royal*. Nor is it natural for the *familles* to lose their grip, from father to son, on their investments. But it does happen occasionally, and it seems that this strange character—the *noble homme* of good gentry background who slides toward genteel poverty—does retain his social status as long as he does not, in desperation, undertake some clearly unacceptable activity, such as *marchandise*.[6] Even among the most economically marginal segment of the gentry—the professional intellectuals—one can find wealthy men. The poet Philippe Desportes is a good example of this. He came from a Chartres family with *marchandise* and *échevinage* on both his father's and his mother's sides, received an excellent classical education, and began his career, like le président d'Ormesson, learning *escriture* in a *procureur's* office. But it was his talent as a poet which propelled him into success. Enormously popular at court, protected by Villeroy, and a first-rate businessman to boot, Desportes eventually found himself hoarding the wealth of several abbeys. He may in fact have achieved an annual income not so far removed from the thirty thousand livres death was said to have parted him from.[7]

Another sensational intellectual's career was that of the classicist Jacques Amyot. Like the Desportes, the Amyots were prosperous provincial merchants whose sons would have been propelled beyond *marchandise*, in the 1530s, with or without talent. Amyot's father, a merchant of Melun, who owned a house worth six hundred livres on the main street, was able to send Jacques to a good *collège* in Paris. In 1532, at the age of nineteen, Jacques had a master's degree from the university and followed the lectures of the royal professors.

At that point in life, he could just barely be said to be leaving his family's *condition*. In Bourges, in 1535, when he took up teaching at the university, Théodore de Bèze remembered him as a "man of low *condition*." The professorship of Greek, at two hundred livres a year, led to the patronage of Morvillier, and Amyot became known to the king. In a great classicist like Amyot, mediocre fortune and a *marchand* father weighed little against a celebrity comparable to that which envelops virtuosi in our time: in the salons of the gentry, Amyot was like a Rubinstein or a Menuhin.[8] He became tutor to the royal family, at a yearly salary of five hundred livres. As his pupils reached the throne, Amyot was named grand almoner to the king, with a salary of twelve hundred livres; he also received the deanship of the Orléans cathedral chapter—a Morvillier fief—and the income of a Burgundian abbey. In 1570 he received the bishopric of Auxerre. With the accession of Henri III his fortunes rose even higher: an office in the *chambre des comptes* for his brother Jean, two houses in Paris, a château, and finally a knighthood in the Order of the Holy Spirit, which was rated more noble than the Order of Saint Michel, even if "there were more *chevaliers* than *chevaux* at Court."[9]

Desportes and Amyot represent exceptional success stories. For both, however low the *condition,* there was nevertheless sufficient capital in the family to back a claim to political nobility (*noblesse politique*). Desportes and Amyot were both trained to be *rentiers*—clerical *rentiers.* Amyot's life and Desportes's would have followed a quiet course, drifting along on prebends and *rentes.* Favorable circumstances allowed them to hoist their talents like sails in the wind: a strong puff from the Louvre, from Fontainebleau or Blois, and their little barks were off, speeding for El Dorado. There is no reason to think, however, that abbeys and pensions raised the esteem in which they were held. Once past that difficult shoal which separates low condition from living nobly, it is smooth sailing all the way; becoming lettered only helped to efface the memory of a difficult passage. Neither Ronsard nor Malherbe knew how to catch the prevailing winds with Desportes's uncanny skill, but they were not, for all that, held in lesser esteem. On the contrary, I have the impression that Desportes's well-known business sense served him badly in this respect.[10]

We know the importance of letters. Lefevre d'Ormesson had everything else in abundance—and remained a *bonhomme.* Could it be that letters alone can propel a person into the gentry? Let us consider the celebrity of the Des Roches ladies—les dames des Roches—of Poitiers.[11] These women, mother and daughter, held one of the most famous salons of the gentry. Their house, in Saint Michael's parish in Poitiers, was the rendezvous of the city's literati. Here, almost daily, the two women held court in the *salle basse.* Local celebrities, such as Scévole de Sainte-Marthe and Scaliger, were to be found at these receptions, in a crowd of poets and playwrights, physicians and university professors, erudite canons, *advocats,* and *officiers.*[12] Sainte-Marthe remembered this salon as a place where "there were, every day, a great many people, lovers of letters and good taste, who came

together at their house very avidly as in some academy; and there was
not a single one of them who did not leave their house more
civilized."[13] Scaliger, who rarely spoke well of anyone, went on
record that the elder dame des Roches had "read and remembered
more history than any Frenchmen he knew of (and was more
learned)." Further, he was willing to certify that she was "the most
learned person in Europe, among those who know only one language."[14] It was to this house that one repaired, immediately after
arriving in Poitiers, if one wished to meet good company and find
brilliant conversation. The ladies published their *Collected Works* in
1578. From that moment their fame knew no bounds. When, in the
following year, legions of *présidents*, *conseillers*, and *advocats* poured
into Poitiers for the Grands Jours, the Des Roches house naturally
became the rallying point of an almost national collection of wits and
pedants, amateur poets and classicists, all singing the praises of the
dames des Roches.

And yet these *dames* were very humble folk. The mother,
Madeleine Neveu, had been the wife of maistre Fradonnet, *procureur*,
taxed at 7 sols: definitely not among the *familles*, definitely no pretensions to living nobly. When Fradonnet died, Madeleine married
maistre Eboissard, an *advocat* at the *présidial* court, owner of a seigneurie, and taxed at 50 sols—a considerable leap upward in the social
scale, but not yet within reach of notability. Eboissard achieved the
status of bourgeois in Poitiers only in the 1560s, when Madeleine was
already middle-aged. Toward the end of their lives, Madeleine and
her daughter Catherine owned their house and a few lands, whose
revenues were negligible: 66 livres a year and some eggs, cheese,
cherries, and chickens. On the other hand, their income from
moneylending in a single year (1580–81) amounted to 551l. 13s. 4d.
for an invested capital of 6,618 livres.[15] It would be far-fetched to see
in this modest but sufficient income—roughly the equal of
Gouberville's—the source of Madeleine's status. Married to a *procureur* or to an *advocat*, worth 60 or 600 livres of income, she would
have been a *dame* nevertheless, and celebrated by the Pasquiers and
Scaligers. Her *qualité* was of a spiritual kind, totally separated from her
husbands' means and positions. The husbands are never mentioned.

Still, the Des Roches ladies were able to keep a salon and did not
engage in menial activities. Their income, however modest, came
from approved sources: land and banking. What of people who lived
on wages? They clearly could make no claim to living nobly. An
exception is made, however, for intellectuals. The lives of any
number of brilliant adventurers come to mind, that of the poet Jacques

Grévin, for example, whose short, tumultuous life is a picaresque novel: tall, blond, charming, and precocious, we find him in Ronsard's entourage in his teens, passionately and hopelessly in love with the sixteen-year-old Nicole Estienne, granddaughter of the publisher and classicist.[16] The purest example of a man who lived nobly and whose only asset was his learning may well be François Brouard, who appears as Béroalde de Verville in encyclopedias and biographical dictionaries. Born in 1556 to Matthieu and Marie Brouard, the infant's only assets in this world were his parents' learning and the prestige of their relative, the well-known professor Vatable.[17] François's father was a professional teacher who had been on the staff of the Bordeaux and Agen *collèges*. His mother was Vatable's niece. Her husband was also related to Vatable, whose shadow loomed over the Brouard household. François was named after this famous relative. If pedagogy has a muse of its own, surely she watched tenderly over young François's progress from the start. His baptism was attended by Mercier, professor of Hebrew, and Chesneau, principal of the *collège* of Tours. He lived, naturally enough, in his parents' *pédagogie*, on the rue des Ecoles, where Professor Brouard supervised the education of distinguished young boarders—Pierre de l'Estoile and Agrippa d'Aubigné among them.

After his father's death, François Brouard—who was making a living as a clockmaker and jeweler in Basel and also may have earned a medical degree, among other things—began his career as a professional writer and changed his name. Brouard was transformed into Beroalde, the name Vatable used to call his father. Verville was the name of a village near Montargis where the Brouard household had once lived for a short time. "Beroalde de Verville" sounded noble enough that François could be described as a *"gentilhomme Parisien"* in La Croix du Maine's *Bibliothèque françoise* of 1584. In truth, François himself was an expert in the field of tacit ennoblement: he had written the captions for *Blason des Armoiries*, a commercial venture full of invented coats of arms that was published in 1579. Continuing his career as a commercial writer, François published a mathematics textbook, a novel, and some translations. He can be found briefly back in the Latin Quarter, at the sign of the Cross on the rue Saint-Jacques, and later in Tours, during the worst years of the League, together with his patrons, his publishers, and his friends and readers. Protected by powerful gentry families—among them the La Guesles, *procureurs généraux* of the *parlement* and archbishops of Tours—Brouard-Beroalde acquired a canon's prebend and continued to celebrate the joys and powers of learning: "There is no pleasure to equal that of always learning ... it is my only passion."[18] This born pedagogue in his later works gave hints on the ways to success through learning. His last and most perverse book was fittingly entitled *Le Moyen de parvenir.*[19]

A university degree, a reputation for wit in *rencontres*, the possession of learning—such assets could override other considerations. Bohemian, heretic, insolvent teachers can be found everywhere in the kingdom, with books, a gown, a dagger, and a broken guitar as their sole possessions. They are treated as equals by wealthy magistrates. It never occurs to Monsieur de Montaigne to look down upon such teachers as Amyot or Pelletier.[20] Nor does it cross Pasquier's mind to give anything but a place of honor to his much-publicized friendship with Catherine des Roches, the daughter of a *procureur*. Letters, we can see, place a man, or a woman, hors concours in French society, then as now.

If wealth is discounted as a source of esteem in this case, can it weigh absolutely in other cases? Is a gentleman worth six thousand livres the inferior of a gentleman worth sixty thousand? Or even six hundred thousand—other things being equal? Here again we are asking a question to which no contemporary could have given a satisfactory answer. And yet, we cannot escape an over-all impression that money does not count.

There is no sympathy for the poverty of the improvident and incompetent nobleman, who, wasting his life in useless pleasures, hunting, gambling, and quarreling, is the perennial target of the gentry's scorn. But there is such a thing as honorable poverty. To be born poor is no vice. And admirable is the life of the man who remains poor to devote himself to higher things, to letters, to civic duty. Such a man expresses through his actions a saintly contempt for money, which the gentry as a whole only talks of imitating. The teacher or professor, beginning with Socrates, is naturally the most common type of gentry saint. But the gentry reserves a special place even among the highest offices of the realm for admirable, selfless "poor men." The chancellor of France, Michel de l'Hospital, provides a most suitable example.

To ask whether the gentry admires wealth in general is not, then, a useful question, since we know that some kinds of wealth are scorned, while some kinds of poverty are admired. Still, it does cost money to live nobly. Rare is the artisan or peasant who can give up his work and retire on an income of several hundred livres a year: enough for decent housing, simple dress and food, and the upkeep of a library.

There is no escaping the fundamental truth that political nobility is a condition which presupposes the ownership of a certain minimum of capital, preferably inherited capital, so that one cannot be accused of having soiled his hands and endangered his virtue in the process of acquiring it. Even the *collège* teacher, who depends on his salary, often fulfills this requirement. He is easily distinguished from the merchant, inasmuch as he is not, in principle, trying to get rich. Like the *officier*, the *rentier*, and the seigneur, the *régent*, or teacher, in his modest way, can be described as living off his inherited capital. In lieu of lands or *rentes*, his investment is in letters. His family, one can argue, invested a not negligible sum in his education, anywhere from one to three thousand livres, over the years. This capital, invested in land or *rentes*, would have produced an income of sixty to two hundred livres a year, enough to live on and more or less the equivalent of a teacher's salary.

The gentry as an economic group may be hardly more homogeneous than the nobility. But what a world of difference between the two social types! Everything separates the threadbare teacher from the equally threadbare *gentilhomme des champs*. Within his own class, however, each of them can find respect and understanding. Within the gentry's world, the poor and the rich behave essentially in the same way. Even very great wealth rarely leads to a betrayal of the gentry's values.

The very richest *présidents* remain loyal to the traditions of their class. They respect learning, they believe in hard work, they are family men, nothing can turn them into courtiers. Le président de Thou is presented to us by Estienne Pasquier, who knew him well, as a "studious" man who reserved certain hours each day for private study. "I came upon him," Pasquier tells us, "reading Cicero's orations against Varro, the book on one side, his notes on the other." Despite the enormous pressure of business on a man like De Thou, he found time to read difficult and purely academic books, like the three volumes of Turnèbe's *Adversaria* which he borrowed from Pasquier and managed to study and return in less than a month. At work, in the Palais de Justice, De Thou "was the first to arrive and the last to leave." He always ate dinner at home after walking back from the Palais with none of the pomp of a *grand* seigneur ("I have seen him, sometimes, walking home alone," notes Pasquier). As soon as he entered his home, the *président* "rid himself of everything connected with the grandeur of his position" and joined his family and friends at table, where he could be found "laughing easily" and surrounding himself ordinarily with "men of mediocre condition." Early to bed and early to rise, the *président* had no time for dancing, gambling, or other entertainments; he always went to bed by nine o'clock and rose early, dressing without the help of a servant.[21]

One of the wealthiest *présidents*, Séguier, is a man worth taking a closer look at, and this we can do thanks to Denis Richet's monograph.[22]

The Séguiers, who were apothecaries in the fifteenth century, were to be found, by 1500, in the Parisian *échevinage*. One of them was still "honorable homme marchand epicier et bourgeois de Paris" as late as 1510, when others in the family were beginning to acquire seigneuries and offices. Following the usual pattern, the Séguiers used their commercial profits to acquire a stake in royal finance. As notaries, as *receveurs des aides*, as *élus*, they abandoned the merchant world, moved into more respectable neighborhoods, and contracted marriages with gentry families. In 1507 Nicolas Séguier, son of a merchant-bourgeois, married into a family of *advocats* and teachers as well as *notaires et secrétaires du roy*, the Le Blancs, who were allied to the Budés. With the Le Blancs's help, Nicolas Séguier rose in municipal politics and in prestige. His house, at the Sign of Our Lady, cost twelve hundred livres, and his tombstone described him as "noble homme maistre Séguier." Of Nicolas's many children, one became *président* at the Châtelet, another *maistre des comptes*. At the third generation, we find a Séguier *président* in the *parlement*.

Le président Séguier, whose fortune Richet estimates at 600,000 livres, runs his affairs in the same way a merchant *laboureur* might.[23] As a moneylender, le président Séguier usually goes after bigger game than the small-town merchants or *advocats* we have come to know, but the method remains the same. When the duchess of Nevers faces financial difficulties in March 1542, she borrows 5,334 écus from Séguier and contracts to pay 1,000 livres annual *rente*. Seven years later her affairs have not improved; once again desperately in need of cash, she sells an immense seigneurie near Dreux to Séguier for 9,000 écus. But after back payments and arrears on the original transaction, she gets only 3,600 écus of this sum. She is hooked, as surely as Marques of Chenonceaux or the small-time *laboureurs* of Poitou, whose fate we followed in an earlier chapter. The sale, probably made at a great loss, is softened by a provision that permits the repurchase of the lands at the original price within three years. Three months later, however, the duchess gives up her right to repurchase the property in exchange for an additional sum of 1,500 écus. The property will be estimated, a few years later, at 60,000 livres.

Another example: in 1567, Princess Henriette de Clèves, desperate

to raise cash, publicly offers a very large group of properties near
Gien for sale. In the absence of serious bids, she is forced to accept
Séguier's offer. He buys the properties for 84,000 livres; they will be
worth 135,000 livres twenty years later. A further example: Montmorency borrows 12,000 livres from Séguier in 1561 against the payment
of an annual *rente* of 1,000 livres, which is still being paid in 1640.[24]
Séguier's loans, it should be noted, were not necessarily made with
his own capital alone, since he acted as banker to a number of great
gentry families who were his allies; the Bohiers and Duprats were
among those who kept their écus in his safe.[25] The very same Président Séguier who buys 84,000 livres' worth of properties from a
princess, who weaves his patient web around a duchess and her
lands, is quite capable at the same time of preparing the ruin of
laboureurs, as we can see from the case of Guiboust, *laboureur*, who sells
a half-interest in a house and garden to the *président* in 1565 "to pay
off 400 livres of a total debt in the amount of 561 livres" which he
owed to the *seigneur président* as a result of the "accounting made
between them concerning the harvests of his farm and lands due
these 40 years."

The Séguiers continue to set traps for peasants and to swallow up
small parcels of lands, almost mechanically. Soon after a Séguier es-
tablishes a bridgehead anywhere, the neighboring *laboureurs* find
themselves in debt and forced to sell out. The process is inexorable:
one-fifteenth of a house and 37 *arpents* of land bought for 78 livres
(1540); 5 *arpents* bought for 100 livres (1541); 6 *arpents* added for 120
livres (1544); 4.5 *arpents* of ploughland for 78 livres (1550). This is a
sample, at random, of a Séguier penetration. As Richet points out,
these purchases, made to round off and extend a first purchase, are
usually disguised usury: a *laboureur* borrows grain or cash, signs a
rente, and then, unable to keep up payments, he must sell his *héritage*, piece by piece, to pay the arrears and fines. The Séguiers's prey
consists not only of independent *laboureurs* but of sharecroppers and
entrepreneurs as well. An enterprising *laboureur* leases a Séguier mill
for 100 livres a year: it soon turns out that the exploitation of the mill
is not profitable enough to cover the cost of the lease. We find the
laboureur, unable to make his payment, selling 8.5 *arpents* of his own
land to Séguier to cover the deficit in his lease payment. Instantly,
Séguier leases the land back to the *laboureur* at a rent of 8l. 6s. annually, on the principle, evidently, that capital must not be allowed to lie
idle.[26]

Capital invested in land does not on the face of it produce spectacular profits: 5 or 6 percent usually, a meager return compared to the 10

or even 12 percent produced by moneylending in the form of *rentes*.[27] There are, nevertheless, solid reasons for investing in land. Le président Séguier, who has sunk about a third of his capital in land,[28] knows what he is doing. Land is a safe investment—inflation-proof and sheltered from the slings and arrows of outrageous Fortune (for who knows whether princes and kings may not at any moment turn against their creditors?). Land is an investment whose profits cannot be calculated merely on the evidence of the lease and sharecropping contracts, for land produces not harvests alone, not rents merely, but also opportunities, as we have seen, for accelerating the bankruptcy of the peasants of the neighborhood and gradually adding their lands to the original estate, which is like a yeast in the expansionary process. The acres thus accumulated, year after year, through the clever use of rural credit, must be added to the wheat harvests, the fattened calves, and the sought-after timber. Gains, these, which do not enter ordinary calculations. Here land gives dividends, not in the form of crops, but in the form of more land. In these transactions, the Séguiers are on the lookout for timber in particular, for the obvious reason that it is very profitable.[29] The care they lavish on reserving manor houses for themselves is also noticeable. Here the reasons are not so obvious.

The manor house is always reserved for the seigneur, together with stable space for his horses, a dovecote, and a private garden within the walls that surround the manor house.[30] Surely the Séguiers do not require that many imposing houses for their personal use? Is it not rather a carefully considered public relations need which obliges the Séguiers to surround themselves with all the trappings of lordship at the center of each of their growing landed empires? An agreeable and imposing façade, designed to inspire confidence among the local clientele, to assure them that the new seigneur is not a Parisian banker but rather a well-meaning and powerful neighbor?

One might easily read into the Séguiers's manorial arrangements a natural snobbism designed to prepare their claim to nobility. But one château is enough for such claims; and besides, the Séguiers, except for one branch of the family, do not seem anxious to mix with the nobility. Pierre Séguier, although *président* of the *parlement*, remained *noble homme et sage maistre*—that is, a commoner—until the last year of his life.[31] His four daughters were all given in marriage to rich gentry families and not to noble families,[32] a strategy which was not only profitable but also, as Richet notes, eminently satisfactory in all other respects, for the Séguiers sealed alliances through these marriages with the Hennequins, the Viallarts, the Danès, the Laubespines, the

Lhuilliers, the Bérulles, and the Huraults—that is, with *conseillers*,
maistres des requestes, and other powerful *officiers.* These connections
were precisely the kind of connections the Séguiers wanted. Avoiding
both the merchant-bourgeoisie and the nobility, the Séguiers in their
alliances were entirely typical of their class. The one branch of the
family which showed signs of wishing to acquire more noble connections did not prosper.[33]

What is striking about the Séguiers and their peers is that their
immense successes, their wealth, and their seigneurial privileges and
honors do not change their life-style, their mentality, or their sense of
belonging to a social class that keeps its distance from the nobility.[34]
There is nothing humble about their sense of their own social status,
but they display, as Richet notes, the vanity of *robins,* not the pride of
the nobility.[35] Theirs is the pride of possession in lands, manors,
rentes, and in their houses in the city—solidly furnished *hôtels* reliably
supplied by their *fermiers;* pride in good management, which they
never delegated to agents (the Séguiers collected their own seigneurial dues, no matter how slim);[36] pride in their children's establishment, their daughters' dowries, their sons' offices; pride in the galleries of worthies collected as godfathers at the baptismal fonts.

This separate pride of the gentry is as solid as the masonry of their
hôtels and quite as capable of surviving for centuries without suffering
serious structural damage. There is a kind of correspondence between
buildings and families and a permanence which would no doubt inspire awe in the mind of a sixteenth-century *président* were he to come
to life again. The very buildings in which the French National Archives are housed—and the archives themselves, for that matter—are
the work of sixteenth- and seventeenth-century *présidents,* financiers,
and their attendant legions of *conseillers, advocats,* and *notaires.* The
Hôtel d'Assy, now 58 *bis* rue des Francs-Bourgeois, sits on a parcel of
land which used to belong to a Briçonnet, *président* of the *chambre des
comptes.* The *hôtel* itself was built by a *président* of the *parlement* in the
early seventeenth century, when this street, fittingly named rue du
Paradis, was filling up with the gentry's palaces.

The succession of owners reminds us that even when, on occasion,
the property went to families with mere money—like Denis Marin,
trésorier général des fermes and relative of Colbert's, who bought it in
1641 for forty thousand livres—the *hôtel* knew how to take its re-
venge, for soon enough the financier's grandson became a *président* at
the *parlement* of Aix.[37] A stone's throw away from the rue du Paradis,
on what is now the rue des Archives, the beautiful pink brick *hôtel*
built by the financier Jacques Coeur in the fifteenth century became

the property of the Lhuilliers—themselves great builders—through marriage. Everywhere on these old streets of the Marais neighborhood the presence of the gentry's wealth is overwhelming. And yet, it is only very recently that we have been able to see these old *hôtels* in their real context. Their physical presence had been hiding under some grimy façade or other—as was true of the Coeur house, for instance, which was rediscovered in 1971. Worse, their very spirit had been buried, hidden by some noble-sounding tradition started in the late seventeenth or eighteenth centuries. Associated, at some point, with a noble family which, for a moment, graced its halls, the *hôtel*, as often as not, acquired a grand name and kept it even when occupied once again by bankers, *présidents,* or even jam manufacturers.[38]

Gentilshommes, even when they were dukes, were, needless to say, rarely in a position to build expensive *hôtels.* Little wonder if courtiers allowed themselves a deep, nervous laugh at the expense of the first Séguier who was naive enough to put up a tablet at the entrance to his house, grandly designating it the Hôtel Séguier.[39] The Place Royale, now Place des Vosges, is vaguely associated in our minds with noble names—Rohan, Richelieu, Bassompierre; but such *grands seigneurs* in fact figured only as tenants. The Place Royale was developed by a consortium headed by Achille de Harlay and including Jeannin—a crowd of *présidents* and financiers who had Henry IV's backing for their project.[40] The original plan even called for the building of a bourse, a stock exchange, as part of the complex.[41] The *hôtels* of the Marais survived through the centuries as the showplaces where *présidents* and *trésoriers* lived when they had reached the height of their dynastic fortunes.[42]

The great gentry families held onto their offices as tenaciously as they kept up their *hôtels,* nurturing their fortunes with a tenderness one can only describe as paternal. An instructive example of this is the Nicolay family, which held onto the office of *premier président* in the *chambre des comptes* from the first years of the sixteenth century right up to the Revolution, from father to son.[43] Not that these three centuries are sufficient to encompass their story, for the Nicolays were *rentiers* and politicians long after the demise of the monarchy. As early as 1412 we find a Nicolay holding office as lieutenant of the *bailli* of Bourg-Saint-Andéol, a small trading town near Pont-Saint-Esprit along the Rhône. The Nicolays are bourgeois and merchants of the town—Jean, *honorabilis vir* and *mercator* in 1450, *honorabilis vir* and *burgensis* in 1471. In the 1480s the family moves into finance. They acquire the rights to collect tolls on the salt barges which pass Bourg-Saint-Andéol as they come up from the Rhône Delta. This is when the

Nicolays leave the bourgeoisie. Jean is *noble homme* in 1488;[44] another Nicolay is *licensié en chascun droit* and *conseiller* of the Toulouse *parlement* in 1491 and eventually becomes *maistre des requestes* and *premier président* of the *chambre des comptes* of Paris. It is this maistre Nicolay who transposes the family fortunes, at the turn of the century, from the municipal financial and political sphere of Bourg-Saint-Andéol to the national level.

At his death in 1527, this first *président* in the Nicolay family had accumulated a true monopoly of financial rights along the Rhône. A specialist in salt tolls, he had four hundred livres coming in annually from the *grenier à sel* of Pont-Saint-Esprit and a collection of smaller salt tolls bought up along the river from various individuals or institutions.[45] To these salt tolls he had added "pensions" and *rentes*, in addition to the lands, vineyards, mills, manors, castles, and houses he owned outright.[46]

The Nicolays' *hôtel* in Bourg-Saint-Andéol is a monument to their aspirations and the envy of the whole town. In its capacious chambers, heavy, carved walnut buffets hoard, under lock and key, the wealth of generations of usury. To put it more sympathetically, the Nicolay house is really a bank. We enter the living room—the *sale basse* on the ground floor—where we find a *buffet à deux guichets fermans à clef* (a wooden safe with two locked doors). There are also a bench, a table, and a pine-wood screen (behind which discreet transactions can take place), a few chairs and stools, a tapestry, and a painting (*Ecce homo*). The small room also contains a safe (a *coffre à clef*) and an edifying painting on the wall (*Noli me tangere*). Upstairs, the bedrooms are equipped with more heavy wooden safes and *coffres à clef*. I count at least twelve rooms, and each contains at least one such *buffet* or *coffre*. In some rooms there are several safes and chests, all with locks. Comfort everywhere: a profusion of luxurious beds, with *ciels* (silk-covered shelters) and sumptuous white Catalan bedcovers; green rugs covering tables; tapestries; and chairs upholstered in embroidered stuffs. The kitchen and larder are filled with food, and we can even find that ultimate comfort, the *chaise percée*, in the upstairs bedroom. But the soul of the family, its very core, lies buried in the chapel, where six locked *coffres* and one special *grand coffre fermant à trois clefs* contain all the contracts certifying to the family's ownership of lands, houses, *pensions, rentes,* and *péages.*[47]

Nothing could be more solidly entrenched than the Nicolay's wealth in Bourg-Saint-Andéol. Nevertheless, at the time of the first *président*'s death in 1527, the family's interests have already shifted to Paris. The late *président*'s son, *noble homme et sage maistre* Aymard, has already entered into possession of his father's office at the *chambre des comptes*. Installed in the Nicolay's Parisian *hôtel* on the rue de la Bretonnerie, practically next door to the Coeur house and within an easy walk of the other *hôtels* of the Marais, Aymard Nicolay has to make some difficult choices: Can he manage his Rhône Valley interests from Paris? He tries to. At his father's death in 1527, he leases out his lands and seigneuries, reserving only the right to come and live in his principal château, that of Saint-Victor.[48] By 1541 he finds it is too difficult to keep track of his various sharecroppers and agents—who steal the absentee landlord blind, no doubt—and so opts for a single sweeping contract with maistre Vallet of Bourg-Saint-Andéol to manage all his properties. Maistre Vallet is required to live in the Hôtel Nicolay (and take good care of all those safes); he is given full powers of attorney, and he contracts to pay the *président* 1,080 livres annually.[49] The Saint-Victor property, minus the château itself, meanwhile, is sold to Thomas Gadagne for 5,000 livres, while the salt tolls are kept in the *président*'s care. Now the *président* feels free to invest in lands near Paris. Following the same developer's pattern that had served the family well in the Rhône Valley, the Nicolays buy up properties north of Paris, in the direction of Chantilly. The seigneuries of Goussainville, Louvres, and Orville form a new axis of penetration along the Flanders road: château, barns, and stables at Goussainville, with dovecote, gardens, woods, vineyards, "le tout clos et fermé de murailles"; marshlands, a mill on the little river which crosses his lands; a windmill and meadows for pasture. The seigneurial *hôtel* at Goussainville is the headquarters of the new Nicolay empire. Like the Séguiers's châteaux, his manor is really a disguised bank. Behind the walls that guarantee the privacy of the gardens and terraces, the knowing visitor will not be distracted by the bucolic touch provided by the little stables, the compost heap, the rooster, the two real cows—brown, ten years old—the two or three calves and one pig. All this comes under the heading of decor; it sets a reassuring mood for the customer who is headed for the office. Behind the noble old walls, and right beyond the cows, there is a real *comptoir*, a business office, where the customer will sit down in the welcoming heavy oak chair covered in tapestry—roses on a green background—to face the two writing-stands and the ivory escritoire, where his leases and loans will be consigned.[50]

So far we have seen how bourgeois *familles* rise in the world, how they acquire university degrees, seigneuries, *rentes*, real estate, offices, dowries, and alliances. We have noticed, too, that, once they have arrived, these dynasties tend to cut their more visible ties with the world of *marchandise* and adopt new ways of behaving, designed to set them apart from the bourgeois world. The new gentlemen insist on living elsewhere, away from the streets where their houses are connected with the grocer's, fishmonger's, apothecary's, or tanner's trade. They move out into the countryside, into manor houses and châteaux. They build elegant mansions in town, surrounded by walls, whose galleries and inner courtyards, embellished with antique statues and small formal gardens, keep the bourgeois world at bay. Whenever possible, the *hôtels* of the gentry crowd together in some special, elegant neighborhood which grew up naturally around the cathedral and the Palais de Justice and where the town houses of *présidents* adjoin those of their relatives, the canons and abbés. In Paris the Ile de la Cité is the natural setting for the gentry's *beau quartier*, and the fact that space is limited there explains the expansion into the Marais neighborhood, across the river.[51]

The escape from the bourgeoisie is an established pattern. The reluctance, in general, to form close alliances with the nobility is an established pattern too, which will be broken only by the most prominent of the great *parlementaire* families, and that rather late and not without misgivings. The record of the Nicolays in this respect is probably not unusual. The family will remain firmly rooted in the world of banking and officeholding for centuries, with few deviations. *Président* after *président, seigneur* and *messire* though he may be, possessor of princely *hôtels* in Paris and in the countryside, remains loyal to the gentry's ideals: education, officeholding, finance, and property management.

"Monseigneur," writes the Président Aymard Nicolay to the chancellor of France, "I have a son who, thanks be to God, has done rather well in his studies at the universities he attended. For two years now I have had him work at the Palais [de Justice], pleading causes and consulting [that is, working as a lawyer], as young men of his condition should [*comme jeunes gens de son estat doibvent faire*]." The purpose of the letter is to offer three thousand écus for an office to establish the son. It never occurs to the *président* that his son might bring more honor to his family by taking up a military career and marrying into a noble family.

Aymard's wife, Anne, the daughter of the Président Baillet, makes it clear in her testament that no expense is to be spared in raising her son to be a jurist: "She wishes and orders," expressly, "that as long as her son Thibault wishes to study law, he should be supported," out of her income, "up to the age of 26 years."[52] Aymard's daughter,

Renée, marries Jean Lhuillier, *président* at the *chambre des comptes,* and
his son, Antoine, who inherited the family's presidency, marries
Jeanne Lhuillier. Anne, the *présidente,* may be addressed as Madame
de Saint-Victor—after the Rhône Valley château which had been kept
in the family for prestige, even though the surrounding lands had
been sold in 1541. But she is in fact a superbly competent businesswoman. To be convinced of this, one need only read the business
memorandum she drafts for her daughter-in-law on the management
of her lands.[53] Her capital is prudently invested with her son the
président and her daughter the *présidente,* who promise, in front of a
notary, "to employ the funds she has entrusted to their care with
fidelity."[54] No doubt she was well advised in her placements (by our
old acquaintance, Monsieur le Pelletier, grand maistre of the Collège
de Navarre and her testamentary executor), and her son, Antoine,
was well prepared for his task: we can read a dissertation he had
written in 1545, entitled "On the Power of Money."[55]

Among the difficult financial decisions Antoine was to face was the
liquidation of the Nicolay interests in Languedoc and Dauphiné. This
process had started in 1527, but its final stages were being accelerated
by the civil wars, during which the cherished old family house in
Bourg-Saint-Andéol, "a large house, well built, honorable, and *de
marque seigneurieuse*" was burned and looted. Alas, even the "titles
and papers" which had been kept in *bon coffres fermans* in the chapel,
"as the safest place in the said house ... and locked with three good
keys"—those *escritures,* which the *sieur président* held "as dear to him
as is possible"—disappeared during the looting.[56] Clearly, the
Nicolay's sphere of influence having shifted to the north, they could
no longer protect their southern investments. As a result, Antoine
makes the difficult decision of selling out in 1583. Even the old *rente*
on the *grenier à sel* of Pont-Saint-Esprit has to go this time. It is sold to
Flèchard, bishop of Grenoble, and his brother, *conseiller* in the *parlement* at Grenoble. Presumably the Flèchards' local alliances will en-
able them to hold on to these investments. All the other Nicolay properties in the south are sold as a single lot to the duc de Ventadour,
lieutenant general of the Limousin, who will know how to protect his
interests. The Nicolay-Ventadour settlement is made against 2,333
livres of annual and perpetual *rente.* For his part, Ventadour signs
over to Nicolay his rights on *rentes* assigned to him by the city of
Paris and to be taken on the salt taxes of Joinville, Langres, Laon, and
other localities in the Paris region and on the *aides* taxes of Picardy and
Normandy.

As we can see, the Nicolays remain salt-tax specialists: they have

merely shifted their zone of operations to a region where their political alliances, which date from the beginning of the century, give them
the strength required to deal with local tax collectors and aldermen. It
is not enough to have *titres et papiers*. To collect on one's investments
requires a well-oiled political machine, put together through marriage
alliances with Lhuilliers, Hennequins, Du Tillets, and other Parisian
magnates.[57] The soundness of the Nicolays' business and political
strategies was to be confirmed during the worst years of the League in
Paris. The reader may remember how le président d'Ormesson's
properties came out unscathed during the siege of Paris because of his
alliances on both sides. The Nicolays also survived the cataclysm
rather well, as I think one can deduce from their unshaken prosperity
and from evidence such as this passport, issued by Henri IV in July
1590, which allows Antoine's widow, Jeanne, to ride through the be-
sieging army unmolested, accompanied by "a *demoiselle* in her service, her *femme de chambre*, three servants, her coach, horses,
coachman, and a *mule loaded with coffers*"! On top of that, she also
carried a similar passport from the Ligueur Hôtel de Ville. That, in the
summer of 1590, is power![58]

We can appreciate how sound the marriage strategies of the gentry
really were when we are faced with the occasional aberration. The
Nicolays were tempted, on at least one occasion, to depart from their
normal policy. The results were disastrous. Antoine's son Jean married Marie de Billy, a young orphaned girl from a noble household.
This marriage, which took place in 1578, went against all common
sense. I do not know why it was contracted for. The girl, I believe, was
unusually young. Perhaps it was a case of passionate love, and the
Nicolays were moved to abandon their usual caution. Or perhaps it
was vanity that blurred their senses. Whatever the reason, they must
soon have regretted this rash alliance. They may also have thought
they could avoid the most obvious kind of friction because Marie was
an orphan and young enough to be trained. The Nicolays took the
bride without dowry, an unheard-of concession. Her grandfather and
guardian, Lancelot de Rosny, insisted on a clause in the contract
which specified that the Nicolays "would not ever ask him for anything." Marie's parents had left her nothing but debts. The Nicolays
were prepared to take her under these conditions. No sooner had
Marie joined their household than they started to receive letters of the
most disagreeable sort, and written in the most barbarous prose, from
her grandfather: "Issued whence she is [of noble birth, that is],
she would surely have found an equally advantageous match,"

whines old Rosny. "Besides," he adds, "you could never have found a girl of better birth to enter your family; and further, her hand was being sought by a *gentilhomme* of ancient house." Doubtful statements, every one of them, and how they must have grated on the Nicolays' nerves. "If I want to see her," complains the grandfather with undue exaggeration, "I have to go to Paris and spend five hundred écus on each journey—money, this, which I cannot recuperate as quickly as you can."[59] These gratuitous insults were not the last offense from the Rosny family. As young Marie developed into a reliable businesswoman under her husband's tutelage,[60] her relatives' aggressions soon went beyond mere insults. The Rosnys used Marie to hold the Nicolays up for ransom in more than a figurative way. Not only had they unloaded the girl without paying a penny's worth of dowry, but they must have tried to get money out of their new relatives in a number of clumsy ways until they were moved, at last, to the desperate expedient of actually kidnapping Marie in the course of a visit she made to her sister's house.[61]

No wonder the Nicolays kept away from the nobility thereafter. Jean and Marie's son Antoine, born in 1590, had Villeroy as his godfather and married an Amelot woman with a dowry of 190,000 livres. Later Nicolays chose wives from among equally suitable families: the Fieubet, the Le Camus, and the Lamoignon.[62] It is only after the Revolution, when the class structures of the *ancien régime* lost some of their significance, that we find the Nicolays ready to marry outsiders. Not that the Revolution put an end to the Nicolays' wealth and power. They suffered the loss of the presidency, to be sure, and some momentary unpleasantness, but le président Aymard Charles Nicolay was still capable of leaving a sixty-thousand-livre dowry to his illegitimate daughter in his testament of 1792.

A year later, the *président* was turned into a *citoyen sans profession* but was not seriously threatened, even during the worst months of the Terror, and he died in his bed in his own *hôtel* in 1794. His son was named Count of the Empire in 1810. No longer seigneur of Goussainville, M. le Comte Nicolay became simply mayor of Goussainville and a member of the electoral college of the *département* of Seine-et-Marne. Notability under new names. He was ambassador at the Court of Baden in 1811, under Napoleon, and a peer of France under the succeeding regimes (1815–32). Emperors and monarchs come and go, but the Nicolays stay. Of the mayor of Goussainville's two brothers, one was made baron under Napoleon, the other, having married into the ancient noble house of Lévis in 1809, died peacefully, at the age of eighty-nine, in Geneva, where his profession is neutrally but no doubt accurately described as that of *rentier*.

How do the Nicolays—and so many other *rentiers* of their kind, big, middling, or small—manage to hold on to their wealth and influence for centuries? The permanence of these gentry fortunes can be hidden by name changes. The families can die out without leaving male heirs; but the fortunes remain, adopted, so to speak, by relatives. Lands, *rentes,* and offices, combined according to well-tried methods, carry on their irresistible lives, as if gentry fortunes were some kind of natural organism necessary to the life of the nation.

The longevity of gentry fortunes requires some explanation. While these fortunes are in the making, it is easy enough to follow the commercial operations, the shady financial deals, the rapacious land swindles, the speculations. But, once achieved, when the *bourgeois et marchand,* the *banquier,* the *élu* has turned into a respectable *conseiller,* a *noble homme* far from *marchandise,* it seems, at least on the surface, that we are no longer in the presence of growing fortunes. The estate achieves the kind of stabilization evoked by contemporaries as an ideal and verified by economic historians, some of whom even speak of decreasing fortunes.[63] The management of seigneuries never produces really spectacular results. In the hands of authentic noblemen, the seigneurie seems to doom the owners to certain bankruptcy.[64] But even when seigneuries are controlled by sharp-eyed financiers, the income from land alone is nothing spectacular.

What happens to the merchant or financier who swallows noble fiefs and becomes a *gentilhomme*? Does he escape the fate of his predecessors, the *ci-devant* seigneurs? Maistre Tristan of Beauvais is a classic example of a *rentier* playing havoc among the nobility of the region, a wolf let loose among sheep. In 1649 he has a capital of some fifty thousand livres in the form of *rentes,* most of it in obligations signed by noble landowners.[65] But let two or three generations pass, and we shall find the satiated beast of prey transformed into a victim in turn; for the Tristans succumb to the attractions of the noble life, abandon their prudent habits of management, live on their lands, pass for noble, and, soon enough, find themselves so deeply in debt that they have to sell out.[66]

The same thing happens to the De la Haye family. These Parisian goldsmiths install themselves in the suburban seigneurie of Vaudétard in 1589. By 1638, having lived too nobly, Jean de la Haye leaves his widow nothing but debts. In 1662 she is forced to sell the seigneurie at public auction. Fortunately not all the De la Hayes had lost their heads, for one branch of the family had remained goldsmiths in the rue Jacob. The late noble wastrel's nephew, Charles de la Haye, a goldsmith, buys up the seigneurie and saves it for the family.[67]

This is no isolated case. It seems likely that, in the middle and lower range of gentry fortunes, families protected themselves against the economic consequences of living nobly by keeping their hand, discreetly, in some profitable business or other. This seems to be routine behavior in a small Burgundian town like Varzy in the seventeenth century.[68] How widespread the kind of commercial enterprise found in Varzy may be among small-town notable families with gentry pretensions I cannot say. It may well be that the situation in Varzy or even in Beauvais is typical of mid-seventeenth-century conditions and less common a century earlier, when it had been easier to break away from the bourgeois condition.[69] Not that the attraction of living nobly had diminished in the minds of merchants. But the social and economic realities of the early seventeenth century required painful compromises. I can think of no more eloquent testimony to this than the autobiography of Jean Maillefer, of Reims, written in 1667.[70]

Jean, the son of a silk merchant, was put to study (*mis aux études*) at the local *collège*, where he did his "seventh, sixth, and right up to the third class" and remembers, fifty-six years later, with great pride, that he won a prize in Greek composition. He remembers being a gifted scholar with a great inclination toward study. But he was obliged to leave the *collège* at the age of 14, the year of his father's death,[71] and he was never graduated and never went on to a law degree. Not that it would have done him much good to become a lawyer in the late 1620s, as we are reminded by Robert Angot's reflections.[72] Maillefer remembers his bitter disappointment when he was taken out of school and apprenticed to a tailor. He spent two years with the tailor, then went on to learn to "write": one year with a *greffier*, and another two years working for a Parisian cloth merchant—all these were wasted years in his estimation.

Hoping to resume his studies, he came home to Reims at the age of 18: because "the pleasures of the mind are pure, agreeable, eternal; one walks head high, one's conscience is free of guilt."[73] His years at the *collège* had spoiled him. He had learned contempt for the merchant's life.

But his resistance was of no avail. Circumstances in 1629 did not permit him to abandon *marchandise*. Making the best of it, he convinced himself that there were some aspects of a businessman's life which were not entirely contemptible. In Lyon, working for a wholesale silk merchant, he learned to write business letters, to keep accounts, to deal with money and credits. At last he began to see possibilities in a business career and convinced himself that wholesale commerce could be said to have "something noble and attractive about it, which was not to be found in retail selling," where "one has to show deference" in a way not suitable in an educated man with aspirations to live nobly.[74]

Young Maillefer's concessions did not come easily, though. The ideas learned in the Roman authors and from his *collège* classmates had taken hold forever. At the age of twenty-five, back in the family's shop in Reims, Jean could not bring himself to serve customers; he stayed out of the shop, "feeling no attachment to it, nor wishing to feel it." Instead, he would hole up in his room and read books.[75] It was this moment Fate chose to strike at him through the appearance of a young woman. She entered his shop as a customer. He fell madly and instantly in love with her, and, despite his great embarrassment at being seen at work in his shop, he proposed to her—for, after all, the Maillefers were well-to-do, and Jean was not a bad match.[76] Maillefer's proposal reveals very candidly the feelings of a merchant wishing to live nobly: "I told her that if she found the condition of merchant displeasing, in which she has seen me, she ought to consider me a blank slate [*une table d'attente*] on which she should feel free to trace whatever she wished. In fact," adds Jean, lying through his teeth, "my parents are more inclined toward buying me an office than setting me up as a merchant."[77] Fortunately for Jean, the woman saw nothing wrong with his condition, and the young merchant's passion was soon rewarded. "A beautiful and pleasant day," writes Maillefer, remembering his wedding night; "oh, how I wish it could have lasted millions of years! New heart, new caresses, how inestimable your value! All the gold of a thousand Indies is as nothing when compared to your felicities! Ah, how I remember it well, my mouth waters when I think of it! So then, I was married on April 27, 1636."[78]

Maillefer was to remain a merchant all his days, but his aspirations to live nobly never quite left him, so strong was the influence of the world he had half-entered in his youth, through the *collège*. He would never be able to face situations in which he was required to show deference to social superiors, he would never acknowledge that his *condition* was lower than that of someone else. Having the military quartered in his house was something he could never bear, "not because of the expense, but because this was a humiliation to me."[79] As for money, he makes a big show of being above such considerations. His heart just was not in his business. "Jean Maillefer, why don't you do some work?" his mother used to ask him, in his younger years, before he had any children. "Whom should I work for?" Jean used to answer. A pretext, it soon turned out, because, once he had children, he still did not meet his mother's standards. She kept asking him, "Jean Maillefer, why don't you work harder?" "I have to conserve my strength for my children," he would reply now.[80] Whether his *collège* years had actually spoiled him for life or whether Maillefer simply poses for posterity, the fact remains that a life of leisure and letters, far away from commerce, was an ideal which continued to exert its languid charm among the more prosperous bourgeois. The two kinds of life were not easily reconcilable.

Marchandise inspired horror in those who had aspirations to live nobly. But we must not conclude that gentry fortunes, cut off from commerce, were therefore doomed to eventual extinction. There are wastrels among the gentry,[81] but they are likely to be the exception. The typical gentry family remains wealthy without touching commercial or industrial investment. Their capital is invested in land, for security; in offices, for political power; and in *rentes*. This last form of investment is the least understood and almost certainly the most important.

The *rente*, in its various forms, is shrouded in a kind of secrecy which has followed it since its medieval origins. It is a form of moneylending at fixed interest rates. In the sixteenth century it received the approval of respected jurists: "This manner of disguised usury is quite ancient" and quite legal, explains Jean Papon's influential legal handbook.[82] Openly practiced "without scruples or any fear," the *rente constituée* nevertheless carried with it an aura of evildoing. Officially condemned as a social nuisance which made bourgeois idle and ruined the nobility,[83] the *rente* had, at the same time, become the chief way of financing the government's expenses. The crown, always in debt and always seeking new loans, made desperate efforts to reduce the permissible interest rate. But the power of its creditors was so strong that these measures failed consistently. It was only when the demand for capital became more moderate, in the early seventeenth century, that interest rates on *rentes* fell back to a lower rate.[84]

We have seen enough examples to know that *rentes* in the sixteenth century were not always written at the legal or generally approved rate of 8.33 percent. Certainly, a 10 percent rate comes up often in contracts. The *rentiers* of this period, whether we are speaking of great bankers like the Séguiers or of small-town lenders like Gouberville, have so many ways of rewriting *rente* contracts, of adding deceptive clauses to them, of maneuvering the borrowers into fines and arrears, that the only safe generalization is that money was lent at whatever rate the traffic could bear. One thing is certain: everyone who lived nobly was a possessor of *rentes*.

Of the three characteristic sources of gentry wealth, the income from *rentes* was the least visible to contemporaries. Offices and lands were not merely visible, they were positively advertised, they were inseparable from a family's *estat, qualité, dignité*, and *condition*. One wore these possessions as ostentatiously as possible; the *nom de terre* replaced the family name, and the office followed as a close second. The *rentes* in one's possession, on the other hand, constituted the private side of one's wealth. Its secrets were consigned to strongboxes and locked chests, opened only on special occasions such as marriages and deaths in the family.

The *rente constituée* had multiple functions. It helped to dispossess peasants. It also helped push the great feudal landowning families further toward bankruptcy. At the same time, in the hands of knowledgeable financiers, the *rente* could resemble modern forms of deposit banking and stock investment; so that the very same person who inflicted "annual and perpetual" payments upon his victims was very likely making *rente* payments to various investors.[85] It was to be hoped that the *rentes* payments one was receiving were at a higher rate of interest than those one was paying out. When the contrary was true, as it was in the hopelessly muddled affairs of the poet Malherbe, ruin was just around the corner.[86]

Of all forms of capital, the *rente* was the most easily negotiable; hence its enormous usefulness. The sale of an office required political approval, and the market price fluctuated almost daily. A seigneurie offered for sale could be subject to all sorts of archaic rights; its value, like that of offices, was determined purely by market demand, while its expected income depended on the honesty and competence of the *fermier* and was in any case at the mercy of acts of God. The *rente* alone could guarantee, if its terms were met, a specific and regular payment. I say, if its terms were met, because hard times affected *rente* payments too. Municipalities and individuals could default on their payments, and the defaults necessitated expensive and interminable lawsuits. In such cases it was best to be a powerful demigod rather than a small-time investor.

This is a home truth which must have come with bitter experience to Jean Bodin, the well-known economic theorist. Bodin was no demigod. Probably the son of a tailor, he had managed to establish himself in the small city of Laon, after a brilliant university career. In

1576, the year of the publication of his famous *Republic*, he married the widow of an *officier* in Laon, Françoise Trouillart. The daughter of an *élu* and the sister of the local *procureur du roy*, Françoise was also, through her mother, related to the Le Cirier family, Parisian demi-gods of the *parlement*. While waiting to inherit the Trouillart family office of *procureur du roy*, Bodin acted as legal adviser and business manager for several great noble families. His experience as superintendent of the affairs of the marquis de Moy was to teach him a lesson. The marquise cajoled him into advancing funds and paid him back with compliments. Bodin, whom the marquise addressed nobly as Monsieur de Saint-Amand, was vulnerable to her social charms: "I promise you that Monsieur [the Marquis] and I, myself, will always feel greatly indebted to you for the courtesy you have shown us in all things." With disarming simplicity the marquise writes "I send you only 20 écus, and I swear to you, Monsieur de Saint-Amand, that this is the best I can manage. In a few days, I hope to send you some more money." Ten years later, the marquise owes a thousand écus, and all she can do is to offer him a hundred livres annual *rente* "until the day comes when we shall be able to reimburse the entire sum." That day will never come, as Bodin by now knows only too well. Furiously he scribbles a comment on the back of the marquise's letter: "The marquise *promises* to pay 400 écus, while she owes 980." He later received a royal order authorizing him to seize her furniture.[87]

Lending money, even in the form of *rente* contracts, had its risks, unless one was powerful enough to intimidate the debtor.[88] No wonder that Bodin, in his investment counseling, has a good word to say for the security represented by land. Writing in about 1584 to his stepson, Nicolas Bayard, who is about to invest his inherited capital, Bodin advises against investment in offices. "You have not yet decided ... whether to sell your land—in order to buy an office." His advice is to sell those of his farmlands which are located too far from Laon to be managed efficiently and to trade these for some good lands near Laon, "so that you will always have something to fall back upon when you have lost all hope." To be in the best possible position in bargaining for a marriage alliance, Bodin argues that "100 livres of *rente* guaranteed by land is worth 1,000 livres of income from offices. If it becomes known that you have put all your money into an office, I fear you will not find it easy to make a desirable match."[89] The next thing is to make a good marriage alliance.

Side by side with *rentes*, offices, and lands, the merger of two families through marriage is a form of investment whose importance cannot be exaggerated. It is the classic way of consolidating a fortune, with each family bringing its capital, in its several forms, into a partnership which will be doubly formidable. Marriage alliances can start fortunes as well as consolidate existing ones. An adventurer like Agrippa d'Aubigné, thirty years old, his escapades and amours behind him, dreams of property. Posing as a *gentilhomme*, a part he plays to perfection, M. d'Aubigné begins to court a local heiress who lives in a château with her uncle. Knowing perfectly well that his own property is not sufficient to weigh in the marriage negotiation, Aubigné declares himself, in the marriage contract of June 1583, the owner of a substantial seigneurie which will be his contribution to the contract. In fact, he had "acquired" this property only a few days earlier, against promises of payment guaranteed by his forthcoming marriage. The trick worked. Soon Aubigné was taking charge of his wife's properties, introducing rational management and rescuing these noble fiefs from the ruinous *"vanité"* of the earlier seigneurs. Broken-down buildings were repaired, useless luxuries (such as hunting) abolished, lands added, until an estate worth eight hundred livres of income when he took over produced three thousand—or so he claims. Many years later, Aubigné, an elderly widower, once again resorted to marriage as a way of refurbishing his fortune. He married the fifty-five-year-old widow of a financier and ended his days surrounded by the comfortable delights of "my books, my exquisite guests, and fine music."[90]

11 *Religion*

Among investments of all sorts, none was more profitable, none more to the gentry's taste, than investment in clerical benefices. Cathedral chapters, replete with fat prebends, attracted the *familles* of provincial cities.[1] The Parisian chapter acted like a magnet for the entire kingdom. Here the elite of the Parisian families—Luillier, Spifame, Hennequin—mixed with the leading names of the Touraine, the Orléanais, and the Auvergne—Beaune, Briçonnet, Poncher, Hurault, Ruzé, Fumée.[2] The canon's prebend was a stepping-stone to higher things: bishoprics and rich abbeys.[3]

It must not be thought that high church office was a preserve of the nobility. We have encountered bishops at every step of this inquiry. It may indeed be true, as Imbart de la Tour guessed, that in the sixteenth century the majority of bishops were recruited from among these families of financiers and jurists which made up the elite of the gentry and that noblemen of ancient lineage had become rare in high church office.[4] Perhaps, sooner or later, a systematic study of the French episcopate will settle the point. But counting has its hazards: the scorekeeper in this case will have to be an astute and rigorous genealogist. Given the present state of the evidence, I am inclined to follow Imbart de la Tour.

Wherever I look, I find bishoprics in the hands of the gentry. The general deputies of the French clergy signed a contract concerning the subscription to an enormous loan on 22 November 1567. Among the bishops whose names appear on the list of signatories only a handful are members of great noble or princely families. There is also an occasional Italian prince or two, but the bulk of the names are familiar to students of financial history: Spifame, Viole, Guilliard, Du Tillet, Bohier, Babou, Neufville, Marcilly, Tiercelin, L'Angelier, and so on.[5]

We know all about the spectacular ecclesiastical careers of the demigods from having watched the Briçonnets and the Beaunes, the Bohiers, the Morvilliers, the Bochetels and the Babous, the Ponchers and Robertets and Ruzés collecting bishops' miters since the early years of the century. Lesser names crop up in most dioceses, too. Even Orléans, with its splendid income, so tempting to great families like the Ganays of the *parlement,* could on occasion fall into lesser hands. When Antoine Sanguin headed this vast ecclesiastical and financial empire, long before it came into Morvillier's hands, the king is said to have asked the new bishop, in a joking manner, "Are you a *gentilhomme?*" "To be sure, Sire," Sanguin replies coolly, sharing the joke, "to be sure, for I am descended in direct line from one of Noah's children."[6]

The king might well joke about such matters. If rich abbeys fell into the possession of bankers, and if even the wealthiest bishoprics and the occasional cardinalate went to a "*gentilhomme*" whose status was based only on his being "descended in direct line from one of Noah's children," what loss was it to the crown? Was not the good will of a single financier like Sébastien Zamet worth more to the king than the loyalty of all his feudal vassals put together?[7]

Clerical appointments were "gifts of the crown" only in an entirely conventional sense. It is neither useful nor realistic, however, for historians to adopt such a convention. More to the point would be the assumption that the crown was rarely in a position to dispense gifts of such magnitude. In most cases, the creation of a new bishop or abbé can be understood as a purely financial transaction. The crown certainly tried to get good value in exchange for its "gift." Some appointments served a political purpose: they bought loyalty from magnates. Others paid off financial obligations: they repaid financiers and tax farmers for the large sums advanced for military campaigns.[8] Among the more established gentry families, the right to receive the incomes of bishoprics and abbeys was already a deeply rooted tradition in the sixteenth century.[9]

Quite aside from the well-known investments of professional financiers, we find that court favorites were not rewarded with abbeys just for their odes and sonnets; rather, such amateur clerics were also amateur investors. They bid for church properties.[10] Their eventual acquisitions of major interests were prepared, over a long period of time, by carefully considered family strategies.[11] The grant of ecclesiastical titles, from the king's point of view, was a financial move which left little room for such considerations as the recipient's social status, to say nothing of his piety.

"My friend," writes Henri IV to his finance minister in 1594, as soon as the news of the Cardinal de Bourbon's death reaches him,

> many people have asked me for his remains [the benefices, that is, which became vacant as the result of the cardinal's death]. I told everyone that they are already disposed of. Will you see if you can persuade the abbé of Tiron [Desportes] to swap for the archbishopric of Rouen, which is worth thirty thousand livres a year at least? He could take care of the chevalier d'Oyse by paying him an annual pension of four thousand écus from the archbishopric's income. As for the abbey of Saint-Ouen, I will reward one of my servants with it; but whoever gets the abbey will have to pay a pension of ten thousand livres annually to you. Manage this business with dexterity, and let me know what happens immediately, by special courier.[12]

Such a letter demonstrates that the crown acted principally as a brokerage firm for investments in church property. A bishopric or an abbey must not necessarily be understood as an unqualified possession. In reality, the new bishop or abbé may be appointed on certain specific conditions requiring him to pay large portions of his nominal income to various investors who need not acquire the benefices in person. The calculation of the gentry's portion in the French church becomes enormously complicated by such common subterfuges.

The documents allow us to imagine the arrival of a newly appointed bishop in his diocese, the new bishop of Séez, for example. Here he is, duly anointed, dressed in the latest court fashion, mounted on a frisky horse, booted and armed. His name is Jean Bertaut, and he does not, on the face of it, have much of the cleric about him. Understandably so: he is a minor courtier, a man in his fifties, a protégé of Desportes, and only just ordained. For many years he had been making a career writing impromptu sonnets and sketching portraits at court. Despite his noble appearance, this aging intellectual and artist is the son of a *collège* teacher from Caen. How could he have amassed the capital and the political alliances required to prompt the "gift" of an abbey *in commendam* and of a minor bishopric? Piety and theological training were not much in evidence in a man like Bertaut or in the circles in which he moved. He never showed up at his abbey, of course. It is only when we look at Bertaut's patrons that we begin to suspect that his role was, most probably, that of a competent and trusted surrogate. He was the loyal servant of a number of *trésoriers*, such as Phélipeaux, Puget, and Gobelin. He was protected and esteemed by L'Aubespine and Loménie.[13]

When the more powerful families ran short of relatives to endow with clerical benefices, they used protégés instead. When the family was not strong enough to accede to the bishop's dignity in name, it bided its time and administered the diocese for the nominal possessor.[14] More direct and more aggressive tactics were made possible on the occasion of the large-scale sales of church lands in the 1560s. The auctions at which these lands were sold were controlled by the *présidial* courts, and the magistrates' relatives and allies naturally came away with the lion's share.[15] It was inevitable that the chief buyers of clerical real estate should be found among the gentry. Such families were in the best position to manipulate the transactions to their advantage[16]—and, besides, "the only kind of people who have plenty of gold and don't know what to do with it are the bourgeois and the men of the long robe, such as *présidents, conseillers, procureurs*, and their like."[17]

Such "persons of the financial or judiciary *condition* and those who were wealthy"[18] occasionally lost patience with their piecemeal inroads on clerical property. In preparing the position papers for the Third Estate, on the eve of the Estates-General meeting of 1561, whose principal purpose was to do something about the huge public debt, the gentry calmly proposed to take over all the church's properties. Estimating the total annual income from church property at 4 million livres, the financiers of the Third Estate guessed that this represented a capital of 120 million. They urged the crown to seize all of the church's property and to arrange to provide the needed 4 million each year by investing 48 million of the total sum and using the interest for the maintenance of priests. Of the remaining 72 million, 42 could be used to pay off the crown's debts, and the balance of 30 million ought to be invested, they advised, in a nationwide banking system, to be administered by the municipalities. This national bank could offer commercial and industrial loans at low interest rates, and the interest itself, some 2.5 million yearly, might be sufficient for the government's military expenditures.[19] This proposal, made in 1561, came to nothing, but it is a fair indication of the gentry's ambitious designs on the Church of France: they wished to own it.

The gentry's consuming passion for the church as a worldly concern was matched by its serious involvement in the spiritual realm. It may be difficult to picture the men who traded in abbeys and bishoprics as moralists and reformers. There is certainly no trace of reform in Guillaume Briçonnet, bishop of Lodève, when he arrives with his numerous followers at Reims in the summer of 1497 to help out in his father's high-pressure campaign to win the nomination to the archbishopric. His father is already bishop of Saint-Malo, abbé of Grandmont, and a cardinal of the church. The Reims archdiocese is vacant because Guillaume's Uncle Robert has just vacated it. The campaign conducted by Guillaume was scandalous even according to the standards of the time. "Never were electors so hardly pressed for their votes," said the royal *advocat*. The Briçonnet party let it be known that the king would be most angry if the canons refused to elect their candidate. The rumor went about that, "if the king's will were obstructed in this matter, the canons were likely to be thrown over the walls of the city by mobs of the people." Meanwhile, Guillaume wined and dined the canons day and night and gave each of them a present of one golden écu. When his father failed to carry the election, by one vote, the recalcitrant elector, Biguet, fearing for his safety, fled the town. "His relatives were telling him that he was ruining them, that the people in the streets were out to get him, that his relatives were being threatened everywhere by mobs calling for them to be beaten and given to the dogs to be eaten."[20]

That same Guillaume Briçonnet reformed the abbey of Saint-Germain-des-Prés, and in his diocese of Meaux he was the first French bishop to introduce evangelical reforms. "The episcopal ministry is entirely evangelical," he proclaimed in one of his sermons. "The bishop is an angel sent by Christ, entrusted with his message; he performs the angel's office of purging, illuminating, and perfecting souls." These were not empty words. Briçonnet resided in his diocese, inspected its parishes, reformed its abbeys and hospices, and, above all, introduced preaching by appointing a diocesan preacher at six hundred livres per annum and getting rid of mendicant friars whose raids "poisoned the diocese with their impostures." Briçonnet set out to "hunt for souls and catch them in the nets of Jesus Christ." He demanded of his parish priests that they reside in the midst of their congregation, and he outlawed dancing and other popular festivities on Sundays. Undaunted by the resistance of special-interest groups, in particular the friars, he pursued violators in the law courts. In all this work he was aided by such men as Lefèvre d'Etaples, his vicar general, and Professor Vatable, the classicist, whom he appointed to a *cure* and a canon's prebend.[21] The same talents and energies that were applied to the acquisition of the church's property could be applied, with the same admirable efficiency and sureness of purpose, to church reform. The ecclesiastical empire-builders we encounter so frequently among gentry families, however, consider their benefices quite separately from their piety. Possession does not dictate piety, neither does it form an obstacle. Clerical wealth and clerical virtue are equally desirable.[22]

No one has summed up this position more tellingly than Jean Orcibal in his sketch of the Duvergier family of Bayonne. Jean Duvergier (1542–96) was the head of the second-most powerful family of this city of ten thousand. Butchers not so long ago, the Duvergiers had risen to notability and wealth through city contracts for meat supply and through tax-farming, wholesale trade, and banking. Jean was the most influential man on the city council, and, naturally, he was related to just about all the other local families of importance.

The notables of Bayonne struck the nonresident and Ligueur bishop as heretics one and all. Some of these men had, in fact, been attracted to the evangelical reform movement in its early stages. Later, the same men resisted organized Protestantism when it became politically dangerous. In the same way, they had fought off the radical conspiracies of the Catholic League, which had found fanatical support among the common people.

A man like Jean Duvergier found himself in conflict with the ecclesiastical authorities as a matter of course. Among his duties as a public official was the supervision of the city's *collège*. He was charged with enforcing attendance.[23] He was also charged with obtaining the ubiquitously disputed income from a canon's prebend for the *collège*. This income, granted in principle by the royal edict of 1560, was no more eagerly given up in Bayonne than elsewhere. In the course of a city-council meeting on 28 March 1580, Duvergier was given the responsibility of sounding out the taxpayers on the question of a concerted tithe-withholding action, a boycott designed to pressure the cathedral chapter into fulfilling its legal obligation toward the *collège*.[24] At the same time, Duvergier, who had thirteen children to provide for, found it entirely natural to settle clerical benefices on at least one of his sons. Jean-Amboise was tonsured at the age of ten and was invested with a benefice when he was fifteen.

In all this, Duvergier's experiences with the church touched only upon material aspects. As Orcibal explains, Duvergier "views the church, in practice, as a great social institution whose chief use is to help him provide for his too numerous children."[25] But nothing says that the very same man could not also be deeply religious in a traditional sense.

On the day Duvergier was asked to organize a tithe boycott, his wife was asked to head up a drive to raise money for an order of preaching friars.[26] Duvergier's public functions brought him into a bitter adversary relationship with bishop and cathedral chapter, but were these not moves for reform? Was not support of the *collège* the most concrete way to instill Christian virtues, together with good letters? "Duvergier is a Catholic, but he raises an impenetrable barrier between two domains: religion should act only upon conscience, while action is concerned only with temporal aims."[27] This attitude was typical of the *familles* of Bayonne, as Orcibal points out. It was an attitude shared by the urban elite everywhere in the kingdom. The mentality of these people allows them to exploit the temporal possessions of the church in the most brutal way and at the same time wish most sincerely for religious reform.

Their position was only apparently paradoxical. Nor was it a new position, devised for the needs of the moment during the Wars of the League, when their enemies began to describe them as *Politiques*, as men, that is, who were willing to modify the traditions of the church for the sake of political expediency. In reality, as Orcibal suggests, their attitude had already been established among the *"classe dirigeante,"* early in the century.[28] There is no essential difference in this respect between the Briçonnet of 1500 and the Duvergier of 1580: it had been the natural attitude of the gentry all along. It was a consistent point of view.

No shame was attached to the appropriation, by dubious means, of church property, because property was not seen as an essential part of the church. Church property was an accidental accretion of capital—badly managed and in need of better management—which anyway belonged to the public. From the perspective of city councils, *rentes* and taxes collected by absentee bishops and abbés were a pure loss to the city and a pure loss to God's purpose as well, especially if the ecclesiastical authorities refused to assume the cost of education, public welfare, and public preaching. Clerics required public funds only for purposes beneficial to the public. Aldermen, mayors, local officials, and magistrates were more than willing to pay for the maintenance of education and public morality, but they wanted their money's worth. Instead, they saw nothing but mismanagement and corruption. The pope could not be expected to reform the French clergy. Hence the position that such matters as the administration of poor relief, hospitals, and schools had best be taken over by lay authorities. What did the church, stripped of its duties in this world, require money for, except the decent maintenance and housing of worthy priests, whose duty would be to preach the word of God? This distinction between the needs of the worthy preacher and the possession of unnecessary real estate allowed the rich and politically powerful families to buy ecclesiastical property with the greatest insouciance and to treat benefices as mere investments while waiting for the crown to sever the connection between property and the religious calling. Even though the crown failed to heed the daring proposal of 1560, the gentry lost no opportunity for acquiring church properties put up for sale, either legally, in auctions supervised by *messieurs* of the local *présidial* court, or illegally, in the wake of expropriations achieved in towns dominated by Huguenot force of arms.

At the same time, it was among gentry circles that the earliest and most consistent demand for religious reform was heard. It would be natural to ask what happens in the mind of a devout Christian who, in effect, buys or inherits ecclesiastical benefices and thus finds himself, perhaps against his will, coiffed with a bishop's miter and committed to the care of souls. He may well tell himself that his nomination to an abbacy *in commendam* is a purely financial act or that his distant diocese is merely a purchased right to collect certain revenues. He may still feel obligated to the care of souls, as did Briçonnet at Meaux. The bishopric as a financial investment may be separated in a man's mind from his Christian duty, but who will fulfill the bishop's or the abbé's duties if the incumbent is a politician at court? And how seriously can one attack the church for its abuses if one happens to hold a portfolio of clerical benefices?

The problem can be shrugged off with a joke, such as the one attributed to the abbé of Tiron, whom we know as the poet Desportes, who is said to have turned down the offer of a bishopric to avoid incurring the heavy moral responsibility of the care of souls—"pour n'avoir pas charge d'âmes." But was he not already burdened with the same awesome responsibility in his function as abbé of two monasteries? "Oh," Desportes is said to have replied, "monks don't have souls."[29]

A more serious way of solving the problem, and a fairly common one, was to absolve one's conscience by placing worthy, pious, and learned Christians in positions of leadership and responsibility in the diocese one simply could not take the time to visit. Thus, while exploiting the revenue of the diocese through trusted financial agents, one could at least make a serious gesture, and a fairly inexpensive one, by establishing reputable scholars in one of the diocese's *cures*.[30]

That the gentry should be receptive to reforming ideas is to be expected. Their education set them apart even before they began to build classical grammar schools. They had learned very early to admire the wisdom of the ancient philosophers together with the piety of the Church Fathers. They read the Holy Scriptures in Latin, Greek, and French. As members of the universal republic of letters, they shared in the most powerful intellectual currents of the time. In the early years of the century, it was Erasmus whose call to evangelical reform reached the Budés, the Ponchers, the Ruzés.[31] From Louvain or from Basel, in Latin and in French, the prince of learning dictated to his French subjects. His message appealed to the educated notables, from the city councils of Bayonne to the Olympian heights of the Briçonnet empire. It was a view of reform which separated religion from observances, divine law from ecclesiastical regulations, the work of God from the work of men.[32]

The evangelical doctrine as preached by Erasmus or by Lefèvre d'Etaples may have been at first the rare and fragile possession of small avant-garde circles protected by powerful prelates. But it soon spread to a wider audience.

Lefèvre's French New Testament of 1523 was addressed "à tous chrestiens et chrestiennes." A French Psalter followed in February 1524. Until then even Latin Bibles had been rare; there were a few, at best, in each diocese, in manuscript on parchment, and these were jealously guarded. Suddenly the Gospel was there in French, available to everyone—little practical volumes in everybody's hands and pockets. Briçonnet of Meaux handed them out to the faithful, free of charge.[33]

The sober *advocats* and *conseillers*, who hoarded books in their provincial studies, had not had to wait for Lefèvre. Their kind of active piety had been fed for some time already, clumsily perhaps, by such printed books as a collection of *Hymnes en françoys*, published around 1498, or *The Imitation of Christ* (*L'Imitation de Nostre Seigneur en franchois*), which sat side by side on the shelves of their libraries with works by Gerson and French translations of Brant's *Ship of Fools* (circa 1500), of Cicero's *De officiis* (1502), and of such traditional manuals of morality as the *Doctrinal de sapience* or the *Miroir de la vie humaine*, titles which I pick up at random among the fifty or so books in the library of a *conseiller* in the *bailliage* of Amiens.[34] In the libraries of the most

notable families we will soon find French Bibles and commentaries by
Erasmus, Lefèvre, and even by Melanchthon; Greek New Testa-
ments; the works of Plato and Plutarch; and the inevitable Cicero and
Josephus standing next to legal treatises by Tiraqueau, Budé, and
Zazius.[35] Meanwhile, the evangelical passion is carried to the schools
by enthusiastic instructors (régents).[36]

Through the printed book and through formal education, evangelical doctrines reached the gentry's sons perhaps more profoundly and
more quickly than any other group.[37] The very success of the reforming ideas, however, brought on the most severe repression. It was
one thing for a président to correspond with Erasmus and another for
the sons of merchants and artisans to be exposed to heretical ideas.
For heresy had become a real danger. The peasants were on the
march in Germany. Who was to draw the line between evangelical
doctrine and Lutheranism? Who was to say when new ideas and
books in everyone's hands might not lead to open sedition in France?
"There are many Lutherans in this kingdom," writes the king's
mother to le président de la Barde in November 1525 to explain her
fear lest these heretics, "once they have done everything they can
against God, may do something against the king and myself and the
state."[38]

Once again we shall be confronted with what appears to be a
singular contradiction. Powerful magistrates, who had been savoring
the Erasmian attack against the clergy and who may have personally
sympathized with the call for evangelical reform, suddenly became
Inquisitors. These men of Luther's generation made a natural distinction between the inner life of the Christian and worldly action. For
them there was no connection between the worldly church and true
piety. It stood to reason, as they saw it, that wool-carders who trou-
bled the public order by breaking statues or holding seditious meetings could not be acting out of truly devout religious motives. Erasmus and Luther would condemn such actions. The troublemakers in
the kingdom, like the peasants in Germany, were dangerous from the
gentry's perspective, not because they held allegedly evangelical doctrines but, on the contrary, because "adding their own opinions and
errors," they misunderstood the Gospel, misunderstood the intentions of the reformers, misunderstood even Luther.[39] Motivated by
ignorance or malice, the seditious elements seemed to be growing in
numbers daily. The danger was new and acute. It had to be confronted immediately and ruthlessly.

It was one thing to approve of the call for reform in 1520, to nod
with agreement as one read The Praise of Folly between sessions at the

Palais de Justice, to admire the purer texts of the Gospel, to offer financial support to learned men and serious preachers. It was another thing altogether, five years later, to stand by and let fanatic sectarians disrupt religious ceremonies and challenge law and order. In the course of these five years, Luther had happened; and in the wake of his inflammatory tracts and sermons, religious reform had moved from scholars' studies to the peasants' fields. Doctrine had ceased to be a private matter, and it was no longer the church alone but the government itself, at all levels, which was threatened.

The magistrate had no choice: he had to move quickly to exterminate heresy when it led to rebellion, even if the evil had insinuated itself among his own kind and would thus be the more painful to extirpate. It was a matter of waking up suddenly to perceive a danger which had been there for all to see all along. The reformers at Meaux, Erasmus in the schools, the Greek texts, and irrefutable arguments with which their own libraries were equipped: what had seemed worthy and admirable only five years ago now stood revealed as sinister. The peaceful and private message of the Gospel had been transformed by some sort of sorcery into diabolical wrath in the minds of "certain private persons." It was high time to arrest offenders. The time had come, as well, to quarantine those who had, albeit innocently, inspired the evil. The *parlement* of Paris moved swiftly to repress heresy.[40] The state was endangered. Henceforward, it was hoped, unorthodox ideas could be confined to safe places: to the salons and libraries of the rich and to the esoteric lecture halls and books of avant-garde intellectuals.

This is the perspective from the *palais de justice* and the *maisons du roy*. It is pointless to ask whether the gentry favored Protestantism or Roman Catholicism. Even if it were possible—absurd suggestion—to add up two columns of figures in answer, the result would be trivial. If we knew, for instance, that 70 percent of royal *officiers* never formally renounced regular Roman Catholic observances, this evidence would tell us only that they were cautious men of property always in the public eye, like that paragon of gentry virtues, Monsieur de Montaigne, or the more humble Monsieur de Gouberville. Did Lefèvre, did Briçonnet, abandon observances? Did the hunted reformers of the 1520s join Protestant congregations? Was there such a thing as a Protestant Church in France in the early decades of the century? Is it useful, at any time, to employ formal adherence as a test of beliefs?

What other tests can there be? It is hardly a novelty, after the splendid researches of Imbart de la Tour, Lucien Febvre, or Jean

Orcibal, to speak of the existence of a third party closely identified with the university-educated leadership of the *consulats* and *échevinages*, the *jurades*, *présidiaux*, and *parlements*. [41] Such a party cannot be identified through its doctrines. It did not create militant organizations. Only very late in the century would it be represented by an effective, if ephemeral, political coalition labeled as the *Politiques* by adversaries on both sides. Most of the time this third party can be defined only by a state of mind, capable of veering in one direction or the other but always suspect to Papists and Huguenots alike.

As fine an illustration of this state of mind as I know of is given by le président de l'Estoile when he recommends his son Pierre to Professor Brouard, who is to take full charge of his education. Brouard, a Protestant, agrees to take the Roman Catholic *président*'s son into his *pédagogie* and scrupulously observes the *président*'s charge to him, which Pierre reports in the following words: "Maistre Matthieu, my friend," says the *président*, "I recommend my son to you. In the matter of religion, I do not want you to take him away from this [Catholic] Church: I forbid you to do that. But on the other hand, I do not want you to raise him so that he will be oblivious of its abuses and superstitions." [42]

Reviled in times of conflict as secret Nicodemites or libertines, men of property and erudition sought to hold on to a difficult neutrality against both "outright Catholics" and outright Huguenots. "What shall we do now, among these tumults?" writes Estienne Pasquier to a friend at the Rouen *parlement*. "Should we imitate Diogenes" and retire to our own affairs? "Our pens serve as our swords. Should we use them as one does double-edged weapons? [That is, strike out against both Catholics and Protestants.] We could not do so without being accused of impiety." Pasquier observes the formation of Catholic and Protestant parties, from a spectator's perspective, "as a tragedy which will be played in our midst and at our expense, and God willing we will lose nothing more serious than our purses." Pasquier might well be speaking for the gentry as a whole when he formulates the fervent wish to exile himself somehow from the coming confrontation "in a foreign country, as a kind of parenthesis," while waiting for this madness to exhaust itself. Alas, too many things were at stake—property, family, offices. A man in the prime of his life could not retire from the fray: "We must resolve to live and die with our state, as good citizens."

The resolution is not easy to carry out. Pasquier, like so many others of his kind, may privately admire much in the evangelical doctrines and count many confirmed Protestants among his closest

friends and correspondents. He may admire the personal and intellectual qualities of a Protestant leader like Coligny, but he "will not
speak of the quarrel he supported, because, as a good Christian," he
will always be "for the Catholic, Apostolic, and Roman Church."
Why is that, when he complains so bitterly about "the majority of
bishops and abbés who trade and barter benefices"? Because, "as a
good citizen," he will "abhor the changes in the state which ordinarily result from the changes in religion." Pasquier sums up the Paris
parlement's position as a belief in the principle that "the general foundation [of a republic] is principally dependent on the establishment of
religion, because the fear and reverence of religion keeps all subjects
within bounds more effectively than even the presence of the prince;
therefore, the magistrates must above all other things prevent the
mutation of religion or the existence of diverse religions in the same
state," which can lead only to "partisanship and internal discord,
which turn into civil wars, which in turn bring about the decline and
fall of republics."[43]

Must the magistrate opt for repression, then? The experience of
previous repressions in moments of crisis, in 1525 and in 1534, confirmed a small majority of the judges in the *parlement* in this course.[44]
Others, like the *conseiller* Adam Fumée, prudently hide their evangelical sympathies to work for toleration: "We think freely," writes
Fumée to Calvin in 1544. "We do not let innocents be condemned. We
even acquit those who are accused for their religious views, to the
extent that we are able to and to the extent that this can be done when
dealing with men who are hostile to the true religion."[45] The gentry is
perplexed: some counsel repression, some toleration; but, as Pasquier
puts it in commenting on the new and severe measures against the
Protestants, "Those who have the most nose"—those, that is, who can
smell trouble a long way off—"predict that all these novelties, introduced to exterminate another novelty, are really the preparations for
a general calamity, from which no one in France will be exempt."[46]

Knowing full well that there was "nothing so much to fear in a
republic as civil war, and of civil wars none more fearsome than those
conducted under the veil of religion," the gentry stood by, helplessly,
while great personages "greatly excited the people to arms."
"Everyone is talking nothing but arson, war, murder, and pillage."[47]
It was too late to repress the Huguenots: force bred counterforce, with
the result that no one was willing to obey magistrates any more.[48]

The republic had as much to fear from one party as from another,
and those who saw the dangers could only retire to their private
consciences and wait for the storms to blow over. The time had come

for caution. No one was safe from denunciation, as Gouberville, for instance, knew only too well.[49] He kept his opinions to himself and went right on with his tithe-farming. He remained on the best of terms with locally important clerics. This was neither cowardice nor hypocrisy. It was the natural course of action for educated men of property who were in the service of the state. Some of them may have desired a purer religion, but few wished to create a new church at the cost of bloodshed and destruction of property. Reform was a private matter. And bringing evangelical doctrines to the common people was, to be sure, a desirable goal in principle, but in reality was probably a lost cause, given the ignorance and superstition of the masses. In any case, no reform should upset the fragile equilibrium of the republic.

The most succinct statement of this point of view, to my knowledge, is to be found in an anonymous memorandum attributed to Montaigne's friend La Boétie. The author of this position paper on the implementation of the Edict of January 1562 addresses himself to the question of reconciling religious reform with legality. "In my opinion," he writes,

> we ought to begin by punishing the insolences [breaches of law, order, custom, and morality] occasioned by religious dissension. As soon as this is done, we must proceed, no matter what else we do, in such a manner as to leave only one church, and this church ought to be the old one, but so completely reformed that it will be seen to be entirely new, and, in its *moeurs*, entirely different from what it used to be. In doing this we must act with such moderation that, on all those points where church doctrine is at all flexible, we must give in to the Protestants, so as to round them up like a straying herd and thus recuperate all those who are not too delicate [in envisaging such compromises] and make it possible for them to return without offense to their conscience. We must under no circumstances tear the followers of Jesus Christ into two sects, a detestable thing before God and ... an unfailing presage of the entire ruin of the kingdom.

The author of the memorandum stresses the purely secular and legal nature of the proposed proceedings: "No person should ever be questioned in any fashion on matters of religion." The inquiry should be conducted by the *parlements*.[50]

In this perspective, the ideal Christian life is that of a man like Jean de Saint-Gelais, the abbé of Saint-Maixent, whose peaceful death, in 1575, at the age of 75, was admiringly recorded by his friend, Michel Le Riche, the *advocat du roy* at Saint-Maixent: "He was

learned in divine, human, and canonical letters. He sought quarrel
with no one, and he lived peacefully with his people." That the learned
abbé also happened to be a Protestant in matters of doctrine was his
private concern. The *advocat du roy* at the local court in Saint-
Maixent made no more distinction between his Catholic and Protestant friends than did his counterpart in the *chambre des comptes* in
Paris, maistre Pasquier. *Cure,* prebend, or abbey could not affect the
inner rectitude of a pious man, nor should one make too much of
conflicting interpretations of papal powers.[51]

Reform is a serious but a private matter. Only the most exceptional circumstances would allow sectarian convictions to be raised
to the boiling point among the *familles* of France. The circumstances
of Calvin's exile, the impetuous decision of Théodore de Bèze—such
accidents of fortune can, occasionally, force men of property and
office to break with their families and to abandon their *pays*. The
gentry, on the whole, found exile too horrible to contemplate. Few
familles participated in the rush to Geneva.[52] Calvin found it difficult
to persuade such people to give up their responsibilities. He denounced them for cowardice; he tried to persuade them that there
could be no compromise between Gospel and papism.[53] Calvin's
success would remain limited. He would have to condone, eventually, the compromise course favored by the gentry. Even when they
accepted the ideas of the Reformation, such men considered it im-
practical to change the outward aspects of traditional religion.[54]

This position, so common among the wealthier families especially,
may strike observers as inconsistent.[55] It is true that, on occasion,
we are tempted to laugh at the way in which some notoriously
greedy beneficiary of ecclesiastical venality hangs on to his revenues
while opting for Calvinism. There is the truly outrageous case of
Antonio Carracciolo, bishop of Troyes, for instance. Carracciolo was a
courtier who made no bones about what he thought of benefices:
"The king gave me this abbey so I could set up my sisters decently,"
he explains.[56] He was appointed bishop of Troyes in 1551, and we
find him, only a year later, conferring with Bullinger in Zurich. Soon
he is in Geneva, where he is received as a Calvinist minister, but he
still claims his rights as bishop of Troyes.[57]

Carracciolo was, however, a most unusual person and the son of
an Italian prince. Much less unusual, in the same diocese of Troyes,
is the course of action charted by the Pithou family. While Carracciolo had been, briefly, the titular head of the diocese, it was in fact
administered largely by the Pithous, one of the most prominent
families of Troyes. It was the lawyer, Pierre Pithou, the son-in-law of

the lieutenant general of the *bailliage,* who managed the affairs of the diocese. The Pithous were in and out of the bishop's residence, they came to dinner, they lent books. And they were also, most of them, among the most prominent secret Protestants in town.[58]

In Troyes there were as many shades of evangelicals as elsewhere, including a handful of people determined and doctrinaire enough to choose exile. Among those who stayed, there were many secret Protestants, who led double lives. Nicole Pithou, one of Pierre's sons, tells us of his scruples rather candidly. He admits to having "wallowed and polluted himself against his own conscience amidst the abominations and garbage of the papacy." He went with the crowd, on Sundays, "to kiss the baboon, that is, to give homage to the beast," while dissimulating his true feelings and "fearing very much to be known and recognized for what he was in truth."[59] Nicole Pithou's anguish may have been sincere, but there were certainly secret supporters of reform in town who found ways of accommodating themselves to such ambiguous situations.[60] In any case, none of the Pithous, so far as I know, chose more than token exile, and none, to my knowledge, pushed scruple so far as to give up any of the lucrative revenues they derived from the diocesan affairs. The power of families like the Pithous survived the worst crises of the civil wars by virtue of coalitions of interest among secret Protestants, liberal Nicodemites, and moderate Catholics, who united to protect themselves and to profit from the church without interference from Rome or from competing *arrivistes* among the lesser bourgeoisie.

In Troyes, as in many other provincial cities, these intense rivalries were fought most characteristically over the issue of public education. Throughout the violences of the civil wars, the city's *collège* had managed to resist a Jesuit takeover. The *familles* protected La Licorne (the school was known by the name of the building in which it was temporarily housed) against the attacks of the cathedral chapter, which wanted to replace it with a Jesuit seminary. A powerful bishop friendly to the Jesuits exerted new pressures in 1605. When the Pithou won the mayoralty election in 1611, the struggle between the *familles*, led by the Pithous, and the pro-Jesuit party, which had wide support among the lesser people, erupted into open violence. The city council named a principal whom the bishop threatened with excommunication. The Pithou *hôtel* was the headquarters of the anti-Jesuit forces. But the Pithous were getting old, and they were childless. Their cause seemed doomed. It now seemed as if the Jesuits needed only to wait. But they had not counted on the resourcefulness of the old Pithous. At his death, in 1621, François Pithou willed his luxurious *hôtel,* including its famous library and all its furnishings, to the city, together with a sizable endowment, for the purpose of establishing a permanent home for the municipal *collège.* The irresistible offer had only one condition attached to it: no Jesuits were to teach in the school.[61]

The enmity between the gentry and the Jesuits was an old conflict by then, and it was destined to continue. Because of the acrimonious polemics it gave rise to, this happens to be a rather noticeable thread of continuity. This hoary duel began when the Society of Jesus was first establishing itself in the kingdom; it was still going strong, a century later, when the gentry's spiritual leaders were labeled Jansenists.[62] The gentry's resistance to the Jesuits, it seems to me, was only one of several continuities in the religious behavior of this social class. Often sympathetic to evangelical ideas of reform from the start, gentry families suppressed their inclinations when it became clear that reform could not succeed without civil war. Henceforward the gentry's strategy was to restrain both factions. Jesuits and Calvinists were fought off as disturbers of the peace. This compromise position, formalized by the Edict of Nantes, addressed itself to the political aspects of the conflict, but it was not without economic implications. The gentry, safe now from the intransigence of both parties, would find it easier to maintain its control over ecclesiastical property.

Had the threat of Calvinism in effect diverted attention from reform? I think it is reasonable to suggest that in the world of the gentry the idea of reform was never abandoned. The gentry had given up on reforming the mass of the people. But it never wavered from the more modest objective of cultivating the *philosophia Christi* within the walled privacy of its own world.

12

Adrift

*Il est temps de nous desnoüer de la
société, puisque nous n'y pouvons rien
apporter.*

Montaigne, *Essais*

The desire to retreat from the world was becoming a noticeable state
of mind among the gentry's philosophers and poets. It has been
argued that this position becomes truly radical only in the 1630s,
with the well-publicized retreats of Jean Duvergier and Antoine
Lemaistre, which led to the foundation of what was to be called
the Jansenist movement.[1] I think it would be more accurate to say
that Jansenism was to be only one form—spectacular because it co-
alesced into a movement, and persecuted because it expressed itself
in theological positions—of a general retreat from society which was
advocated in the gentry's best-loved books as early as the 1570s.

There had been a time when the idea of retiring from worldly affairs
had been little more than a classical topic for literary debates. City life,
on the other hand, offered immense rewards: "the friendships, the
obligations, the alliances of persons which we acquire daily."[2]

This confident mood had existed before the civil wars, when the
world seemed to beckon with all its attractions to young lawyers like
Pasquier. The birth of a son was an occasion, in those days, for pure
jubilation (*Puer nobis natus est!*).[3] One wished to be a *philosophe*, but
not a *philosophe misanthrope* in the Stoic mold. The ideal, rather, was
that of a worldly philosopher, a *philosophe mondain* or *civil*.[4]

All this was to change. The time would come when Pasquier would

have to defend himself against the accusation of being a misanthrope.[5] Even then he will refuse the Stoics' view.[6] He will still get
bored in the country.[7] What he seeks in the solitude of his estate is
not so much the bucolic pleasures celebrated by the poets as his
independence. "Each of us is king of the republic God entrusted him
with. I am king, in my little way, because I know how to control my
passions. And when I speak of myself, I mean all those who would
follow this course." In his private Pantheon, the worldly Aristotle is
replaced by the "three greatest philosophers in the world: Solomon,
Heraclitus, and Democritus."[8]

Maistre Pasquier's transformation is no isolated case, nor can it be
accounted for by the loss of youthful confidence; younger men are
touched by the new mood as much as their fathers.[9] If we are to
understand the origins of Jansenism and of the other varieties of
misanthropy which begin to occur with such frequency in the early
years of the seventeenth century, we should note that the rejection of
the world is not necessarily expressed in theological or even Christian
terms: some retire to their fields, some to their classical authors; some
become saints, others atheists. What we have to seek is the link between Solomon and Heraclitus.

An explanation for the new mood has been proposed—a partial
explanation, to my mind. It is argued that the *officiers*, as a social
group, were increasingly being disappointed in their political and
economic expectations because the crown, beginning with Henri IV
and especially under Richelieu's ministry, had broken the old com-
pact which tied the government to the *officiers*. By the time of the
Fronde, the alliance was shattered. The *officiers* found themselves
hating the "absolutist" state and, at the same time, incapable of attacking it. Their frustration, Goldman argues, was the "infrastruc-
ture" of the tragic paradox in Pascal's and Racine's vision of the
world.[10]

This hypothesis contains plausible elements. Once we agree upon a
working definition of the gentry as a social group, we may find that
its power was to diminish vis-à-vis that of other groups. We may find
that the gentry's wealth was declining and that the social status of the
mass of *officier* families diminished between the wars of the League
and those of the Fronde. Even if these hypotheses were to be confirmed, however, they would not provide a satisfactory explanation
of the loss of nerve implied by that misanthropy which was already
becoming synonymous with *sagesse* in the last decades of the sixteenth century, long before the government could be said to be slip-
ping from the grasp of the *officier* syndicates.

Later, when Nicolas Pasquier complains about "our France" having "reached extreme old age," when he describes the country as "sick," "stumbling along helplessly," and "near death," he does have political circumstances in mind.[11] He was not alone in seeing the assassination of Henri IV as a deathblow struck at the gentry's vital interests and in seeing an even crueler calamity in the regency which followed. But Nicolas is not thinking of catastrophic events alone, nor does the discomfort he expresses proceed merely from political advantages lost.

The intrinsic worthlessness of the nobility is an evil on a grander scale than the misfortunes of a single reign.[12] The other classes of society[13] also seem to suffer from "nonchalance" and "presumption." Merchants, artisans, and peasants, he complains, are leaving their proper and productive work, because they are attracted by the lure of education: "This great number of *collèges* to be found everywhere in the kingdom is nothing but an anthill filled with presumptuous apprentices." The strength of the kingdom is being undermined, he claims, by the "availability of *collèges*, which makes the plowman abandon his plow and the artisan lay down his tools."[14]

This accusation is significant. Pasquier is far from alone in making it: it becomes, toward the end of the century, a commonplace complaint of the gentry. It is a new complaint, and it puts the gentry in an ambiguous position. It was they, and their fathers before them, who had proclaimed the virtues of public education loudly everywhere in the land. It was they who had founded schools in every town, for the good of the republic. Nicolas Pasquier himself, while complaining about the excessive number of *collèges*, was at the same time obtaining royal letters patent for the *collège* in his jurisdiction. The royal chancellor, Bellièvre, even while expediting these documents, allowed himself, according to Pasquier, the remark that "there were too many *collèges* already in France."[15]

Something had changed since the days when good letters were thought to be the salvation of the people. Had the teachers and professors failed in their task? Was classical learning itself on trial? One might receive such an impression from Montaigne, but his strictures against the schools become understandable only when we perceive that he is not alone in expressing his disappointment.[16] The schools have failed to inspire the lower classes to virtuous behavior. This is the charge against them. This is why *collège* after *collège* is allowed to sink into bankruptcy. Only the threat of Jesuit takeover inspires canny rearguard actions against the common enemy. The gentry has not turned against classical education itself; it has simply abandoned its attempts to carry good letters to the masses. For what did education profit the *sot populaire*? At best one could inculcate respect for learning, but the masses could not be taught to admire goodness.[17] The learning acquired in the schools "does not nourish and aliment their schoolboys and children; it is passed from hand to hand, for the sole purpose of parading it, of displaying it in front of others."[18] The boy goes off to school; he comes back fifteen or sixteen years later—to what advantage? All one can say is that his "Latin and Greek have made him prouder and more arrogant than when he left his home."[19] As Montaigne sees it, the purposes of higher education have become distorted. The *collèges* were being used only to make men richer. Were it not for that, the thriving educational establishment would soon shrink back to its erstwhile insignificance.[20] Since "studying, in France, has pretty much only one purpose, namely, profit," we find, "ordinarily, that only persons of low fortune take it up as a full-time occupation," in order to make a living from their learning. Such people have the lowest kinds of souls, "by nature, by upbringing, and by example." The lame are not much good as athletes. Lame souls, in the same way, are not suited to spiritual exercises. Vulgar souls are not worthy of philosophy.[21]

This is the bitter conclusion of the gentry's ideological leaders. They do not abandon good letters, but they remove them from the sight of the vulgar. They shut themselves up in private retreats, where they commune as fervently as they always have with the great books of their youth. "My books on one side, with my pen and my thoughts. On the other side, a good fire," writes maistre Pasquier from his "parenthetical" retreat near Melun. "The day lasts a mere hour, the hours a mere moment." Is this the refuge of a misanthrope? "On the contrary," he explains; his motive is self-love.[22]

But then, not everyone had the charm and natural bonhomie needed to carry off a retreat from the world in such pleasant fashion. Montaigne, in his book of essays ("Je n'ay livre entre les mains que j'aye tant caressé," admits Pasquier), allows himself more somber thoughts. Persuaded of the "nihilité de l'humaine condition,"[23] he has his doubts about the effectiveness of retreating to the country. He does not fool himself into thinking that "ambition, avarice, irresolution, fear, and concupiscence can be left behind."[24] He can find no solace in religious ritual. Prayers are a form of play-acting or, worse, magical formulae.[25] The church and its traditions he can sum up as a charade.[26] If anything could have tempted him in his youth, he admits, it was the Protestant movement, if only because of the difficulties of the enterprise. But how presumptuous all these sectarians are to assume that anyone with the least clarity of mind must needs be at least a secret sympathizer, even if he denies it.[27] What "fantastic imagination" induced these militants to take it for granted that a man with some clarity of mind would necessarily agree with them?[28] Montaigne thought that the church was justified in prohibiting the "promiscuous, daring, and indiscreet" distribution of the sacred Scriptures: they were not meant to be everyone's business.[29] How foolish of the Protestants to think they have made the Bible comprehensible by translating it into the popular language![30] Montaigne, who is as devoted to the Scriptures as he is to the pagan classics, would withhold both of these treasures from the vulgar.

The creation of *collèges* had not served the cultivation of virtue, it had merely created opportunities for social climbing. The evangelical movement, instead of achieving religious reform, had created civil war. The gentry, in sum, had made a fundamental and fateful mistake. Thinking to create a following among the common people by allowing them to share its classical education and its reforming morality, the gentry had merely armed its enemy. Hordes of newly licensed lawyers stood ready to challenge the gentry's privileges, and armies of psalm-singing shop clerks were prepared to kill and burn in the name of the Lord. A generation of brutal social conflict, barely disguised as a religious crusade, taught the gentry that it stood alone in the world.

This sense of isolation, which Goldmann described in cosmic terms and which he attributed to the progress of rationalism, seems to me to be as much a part of Montaigne's world as of Pascal's.[31] The painful retreat from the world undertaken by the gentry during the Wars of Religion was more than a tactical withdrawal: it was a rout, a general *sauve qui peut* which sent the gentry back to their private libraries. "I especially wish that we should be judged separately, each on his own," insists Montaigne,[32] and he recommends that one should "imitate the animals who wipe out the tracks leading to their lair."[33] "We have to reserve for ourselves the back of the shop [*arrière-boutique*] which must be free of encumbrances and where we can establish our true liberty and principal retreat and solitude."[34]

How many of Montaigne's admirers followed his advice—or wished they could! His definition of wisdom was that of an entire class: "To withdraw your soul from all pressures, to hold it in liberty and give it the power to judge freely in all things." As for outward appearances, the wise man ought to "follow the traditional forms, for our thoughts do not concern public society."[35] This course of action became the favorite target of the Jesuits' champion atheist-hunter, Father Garasse. His attacks against the "curious doctrine of the *beaux esprits*," often directed against old Pasquier in particular, called forth a defense from Jean Duvergier, the founder of Jansenism. This exchange of polemics, in the 1620s, provides a link between the "curious doctrine" of Montaigne's generation and the equally curious doctrine of Port-Royal.[36] The dissimulation of Montaigne, in the 1580s, was not at all the same as that of the Nicodemites of the 1550s or that of the persecuted Jansenists of the next century. What all these "curious doctrines" had in common, though, was that they hid in the same *arrière-boutiques*.

Garasse is attacking the "quintessence of atheism," and he knows where to find it. It flourishes among those who insist "that each one of us must remain entirely free to believe what he wishes."[37] Shrewdly, Garasse observes that such people proclaim their Catholicism loudly and that "when they speak of the Bible, they praise it excessively."[38] They hold that the populace must be kept entertained with miracles and that one ought to profess Catholicism *en apparence*, so as not to shock the simple.[39] Garasse castigates the intellectual pride of these *beaux esprits*, who are driven by their desire for originality, always in search of new ideas, always intent on going against the grain of all established customs. Rabelais is their handbook, he claims; and, of Rabelais, "It is impossible to read a single page without incurring the danger of offending God mortally."[40] What did it profit these intellectuals to have gone to so much trouble to "get away from the common opinion"? As for him, Garasse tells us, he prefers the well-traveled road—*le grand chemin battu*.[41]

Garasse's purpose is to prove that, in the privacy of their souls, these self-conscious intellectuals, "who adore all their inventions, their words, their thoughts, yes, even their dreams, which they would have printed if they could," are the enemies of God and the enemies of society.[42] He likens them to "cats walking on roof tiles."[43] This, I think, may be taken as a sharp sketch of the gentry's predicament. Garasse knows his enemies' weaknesses. They are marooned on the rooftops, high above the *"grand chemin battu"* of the ordinary Christians.

The gentry's heroes do not cut their ties to the world out of a sense of failure. On the contrary, these are well-known, successful politicians, still young, with glorious careers open to them, like the *conseiller* Eyquem of the Bordeaux *parlement*, who sells his office in 1570 and opts for one of the best-publicized and most admired retirements in the history of literature.[44] The same is true of the famous retirement of Antoine Lemaistre in 1637: he was only twenty-nine years old, and his career was the envy of the Parisian *officier* circles.[45] Even the most inwardly pious of these men had no intention of "leaving the *palais* in order to enter the church." Even the solitude of Lemaistre's retreat still has much in common with Montaigne's *arrière-boutique*. As Lemaistre took the trouble to explain, in an open letter to his patron, the chancellor Séguier, he did not want his decision to be misunderstood. He was not about to take Holy Orders or shut himself up in a monastery: such a decision was even further from his mind than the continuation of his career as a lawyer.[46]

When such influential and philosophical men repudiated the "servitude" of public office, "in the full vigor" of their age, to devote themselves to the pursuit of "liberty, tranquillity, and leisure," when they retired to a private house "to live without ambition," their decision was profoundly admired by those who could not pursue their kindred inclinations for such practical reasons as having children to push in the world. "To have no business at the *palais*," to be "far from the court," to "have a tranquil mind"—that is happiness as defined, volubly and interminably, in all the poetry conceived in the busy offices of *procureurs* and *advocats; it is "to be satisfied with one's possessions and desire nothing else" and to wait for life to end "without desires, without fears, without worries."[47] "Adieu, city, adieu luxurious house, always accompanied by fear and alarms."[48] This is the recurring theme.

The ideal commonly pursued in this literature is that of a comfortable retreat, whose merit lies in protecting one, not from the sins of the flesh but from politics, which is portrayed as a series of servitudes. "Oh, how much happier is he who, in his solitude, need not beg the support and favor of the dumb masses [*ce sot populaire*]." How happy is he who, "having peacefully retired from the court and from the inconstant world, leaving public affairs alone . . . is his own court, his own seigneur, and his own king."[49] To spend one's life in the haven of one's family, "free of hatred and envy, among the fields and forests, far away from the tumult and the noise of the common people," to be "his own court, his own favor, his own king"—this is the fervent dream of the gentry.

Coming from the pen of our old friend Desportes, the bon vivant abbé, we may suspect that this vision of a retired life is not necessarily to be confused with a desire for mortification. The goal is contentment: "Gentle sheep, my loyal companions," exclaims the worldly abbé, "hedges, bushes, forests, meadows, and mountains, witness my contentment."[50] Nor is there any suggestion of frugality in the lawyer Tabourot's wishes: sufficient goods, "amassed without labor, ... and friends neither greater nor lesser than I."[51] "I live my life quietly," writes the lawyer Durant, "I have neither charges nor offices, I have no benefices, nor do I have more possessions than I need, I am master of my desires and such as God made me: I aspire no higher." "Free of worry, accompanied by my book, I ramble among the fields: *voilà* my life ... isn't it good?"[52]

The gentry wishes to escape from servitudes: the servitude of the royal court—and the servitude of the masses as well. Father Garasse is quite right: these *beaux esprits* are like cats on rooftops, wary of the crowd below. They long for a kind of freedom that will make them immune to the pressures of the social community. They cannot abide the servitude imposed by the ordered social world. They wish to be lords of their own republics, lords of themselves alone, with no one above and no one below. They are tired of competing for status with insolent noblemen; they are weary of the crowd whose favors must be solicited. Their country estates are allegorical republics, El Dorados of the mind, where differences of rank are unknown.

Of the tentative conclusions which can be drawn from this literature of retreat, two stand out. One is that the gentry, in its more introspective moments, sensed its failure as a social class. It was proving impossible, after all, to replace the nobility and to assume the leadership of the nation, in spite of the wistful proclamations of dreamers like Turquet de Mayerne, who could still, as late as 1611, imagine a hopeful future in which "envy shall cease" and "vain reproaches" will no longer be exchanged between "the old and the new nobility." The time when "one would say of someone that he is a new man and this will be a mark or title of honor instead of scorn"—this time was not at hand.[53]

This is not to say that our men had failed, individually, to achieve high status in the kingdom; it is rather that they were failing to achieve it on their own terms. Despising the old nobility for its ignorance, dissoluteness, and violence, the gentry had dreamed of imposing its own values on the nation. The civil wars, that tragedy played at their expense, proved the futility of this dream. The gentry might continue, on occasion, to imagine itself as the natural leaders of the Third Estate, but the brutal fact was that the mob, that "barbaric chameleon," singled the gentry out for its particular hatred.[54]

Was it this realization which put an end, eventually, to the gentry's political ambitions? The *familles* of all the good towns would continue to own the kingdom, in an uneasy partnership with the *grands* and the court; but their role would have to remain a private one. Bereft of the support of the nation, deeply separated from its origins, the gentry was forced to capitulate to the *traisneurs d'espée*. Henceforth it would become necessary to masquerade as *gentilshommes*—or remain plain bourgeois.

The virtues of that ephemeral Fourth Estate, as enumerated by Montaigne—peace, profit, learning, justice, and reason—were not, after all, to take precedence in public opinion over the virtues of the nobility: war, honor, action, valiance, force. In order to achieve the highest honors, it became necessary, once again, to embrace the values of the enemy. There was no choice but to pretend to be what one was not and to become "an amphibious man," to wear the lawyer's gown in the morning and to dress as a *gentilhomme* at night.[55] One could not appear as an *honneste homme* in public without being a misanthrope in private.[56]

The gentry were becoming uncomfortable in their skins. Forced to portray nobility, often *à outrance*, they hated the part. Caught between two worlds, reviled by the bourgeoisie and taunted by courtiers, the more sensitive of them resorted to eccentricity, as did Malherbe, who could have been a model for Molière's *Misanthrope*.[57] The brooding concern about the *humaine condition*, from Montaigne to Pascal, becomes more understandable in this perspective. Was it not the proper worry of those who had no more specific *condition* to call their own?

What I am suggesting, at the conclusion of this essay, is that there may be a connection between the gentry's failure to impose itself as a recognized social class and the elaboration of a moral philosophy which claimed to ignore class distinctions. King or peasant, Parisian or cannibal, each man is to be judged on his own by the worldly philosopher who declares himself the adoptive citizen "of all countries where there is something to learn."[58] If the gentry's most painful and most deeply buried grievance was that there was no place for persons of their kind in the world as it was constituted, then we may begin to understand why the gentry, in turn, resigned from this world and rejected its hierarchies.

For men who want to be neither bourgeois nor *gentilshommes*, it is a misfortune to have been born into a society which refuses to admire any *condition* other than nobility. Ah, to have been born in Venice rather than in Sarlat![59] Republican Venice, presumably, knew how to reward rich and learned magistrates. How much more open to talent was republican Rome, where new men—"who were not noble of race but were beginning to ennoble themselves by their own means and their own virtue"—could rise in the public esteem through their probity and eloquence.[60] Unable to conquer dignity within the contemporary hierarchy of social values, the gentry was tempted to seek its rewards beyond and outside of orders and estates and hence to declare commonly accepted social distinctions null and void.

The differences which separate the nobleman from the villain, the magistrate from the private person, the rich from the poor, all these, in Montaigne's view, are insignificant. Purely external and conventional, these differences mean no more than the color of the trousers a man is wearing. They are mere *peintures*, applied to the outside of a man. They say nothing about his essence. The emperor himself, whose pomp impresses us in public, is, in private, an entirely ordinary man; he may, in fact, be viler than the least of his subjects. How foolish to think that a man of good sense would consider it an advantage to perform his bowel movements attended by twenty courtiers. The advantages of kingship are imaginary. Anyone who stays at home and knows how to conduct his affairs without quarrels and lawsuits is as free as the duke of Venice. No prince enjoys worthwhile pleasures which are not also largely available to men of middling fortune. "Essential and effective subjection" is a servitude voluntarily chosen, and it concerns only those whom pride attracts to the courts of princes. Could it be that the happiest society would be one in which equality reigned among men and in which precedence would be measured solely according to an individual's virtue?[61]

Montaigne is rather candid in admitting his preference, at least academically, for an equalitarian society: democracy seems to him the most natural and equitable form of government.[62] His views are expressed obliquely, as in the conversation he reports having had with an American Indian. Asked about what he found most remarkable in his first experience of Europeans, the Indian replies that he is perplexed to see some men "filled and gorged with all sorts of goods" while others were "begging at their doors, worn out by hunger and poverty." Montaigne notes that in the Indian's language men are spoken of as "the other halves" of other men and reports the Indian's judgment, namely, that he could not see why "the poor halves could suffer such an injustice and why they did not grab the rich by their throats or set fire to their houses."[63]

Montaigne, who finds the cannibal's judgment sensible and rather admirable,[64] is not, after all, very much concerned with the redistribution of wealth. In his view, the end of social organization is to produce virtue. Wealth and poverty are conditions worthy of notice only to the extent that they interfere with the cultivation of virtue. This is the yardstick which allows him to condemn excessive riches as well as excessive poverty. The equality among men which he and others of his kind esteem is a moral and natural equality,[65] the kind of equality which puts simple peasants on the same level with philosophers.[66] Custom may dictate the superiority of warriors or priests, but such notions are to be disregarded by the philosopher. "Certainly if there is anything at all clear and apparent in nature ... it is that nature, which governs men in God's name, has made us all of the same form and, as it were, cast us all in the same mold, so that we may all recognize one another as companions or rather as brothers."[67]

The formulation is too passionate to be Montaigne's; it belongs to his other half, Monsieur de la Boétie.[68] Fraternity is inseparable from liberty and equality in La Boétie's view. "We are all naturally free," he affirms. "It is beyond doubt that if we lived endowed with the rights nature gave us and according to her teachings, we would naturally obey our parents, be subject to reason and be serfs to no one." The very animals shout to us: VIVE LIBERTÉ!

If men could only overcome the voluntary servitude inherited by custom, if they could only see that long habit can never give the right to do evil, then they would follow the lead of "those who have a clear understanding and a penetrating mind." Such men, "who were born with naturally good minds and have improved them further through education, would be capable of imagining liberty and feeling it in their minds, even if it were entirely lost in this world." We are all brothers. If nature endowed some of us more bountifully than others, he explains, it was surely no part of nature's intention to set the stronger or shrewder into the world, like armed brigands in a forest, to prey upon the weak. Rather, we must believe that the inequalities created in us naturally are meant to give rise to fraternal affection, some having the power to help, others the need to be helped. The power of speech was given to us for the purpose of fraternizing among ourselves, so that a common and mutual declaration of our thoughts might lead to a communion of our individual wills.[69]

It is not my intention to suggest that La Boétie's passionate advocacy of liberty, equality, and fraternity ought to be read in the spirit of the eighteenth-century revolutions.[70] Nor do I wish to claim that La Boétie's political theories were representative of the mind of the gentry in the sixteenth century.[71] I do think, however, that the philosophical radicalism of this text is not entirely alien to La Boétie's semblables and frères, who, according to Montaigne, found much to admire in it.[72]

An academic and utopian exercise it may have been. What interests us is not whether this discourse could have led to sedition. The text and its reception tell us only that among the gentry, on occasion, the flight from painful political realities could take astonishing forms. These were clear minds, ready to deplore the iniquities of an aristocratic society in the name of abstract ideals of justice. These were not peasant rebels, driven to despair by hunger and oppression, nor were they religious fanatics come to fulfill millenarian prophecies. It was specifically and only among the *beaux esprits* of the gentry that men could be found who were able to question the social foundations of the *ancien régime* and imagine the possibility, at least, of a fundamentally changed society. Such men were cut adrift from their moorings in the social world.

Unlike the apologists and spokesmen of other social groups, the gentry's philosophers could not simply blame all crises on change and look to the past as a time of harmony and justice. If only taxes were reduced to the level of a previous reign, cried the peasants; if only rich *officiers* were forbidden to rise above the commonalty, explained the bourgeois, in agreement with the nobility—then all would return to its normal state. This kind of normality was profoundly incompatible with the gentry's aims. Their historians hated the feudal society of the past; their moralists hated the nobility; their political theorists imagined, without much conviction, a utopian future in which merit alone, rather than birth, would propel men toward leadership—it being understood that well-managed capital was no mean evidence of merit.

For the time being, these remained private dreams. For a very long time to come, the gentry, lacking a following, could only compromise with the existing order of things. Civil philosophers had no choice but to follow Montaigne's advice and loosen the ties which bound them to society. They limited their goals to the cultivation of their own gardens. Not literally, to be sure. If some could be found who actually chose to retire to the country, they were merely symbolic outriders of a much larger procession which fled from public life without leaving Paris. The gentry gave up all hope of concerted political action. It ceased to challenge the nobility and gave up enlightening the bourgeoisie. Only in rare utopian moments would some continue to dream of conquering the nation for the common good, of ousting insolent noblemen, of taming the barbaric chameleon of the lower classes. Now it was each man for himself.

Families continued to cultivate their capital and their alliances. They guarded their privileges; they continued to buy tax exemption, office, honor, and nobility of a sort. They continued to flock to Paris, the capital of privilege; the provinces were largely handed over to the limited vision of newer bourgeois elites. *Collèges* and universities withered away. Soon there was to be "no civilization outside of Paris."[73]

It would be a mistake, though, to close the books on the gentry as soon as it cut itself adrift. A social class is neither formed nor dissolved as easily as a business partnership. In the sixteenth century, the bonds which held the gentry together as a group were more clearly visible than they were to be later. Dress, speech, life-style, and education set the gentry apart from the three estates of the realm. The gentry was known and understood, then, as being constituted by a separate kind of persons. This was a time when the most powerful *président* in Paris had more in common with a provincial lawyer than with his splendid equals at court.

The most visible of these solidarities were eroded in the course of the seventeenth century. *Présidents* dressed like marquis, spoke like courtiers, no longer bothered with doctorates in law. One began speaking of a *noblesse de robe*. Provincial lawyers found it more difficult to leave *bourgeoisie* behind. They were no longer assured of that commonalty of interests that had cemented the gentry's relations up and down the land.

Change there was. But it would be misleading to exaggerate its extent. The public solidarity of the gentry was moribund. But in private, whether they thought about it or not, gentry families continued to behave in ways which set them apart from the nobility. They continued to seek marriage alliances largely among families of their own kind; this had been true in the fifteenth century, and it was still true in the eighteenth.[74] Even had they wished to mix with the nobility and become confused with them, they would have been snubbed, in the eighteenth as in the fifteenth century. This was as true in provincial cities as in Paris.

When some Parisian magistrates found themselves marooned in Bourges in 1753 and 1754, they observed that

> the noblemen, three-quarters of whom are starving, are nevertheless wrapped up in their genealogical pride and keep their distance from the *robe* and finance milieu; they find it incredible that the daughter of a *receveur des tailles*, married to a *conseiller* of the Paris *parlement*, should turn out to be sophisticated and worldly; as for the bourgeois, they are plunged in the crassest ignorance ... their wives bigoted and pretentious, given to games of chance and flirting.[75]

Even in Paris and at court, someone like the Président de Montesquieu, "a man of considerable standing and known as such in his
province," counts for very little.[76] When *présidents* are to be found
who will claim that "nobility of the *robe*" is indistinguishable from
true nobility, such claims will be sorely tried in real life. They will also
be refuted by theoretical writings such as those of the Chevalier
d'Arcq, which were characteristic of the point of view of the nobility.
"Those who rose to the first ranks of the magistrature," writes
d'Arcq,

> without the aid of high birth, through their own merit only, did
> obtain nobility. . . . However, this nobility has always been kept
> separate from that obtained by arms. The warrior, obedient to the
> judge only in the temple of justice, has kept his superiority
> everywhere else. These two kinds of nobility have kept flowing
> together like two streams in the same riverbed, whose waters do
> not mix.[77]

Was it the exclusiveness of the nobility which kept the oldest and
richest *robe* families from betraying their origins in a headlong rush
toward *gentilhommerie?* Certainly the open arrogance of the *traisneurs
d'espée* must have provoked great irritation. When government regulations were promulgated with the intention of discriminating against
the newer sort of nobility, they provoked nationwide frustration.[78]
But the greatest *robe* families could hardly be kept in their place by
means of edicts and regulations. The requirement of four generations
of technical nobility could not have bothered families like the Joly de
Fleury.[79]

The technical nobility achieved through the exercise of an office in
the *parlement,* from father to son, for generations on end, did not
necessarily make the great *robe* families noble in a social sense.
Whether or not they claimed titles and had themselves called marquis
or barons, contemporaries understood that their *qualité* resided in
their *façon de penser* rather than in their parchment affidavits and
seigneurial rights.[80] The social historian is wasting his time if he asks
whether the magistrates of the sovereign courts were noble or commoners, for the resulting information is useful only in determining
the degree of privilege accorded to such persons by the state. In the
eighteenth-century *parlement,* we are told, an overwhelming majority
of the magistrates were noble before taking office. Does this mean
that the nobility, as a social class, was giving up military careers and
preparing to study law? It means nothing of the sort, of course. It

means only that these magistrates were the sons and grandsons of other *officiers* who had achieved legal nobility through the exercise of their office. The recruitment of magistrates was not essentially different in the eighteenth century from what it had been in the sixteenth. That is, the offices were open, first of all, to those families which already held office in the court and, secondarily, to patient parvenus whose families had sufficient wealth and had lived nobly enough to merit consideration. The *noblesse de race* stayed away from the *parlements.*

If we wish to talk about social classes at all, we may have to abandon the convention of describing the elites of the *ancien régime* as "bourgeois" and "noble." Both nobility and bourgeoisie existed as legal definitions of status. As such, they changed meaning in time and were always ambiguous. Under no circumstances could either of these terms be applied with accuracy to the sixteenth-century gentry defined in this book.

Could it be argued that by the eighteenth century the gentry had lost its public character so completely that its leading families had been integrated into the nobility, while the so-called bourgeoisie had absorbed the rest? The suggestion is not implausible. It does seem that the term *bourgeois,* in late eighteenth-century Paris and Chartres, referred to the same group of notables, living nobly, who would have been called *nobles hommes* in sixteenth-century contracts.[81] It also seems fairly clear that the bonds of mutual interest which had once held the gentry's world together had become dangerously frayed by the end of the eighteenth century. Magistrates in the *bailliage* courts could no longer be counted on to follow the lead of the demigods of the *parlements.* But was this political fissure, driven through the gentry's ranks, due to fundamental social changes? On the eve of the Revolution the *bailliage* families were only very rarely noble in any sense, but this had also been true in the sixteenth century. If they were more readily inclined to accept the Revolution as a group than the *messires* of the *parlements,* this would seem an entirely natural position. They had, after all, so much less to lose.

That there were conflicting interest groups within the gentry is entirely understandable. It may be more significant, though, even in the eighteenth century, to consider the more permanent and more profound conflict which opposed the *gentilshommes* to the rest of society. The most eminent *présidents,* it seems, could be kept at arm's length by courtiers at Versailles and be snubbed by simple *gentilshommes.* On the other hand, it seems that neither wealth, nor power, nor public esteem ever quite erased feelings of bitterness and euphoric visions of public equity and virtue, even in the most well-placed magistrates. "I have often maintained and I still maintain," writes Malesherbes, in 1766, "that a philosophy which would bring men as close to equality as possible would be the greatest good for humanity, or at least one of the greatest. Unfortunately, we are very far from being able to realize such a goal. I view the feudal government as a multiplied tyranny ... and I am happy to tell you that, in this, almost everyone is of my opinion these days." (Not really everyone, of course. Everyone in the salons he frequented, perhaps.) One would not have to go far to find the opposing viewpoint expressed in the name of the nobility.[82]

These are impressions which I gather from another age and which I am not prepared to evaluate. I have been, after all, pursuing a most elusive prey. I think I have tracked it down to its lair, on occasion. I may have persuaded the reader of the existence of nationwide solidarities which, in the sixteenth century, transcended considerations of wealth. We traced the formation of social coalitions; we chronicled, in this last chapter, their dissolution. I am inclined to think of the rise and fall of the gentry as a social conjuncture, akin to those well-known economic cycles which characterize the *ancien régime.* I do not really believe that the gentry disappeared before the Revolution. Rather, it seems to me, its existence as a self-conscious class was muted and hidden, like the presence of a subterranean fault in a volcanic region. The seismic shocks of the sixteenth and early seventeenth centuries seem to have been followed by a long period of inactivity. The violent eruptions of the late eighteenth century might usefully be studied against the background provided in this essay. It may be that we would confirm, once again, that if the Revolution was a conflict between social classes at all, then it was not a mythical bourgeoisie which hurled itself against the nobility. We may discover that it was largely a resurrected gentry which took up its pens and parchments to do battle against its primordial enemy, the *traisneurs d'espée,* and that the fall of the *régime,* in this perspective, is no surprise at all but rather the culmination of a centuries-old tension.

A Note on Sources

I would like to have provided a complete, systematic listing of all the sources cited, but such a bibliography, adding many pages to this volume, would further have increased the already high cost of production. I shall therefore limit myself to indicating those manuscript sources which, though not highly visible in the critical apparatus of my book, were nevertheless as necessary to its making as a foundation is to the construction of a house.

The principle I have followed in my use of sources is the following. Whenever the need arose to demonstrate a point by having recourse to nonliterary sources of the kind which are the staple of social history—private diaries, correspondence, contracts, minutes of city council deliberations, and so on—I have chosen to make the point by referring to published records unless unpublished sources made the point more effectively.

Since this is not the usual practice of academic theses, I should explain that this book was not written to fulfill any academic requirements. Free of the need to demonstrate hard work and the proficient use of unpublished sources, I have been able to devote my efforts to other purposes. In this essay questions are raised which require the cooperative scrutiny of many specialists, most of whom do not have

easy access to French local archives. The evidence presented here
should be as easily available as possible. Hence my preference for
using archival records already printed, however obscurely, in monographs, collections, and proceedings of learned societies. This preference may also betray a touch of piety on my part—my reverence,
namely, for the work, the prodigious, accurate, and inspired work, of
the *érudits* and *savants* who came to maturity before 1914. Their
energy, their craftsmanship, their seriousness of purpose are the
mark of a vanished epoch. They were giants, and their race is extinct.
These antiquarians of my grandfather's generation did not miss
much, as I discovered in following their path through many de-
positories of local archives.

What follows is a selective guide to the unpublished sources which
I looked at and found useful. On the whole, these explorations only
confirmed a general picture which could have been constituted almost as effectively from the enormous—and largely ignored—
accumulation of published sources. Anyone who wishes, as I did, to
test this proposition must go to the local archives. Among these, the
following archives départementales seemed most useful to me.

Basses-Alpes: Series E. 354 (Fauris family, proofs of "living nobly");
    503 (Guibert family); 527 (Isnard); 90 (Barras); also 351 and 352.
Basses-Pyrénées: Series E. 1789 (a *notaire's* papers); 1802 (Lostal fam-
    ily); 1857 (*enquête de noblesse*); 1987 (wills); 1992 (economic activities
    of an *advocat*); 1997 (Gassion, *marchands* and *advocats*); 2002 (Se-
    condat gift to *collège* student); 2003, 2007, 2008, 2013, 2015, 2026 (rise
    of Blair family, *collège* principals); 2027 (catalogue of *advocat's* li-
    brary); 2029 (successes of *collège régent*).
Calvados: Series E. Gosselin family papers.
Charente: Series E. 1512–16 (Nesmond family).
Côte-d'Or: Series E. 102 (Bouhier family); 109, 110 (*inventaire* of fur-
    nishings); 113, 123, 136, 205 (*seigneuries* bought by *marchand*
    families); 741, 742 (Desbarres family, excellent case study); also 755,
    847. Series D. 4 (Godran family); 47bis, 48, 13 (*inventaire* of library).
Deux-Sèvres: Series E. 1306–17; 1981 (*laboureur* establishing endow-
    ment for his son to study in Paris); 1995 (disintegration of *escuyer*
    estate in favor of *marchands* and their allies).
Dordogne: Series E. 2E 1812 (Chevallier family); also 2E 72 and 2E
    1833.
Hérault: Series C. 7834–37.
Indre-et-Loire: Series E. 44 (on Jacques de Beaune); also E60. Other-
    wise disappointing.

Maine-et-Loire: Series E. 1463, 1464, 1533, 1622, 1639, 1650, 1652,
    1697, 1749, 1776, 1831, 1905, 2044, 2319, 2506, 2596, 2677, 2725,
    2802, 3344, but especially 3381–86 for Milsonneau papers, contain-
    ing cost of boys' schooling, letters from the boys, and *inventaire* of
    library in 1588. Also 3385 for Oger family schooling costs.

The archives départementales of the Cher (at Bourges) are very rich.
This is not true of the Var (at Draguignan) or of the Aude (at Carcas-
sonne). I think that those of the Bouches-du-Rhône (at Marseille)
would repay close scrutiny. I did not spend enough time there. The
archives départementales housed in the new préfecture building in
Rouen are surely rich but are deplorably catalogued and inaccessible
as far as the E series in concerned. The archives départementales of
the Vienne and Haute-Vienne may be promising for the study of
collèges (D series).

Notes

Chapter 1. Introduction

1. Marc Bloch, "Sur le passé de la noblesse de France: Quelques jalons de recherche," *Annales Economies, Sociétés, Civilisations* 8 (1936): 366–78.

2. For an up-to-date discussion of the problem—painstaking and candid if somewhat labored—see the long introduction in Régine Robin's *La Société française en 1789: Semur en Auxois* (Paris, 1970).

3. Roland Mousnier, *La Vénalité des offices sous Henri IV et Louis XIII* (Rouen, 1945), p. 58.

4. Ibid., p. 509.

5. Mousnier, "Problèmes de stratification sociale," in *Deux Cahiers de la Noblesse (1649–1651)* (Paris, 1965), p. 39.

6. Mousnier, *Vénalité*, p. 58.

7. Mousnier, "Problèmes," p. 36.

8. Mousnier, *Etat et société en France aux 17ᵉ et 18ᵉ siècles* (Les cours de Sorbonne, Centre de Documentation Universitaire), p. 247.

9. Robin, *Société*, pp. 28–29, is candid enough to admit that a "mode of production" does not exist in reality and that Marx's "feudal mode of production" has little to do with feudal society as described by historians. She sums up recent and older polemics and perplexities easily (ibid., pp. 33 ff.) and tries to establish that the economic activities of the bourgeois of the *ancien régime* cannot be made to fit into a capitalist mode of production since they were typically landowning *rentiers*.

10. Mousnier, in *Le Conseil du roi* (Paris, 1970), p. 20, estimates that in 1665 as much as 13 percent of the total population of the kingdom was made up of

officiers and their families. These 230,235 people—out of a total population estimated at 17.5 million—do not entirely overlap with the category of bourgeois *rentiers* "living nobly," but the figure is a clue at any rate to the size of this group.

11. Mousnier, *Etat et société*, p. 246.

12. See Robin, *Société*, pp. 33–37.

13. G. Lefebvre (*Etudes Orléanaises*, 2 vols. [Paris, 1962], 1:153 ff.) counts industrialists and merchants as "noble," as he does again on p. 179 and elsewhere; all the while, Lefebvre was quite aware of the fact that the "nobility" of his sugar refiners and *rentiers* was not accepted by public opinion and was rejected outright by the assemblies of the nobility; he also notes that the new *anoblis* stayed away from the nobility in their marriage alliances (p. 187).

14. Pierre Goubert, "Problèmes généraux de la noblesse française," *XIII Congrès International des Sciences Historiques* (Moscow, 1970).

15. M. Bloch, "Passé," p. 375. Mousnier makes the same point, more prosaically, in 1970 (Mousnier, *La Plume, la faucille et le marteau* (Paris, 1970), pp. 12–13.

16. Another great medievalist, R. Boutruche, exposing the fragility of these status distinctions as they were perceived in the Bordeaux region in the late fifteenth century, denies the existence of clear lines of demarcation between the high bourgeoisie and the nobility and observes, quite rightly, that "the jurisprudence of the sixteenth century had not yet imposed its mark on the social groups, nor had it yet created among them this well-ordered hierarchy so freely transposed to earlier times by too many historians" (Boutruche, *La Crise d'une société* [Paris, 1947], p. 82).

17. Jean Richard Bloch, *L'Anoblissement en France au temps de François I* (Paris, 1934). In the late eighteenth century, *lettres de noblesse* remain rare, it seems: seventeen per year in the 1770s and 1780s is David Bien's estimate ("La Réaction aristocratique avant 1789: L'Example de l'armée." *Annales Economies, Sociétés, Civilisations* 29, no. 1 [January–February 1974]: 23–48).

18. See J. M. Richard, *La Vie privée dans une province de l'Ouest: Laval aux 17ᵉ et 18ᵉ siècles* (Paris, 1922), pp. 165–66, 303.

19. The first-rate studies by Jean Meyer on the nobility of Brittany and of Monique Cubells on the nobility of Provence, among others, make it clear that a very high proportion of the families which were considered noble in the eighteenth century were descended from sixteenth-century *arrivistes* of bourgeois origin. See, especially, the observations of Cubells in her "Usurpations de noblesse en Provence," *Provence Historique* 81 (1970): 224–301. "It is unquestionably a fact that just about the entire nobility of Provence ... owes its exodus from *roture* or bourgeoisie, since the 15th century, to wealth acquired by commerce" (p. 247). Of the 439 families she considers, only 33 were nobles by 1400 or so, while the largest number, 220 families, achieved nobility in some way between 1550 and 1673 (p. 248).

Chapter 2. What the Jurists Say

1. "En France il y a deux sortes de personnes: les uns sont Nobles, les autres sont Roturiers ou non nobles. Et sous ces deux especes sont comprins tous les habitans du Royaume: soit gens d'Eglise, gens de justice, gens faisans profession des armes ... & autres, ... de quelque estat, qualité & condition

qu'ils soient." This formulation is made by the jurist Jean Bacquet in his *Traicté ... concernant les francs-fiefs* (Paris, 1582). I am citing from the 1625 edition, p. 3.

2. The jurist Charles Loyseau was probably born in Paris in 1564. His father, Regnauld, was an *advocat* at the *parlement*, his grandfather Jean a simple (but no doubt rich and successful) *laboureur* of Nogent-le-Rotrou. It was Regnauld Loyseau, the lawyer, who made the family fortune. He allied himself through marriage to well-to-do merchant families of Dreux and Chartres and managed the business affairs of Diane de Poitiers. His son Charles had the advantage of an excellent education as well as his father's wealth and connections. He is said to have become an *advocat* at the age of 20. By 1593 he exercised the office of *lieutenant particulier* in the *bailliage* of Sens; in 1600 he became *bailli* of the County of Dunois. He married the daughter of Nicolas Tourtier, *conseiller, trésorier,* and *receveur* of the duchess of Longueville. Charles Loyseau's estate, after his death, was worth 146,024 livres, including much land near Dreux, houses in Paris, and a portfolio of *rentes*.

3. Loyseau's treatise *Des Ordres,* which concerns us here, was published in 1613. There were several editions of it in that year. It was never reprinted separately, to the best of my knowledge, but it appeared again in the three editions of Loyseau's collected works in 1666, 1678, and 1701. Roland Mousnier cites a 1610 edition, however, which is unknown to me and not listed in the Bibliothèque Nationale catalogue. By contrast, Bacquet's treatise on *francs-fiefs,* first published in 1582, was reprinted in the eight successive editions of his collected works (1608, 1612, 1625, 1630, 1658, 1664, 1688, 1744).

4. Bacquet, *Traicté:* "Il suffit que les temoins deposent qu'ils ont cogneu son ayeul et son pere" and "les ont veu vivre noblement" (p. 4). "Le meilleur sera que les temoins soient Gentilshommes de race, officiers Royaux et autres gens de qualité, non pas simples marchands" (p. 114).

5. This eventuality is foreseen by the satirist Etienne Tabourot in *Les Bigarrures du seigneur des accords* (Rouen, 1595), pp. 33–37: "Veu que les Iuges les premiers se moqueront au bout de compte & les declareront Gentilshommes pour ce qu'eux mesmes auront parens de mesme farine & seront aises de se preparer par la un degré pour usurper quelque jour."

6. Bacquet, *Traicté:* "Les officiers royaux non nobles de race ny anoblis sont subjects au droict des francs-fiefs" (p. 60). It must be added that there really is no clear law. (See J. R. Bloch.)

7. See Noël du Fail, *Contes d'Eutrapel,* Assézat, ed., 2 vols. (Paris, 1874), 2:264. (Original edition, Rennes, 1585.)

8. Ibid., p. 269. "Vous ne sauriez avoir remarqué un vray Gentilhomme de race entre dix qui en portent les accoustremens et occupent les terres nobles."

9. Michel de Montaigne, *Essais* (Pléiade edition, Paris, 1967), p. 267: "Les armoiries n'ont de seurté non plus que les surnoms," and "il y a tant de liberté en ces mutations que, de mon temps, je n'ay veu personne, eslevé par la fortune à quelque grandeur extraordinaire, à qui on n'ait attaché incontinent des titres genealogiques nouveaux et ignorez à son pere."

10. On the closing down of opportunities, see Mousnier, *La Vénalité des offices sous Henri IV et Louis XIII* (Rouen, 1945), p. 354; Henri Drouot, *Mayenne et la Bourgogne,* 2 vols. (Paris, 1937), 1:33; Pierre Deyon, *Amiens, capitale provinciale* (Paris, 1967), p. 273; Marcel Couturier, *Recherches sur les structures sociales de Châteaudun, 1525–1789* (Paris, 1969), p. 223.

11. Loyseau, *Des Ordres* (in 1666 edition of his *Oeuvres*), p. 32.

12. Florentin de Thierriat, escuyer, seigneur de Lochepierre, *Trois Traictez* (Paris, 1606), p. 13.

13. Ibid., p. 9: "Le gentilhomme est preferable au Noble Politique."

14. Ibid., p. 133: "Je ne suis pas de ceux qui se disent enfans de la Terre. . . . Vous et les autres, vrayment Nobles de Race en Race et de lignée en lignées."

15. If we are to believe Tabourot, who explains that *anoblissement par lettres du Prince* is held in contempt because even the usurpers, "se moquans de ceux qui ont lettres du Roy—les appellent Gentilshommes en parchemin" (*Bigarrures*, p. 32 recto).

16. Thierriat, *Trois Traictez:* "La question est de sçavoir si la richesse ano-blit" (p. 162). "La richesse est une chose vile et la vilité ne peut donner la Noblesse qui est une dignité" (p. 164). "C'est une ferme base pour parvenir à la Noblesse," "celuy qui est riche peut s'exempter des Arts mecaniques." "Mais que sans vertu et sans le benefice du Prince le Riche puisse estre annobly c'est un abus" (p. 165). "Que la Richesse soit un moyen de parvenir à la *Noblesse Politique:* cela est sans contredit, veu ce qui s'en practique jour-nellement" (p. 166).

17. Ibid., p. 38, on the distinction between *gentilshommes, anoblis, roturiers.* Citing Seyssel, Thierriat speaks of "l'estat moyen entre les Nobles et le peuple" (p. 87); on *anoblissement expres* as opposed to *moyens taisibles pour anoblir*, see pp. 168, 183. "Quand le Roy donne à un Ignoble un Estat de President ou Conseiller en Cour Souveraine" (p. 185), Thierriat considers the man to have been *taisiblement anobly.* "Un estat moyen entre la Noblesse et le peuple par lequel ils parviennent à la Noblesse" (p. 87).

18. Loyseau, *Des Ordres*, pp. 34–35. (*Gentillesse* is defined as the kind of nobility which *"excede la memoire des hommes,"* while *Noblesse* comes from *anoblissement du Prince* either by letters or by office or even seigneuries *anoblis-santes.*)

19. Ibid., p. 39.

20. Ibid., p. 44.

21. Ibid., p. 46.

22. Ibid., p. 74: "Il y a plusieurs Ordres ou degrez au Tiers Estat: gens de lettres, financiers, praticiens, marchands, laboureurs, ministres de Justice & gens de bras" among others. Loyseau is clear in his own mind about the total lack of legal or official meaning in the use of a concept like orders: such status ranking, to his mind, "concerne simplement l'honneur" and is not written into the law (ibid., p. 6). Elsewhere he admits that "le Tiers Estat de France n'est pas proprement un ordre" (ibid., p. 74).

23. And Loyseau knows this, naturally: "Ne tenons point pour parfaite Noblesse, celle dont il se peut prouver que la race ait esté roturiere en quelque temps que ce soit" (ibid., p. 33).

24. Thierriat, *Trois Traictez*, p. 39, cites the case of the Estates of Lorraine in which the *anoblis*, while in principle present as part of the noble estate, have no voice in the deliberations.

25. According to J. Russell Major's figures, 35 percent in 1576, 43.8 percent in 1588, 47.3 percent in 1593, and finally at the 1614 meeting of the Estates-General, 49.5 percent of the Third Estate deputies were royal officials, while another 25.8 percent were municipal officials, and only 9.1 percent were plain inhabitants of towns. The same *officiers* who packed the meetings of the Third Estate also claimed noble status. Thus according to Major, 38 percent of the

Third's deputies in 1614 were seigneurs, *sieurs,* or *escuyers,* and an additonal 14 percent stated that they were noblemen.

26. *Discours d'un gentilhomme françois à la Noblesse de France* (1614), p. 9. Whom does the speaker have in mind when he refers to a class of persons who are neither nobles nor *officiers*? Is he challenging the credentials of those Third Estate deputies who are not technically bourgeois, those 52 percent who claim some kind of noble status but are not really *nobles de race*? That would seem plausible, but then why say that they are not *officiers*? Most of them are that too. Perhaps this is an evasive tactic, a way of avoiding direct confrontation with royal officials. Or perhaps just sloppy thinking. "Une autre sorte de personnes, inutiles au Roy et au Public qui ne sont n'y nobles n'y officiers." "Pretendus membres du tiers Estat," "qui est le vray commencement de la subversion des anciennes familles de la Noblesse et l'establissement des modernes qui en usurpent et achetent la qualité." "Detriment du pauvre peuple," "faveur, parentelle, alliance et intelligence qu'ils ont avec les officiers, tant de Justice que de Finance." But I suspect this is a divide-and-conquer technique: the speaker wishes to expose the majority of Loyseau's *nobles hommes* who hold no important office in the sovereign courts and who separate their status from the *parlementaires,* who will soon be referred to as *nobles de robe.* It is a mirror image of Loyseau's distinction between the *simples gentilshommes* and the *grands.*

27. I use the word *class* here not in the special meaning—or meanings—given to it by the Marxists but in a common-sense way, to mean merely one group of people who, on a nationwide scale, have more in common with one another than they do with the rest of the population and who are conscious of this solidarity.

28. Loyseau, *Des Ordres,* p. 46: "Honnestes Bourgeois vivans de leurs rentes, notamment ceux qui ont droict de porter qualité de Noble homme."

29. Loyseau, ibid.: "Plus honnestes habitans des villes."

30. Ibid., p. 45: "Les Nobles ont droit de se qualifier Escuyers ... fussent ils gens de ville & de longue robe, anoblis seulement par leur dignitez."

31. Ibid., p. 100: "il semble que le titre de Baron est la borne & la dernière dignité de la haute Noblesse." P. 101: "Quant à la simple Noblesse, on peut dire qu'il y en a aussi une honoraire & de nom seulement a sçavoir celle dont se qualifient les Officiers de Justice, les Advocats & autres qui ne sont nobles de race & n'ont Office anoblissant."

32. Ibid., pp. 100, 101, 42, 47.

33. Ibid., p. 101.

34. Ibid., p. 102.

35. Ibid., p. 42.

36. Ibid., p. 52.

37. Ibid., p. 35.

Chapter 3. Contours and Solidarities

1. Marcel Couturier, *Recherches sur les structures sociales de Châteaudun, 1525–1789* (Paris, 1969).

2. Ibid., p. 228.

3. Ibid.: "Tous [les 'nobles hommes'] se disent seigneur de quelque terre."

4. Ibid., p. 222.

5. Ibid., p. 231.

6. Ibid., p. 219.

7. Ibid., pp. 217–18.

8. Ibid., p. 229. Couturier's findings lead him to affirm again and again, as if it were surprising, that the essential borderlines between social groups are marked by the epithets of honor. It is no surprise to me, and it was no surprise to other students of sixteenth-century social history in France. See, for example, Paul Raveau's observations made in 1926: "Tous ceux qui sont familiarisés avec ces documents du XVIe siècle, ... savent très bien qu'on ne saurait s'y méprendre, et qu'à première vue dans la lecture d'un acte, on voit à qui l'on va avoir à faire: ... *noble homme maître* un tel, ou encore *noble et honorable homme,* indiquant celui qui aurait bien voulu faire suivre son nom du titre d'Ecuyer, mais n'en avait pas encore le droit" (Paul Raveau, *L'Agriculture et les classes paysannes dans le Haut Poitou au XVIe siècle* [Paris, 1926], p. 218).

9. Couturier, *Structures sociales,* p. 216: "Une charnière capitale des classements sociaux se situe en effet dans cette zone de la société, celle qui souligne la présence ou l'absence d'épithète d'honneur."

10. Ibid., p. 229.

11. Ibid., p. 227.

12. Ibid., p. 228.

13. Couturier's computer figures a coefficient of 3.56 for *laboureur* households, 4.17 for vintners, 3.98 for artisans, 4.28 for merchants. These are seventeenth-century figures; they would be higher, says Couturier, for the sixteenth century. I multiply the *feux* of *nobles hommes* by 4, but I could just as well try 4.5. There is no question of accuracy here; at best we can get a rough idea of proportions. Couturier does not estimate the number of *noble homme* households, and he lacks a term for describing the elite. When he speaks of magistrates, he thinks in terms of about 40 families.

14. The endogamy rate among *honnestes personnes* is practically the same: an astonishing 80 to 95 percent (Couturier, *Structures sociales,* p. 223).

15. Couturier guesses that among the elite of *magistrats* a fortune of 20,000 livres is probably the minimum requirement. A very few fortunes larger than 100,000 can be guessed at. Among the merchant-bourgeoisie he guesses an average range of 3,000 to 30,000 livres (ibid., pp. 147–48).

16. Ibid., p. 125.

17. Ibid., p. 236. This is true of the Mingres, Demeddes, Convers, Michau, Costé, and Rossard families among many others.

18. Ibid., p. 276.

19. Pierre Deyon, *Amiens, capitale provinciale* (Paris, 1967), pp. 272–73.

20. Ibid., pp. 241–42.

21. Ibid., p. 273.

22. Ibid., pp. 266–67.

23. Ibid., p. 275.

24. Pierre Goubert, *Beauvais et le Beauvaisis* (Paris, 1960), p. 321.

25. Ibid., pp. 327 ff.

26. Ibid., p. 343.

27. Henri Drouot, *Mayenne et la Bourgogne,* 2 vols. (Paris, 1937), 1:46.

28. Ibid., p. 43: "Catégorie complexe par ses origines, mais homogène par ses moeurs, qui étaient spécifiquement celles de la bourgeoisie: économie méthodique, mariages fructueux, placements consolidateurs."

29. Ibid., p. 46.

30. Ibid., p. 48. Drouot sums up the feeling of solidarity and class consciousness within this "haute classe où déjà, dès ces années d'avant la grande Ligue, les traits, les moeurs du grand robin d'ancien régime sont nettement ébauchés" in speaking of a "solidarité supérieure à cette préoccupation [nobiliaire]" which dominated "tout le monde robin."

31. Ibid., p. 52.

32. Ibid., p. 71.

33. Ibid., pp. 34, 45.

34. Marcel Bouchard, *De l'Humanisme à l'encyclopédie* (Paris, 1930), p. 37.

35. G. Roupnel, *La Ville et la campagne au 17e siècle* (Paris, 1955 [1922]), p. 134.

36. Ibid., p. 189.

37. Ibid., p. 115.

38. Ibid., p. 196. Roupnel's thoroughly documented conclusion is worth citing in full: "Cette classe sociale, dont nous discernons si mal le contour et le nom, a en effet un caractère spécifique bien autrement précis que l'office. C'est le fief. Cette aristocratie urbaine, qui est née et vit dans la ville, est territoriale, autant, plus encore que l'ancienne noblesse à qui parfois son épée suffisait. Ses droits et sa puissance reposent sur une réalité d'une bien autre évidence qu'un siège en Cour et un titre. Elle possède la terre. Elle est la propriétaire des campagnes."

39. Ibid., p. 187. The Saulx-Tavannes family (see A.D., Côte-d'Or, E 1742), one of the greatest Burgundian lineages, for instance, was rescued from bankruptcy in 1642. Guillaume de Saulx had lost his seigneurie of Arc-sur-Tille, sold for debts to the highest bidder. The count, luckily, had married Françoise Brulart, the niece of Noël Brulart, *maistre des requêtes.* It was this same uncle Brulart who had snapped up the seigneurie for 65,000 livres. He was, it turned out, willing to resell it to his niece at the same bargain price.

40. Ibid., p. 192: "Commencée dès le 14e siècle, la constitution en classe de la bourgeoisie parlementaire se poursuit au 15e siècle, se complète activement au 16e siècle, s'achève au 17e siècle. La construction sociale une fois terminée se ferme alors."

41. Gilbert Martin, *Choses et gens du pays de Montmarand aux XVIe et XVIIe siècles,* 2 vols. (Moulins, 1963),1:117.

42. Paul Raveau, *L'Agriculture,* p. 218.

43. See F. Mireur, *Le Tiers Etat à Draguignan* (Draguignan, 1911).

44. Lucien Febvre, *Philippe II et la Franche-Comté* (Paris, 1911).

Chapter 4. The Pursuit
of Nobility

1. An excellent summary provided in Davis Bitton, *The French Nobility in Crisis* (Stanford, 1969).

2. Noël du Fail, *Contes et discours d'Eutrapel* (Rennes, 1585), reprinted in his *Oeuvres facétieuses,* Assézat, ed., 2 vols. (Paris, 1874), 1:269.

3. Etienne Tabourot, *Les Bigarrures du seigneur des accords* (Rouen, 1595), p. 32 recto.

4. The *pasquil* is printed in the *Journal de l'Estoile pour le règne de Henri III (1574–1589),* Lefebvre, ed. (Paris: Gallimard, 1943), pp. 131–33. L'Estoile provides us with a Parisian example of such a *pasquil,* "very scandalous and libelous, directed against most of the great houses and families of the city,"

printed in 1576 and clearly savored as much among *officier* families as elsewhere.

5. Ibid.

6. How sensitive a matter this was can be deduced from an incident noted by L'Estoile: the son of Semblançay (alias Jacques de Beaune) killed a *gentilhomme* who had doubted his nobility (L'Estoile, *Journal*, p. 130). The Beaune family moved in the same social circles as the Villeroys. They were, in fact, related through the Briçonnets. And of course the accuser was entirely right: Jacques de Beaune appears as "honorable homme Jacques de Beaune, marchant" in a sales contract of 14 April 1490, as I had occasion to confirm in the Archives Départementales of Indre-et-Loire in Tours, dossier E44. For the main facts of Villeroy's biography see J. Nouaillac, *Villeroy* (Paris, 1909).

7. Nouaillac, *Villeroy*, p. 33, cites Sully on Villeroy, who is said to fight "avec des mains de papier, des peaux de parchemin . . . des traits de plume."

8. Ibid., p. 32.

9. See René Filhol, *Le Premier Président Christophle de Thou et la réformation des coutumes* (Paris, 1937), p. 38. The De Thou's wealth and prominence began in the Orléans *échevinage* in the fifteenth century, when they turned from commerce to office and allied themselves with the Viole family, already established in the Cour des Aydes in Paris.

10. La Croix du Maine, *Bibliothèque Françoise* (Paris, 1584), in the article devoted to the poet Jacques Tahureau.

11. For all this see H. Chardon, "La Vie de Tahureau," *Revue historique et archéologique de Maine* 16 (1884): 297 ff.

12. L. Froger, "Nouvelles Recherches sur la famille de Ronsard," *Revue historique et archéologique du Maine* 15 (1884): 90–202.

13. The Chevalier family papers on which this account is based are stored in the Archives Départementales of Dordogne in Périgueux. I am citing from a series of bundles (*liasses*) under the general call number of 2E1812.

14. Ibid., 2E1812 (29) folio 1 recto.

15. Michel de Montaigne, *Essais* (Pléiade edition), p. 369.

16. I am indebted to M. Baratier, head of the Archives Départementales of the Bouches-du-Rhône in Marseille for showing me the information concerning the Albertas family. The papers, recently acquired, await close inspection.

17. H. Courteault, *Le Bourg-Saint-Andéol* (Paris, 1909), p. 183.

18. Fernand Lequenne, *La Vie d'Olivier de Serres* (Paris, 1942). It should be pointed out that for people who have not had access to notarial documents, Olivier de Serres indisputably "belongs to a noble family." See, for instance, H. Vaschalde, *Olivier de Serres* (Paris, 1886), p. 34.

19. Among examples from the south, I should cite the coexistence between commerce and noble status described by Janine Estèbe in "La Bourgeoisie marchande et la terre à Toulouse au XVIe siècle," *Annales du Midi* 76 (1964): 457–67. A typical case is that of Pierre Rognette, who styles himself "Nobilis Petrus de Roquito, dominus Ozivellae et codominus Odarsi, mercator et burgensis Tholosae" (p. 465). In Toulouse, as elsewhere, we observe that the elite of the bourgeoisie, still an open class in the sixteenth century, becomes a nobility one century later (p. 466).

20. Cited in E. Esmonin, *La Taille en Normandie au temps de Colbert* (Paris, 1913), p. 201.

21. Ibid., p. 200.

22. Michel Mollat, *Le Commerce maritime normand à la fin du Moyen Age* (Paris, 1952), p. 488.

23. The Bretel family history is given by the baron d'Esneval in his "Une Famille parlementaire de Normandie: Les Bretel de Gremonville," *Revue Catholique de Normandie* (1924), pp. 186 ff.

24. *Advis, remonstrances et requestes aux Estats Generaux tenus à Paris pars Six Paysans* (1614).

25. Robert Angot, *Les Nouveaux satires et exercices gaillards de ce temps* (Rouen, 1637), p. 100. This is the sad state of affairs in the background of the wistful verses of Robert Angot, sieur de l'Esperonière, who is an *advocat* at the présidial court in Caen in the early seventeenth century. His complaint is that to put one's hope in a lawyer's career, nowadays, is like sowing seed at sea; the men of culture, "the Greek and Roman flowers which used to perfume these halls," are gone now, to be found only in the higher courts. "Why aren't you in a shop, earning money?" he asks. "Might as well, there is no future here," is the reply.

26. Jacques Tahureau, *Dialogues* (Paris, 1572), p. 82 verso.

27. Ibid., p. 84 recto: "Ne meprisent ils pas les armes?"

28. *La Justice aux pieds du roy* (1608).

29. Henri de Mesmes, *Mémoires*, Frémy, ed. (Paris, n.d.), p. 9. Someone like Henri de Mesmes, a distinguished *officier*, claimed descent from "an ancient Scots knight" of the thirteenth century, but he betrays his true origins in a remark like this one: "In France, the men of the sword have *plumes* [feathers or pens] only on their hats."

30. See Molière, *Oeuvres complètes*, 4 vols. (Paris: Garnier-Flammarion, 1965), 3:279–86.

Chapter 5. Land and Lordship: "Ex Labore Honor"

1. The Latin motto used in the chapter title heads a *livre de raison* of 1570 (cited by Charles De Ribbe, *Les Familles et la société*, 2 vols. [Tours, 1879], 1:77). The French quatrain by Claude Mermet is reprinted in *Anthologie poétique du 16ᵉ siècle*, 2 vols. (Paris: Garnier-Flammarion, 1965), 2:322.

2. On the passion for land-buying among the notable bourgeois of Bordeaux, there are useful indications in R. Boutruche, ed., *Bordeaux de 1453 à 1715* (Bordeaux, 1966), in which they are described as unceasingly collecting new lands, "ce qui les amène tout naturellement au seuil de la noblesse, dans laquelle ils se glissent de façon plus ou moins honteuse et subreptice" (p. 169). Speaking of the late fifteenth century, the author concludes that "la marchandise heureuse conduisait à la terre . . . . Du même élan, elle ouvrait la voie à la noblesse" (p. 83). Jehan Gimel (p. 169) and Ramon Eyquem (p. 83) are cited as typical among many others. By the late sixteenth century, the author observes the concentration of lands in the hands of the very rich, office-endowed families. These "marquis de Carabas en robe longue" are already several generations away from *marchandise*. Retired among the delights of their superb libraries (p. 173), they hold title to the most valuable vineyards of the surrounding countryside (p. 177), a fact which did not escape the king's

attention: "Quel est le paysan duquel la vigne ne soit au président ou au conseiller, le pauvre gentilhomme duquel it n'ait la terre?" wrote Henri IV to le président Dubernet (p. 172)—whose own family had been fish merchants not so very far back, like the Montaignes—and who could, one supposes, only smile in happy acquiescence. On the dropping of family names and the assumption of *noms de terre*, note the amusing complaints of Monsieur de Montaigne (né Eyquem) himself: "C'est un vilain usage," he tells us in all seriousness, "et de très-mauvaise consequence en nostre France, d'appeller chacun par le nom de sa terre et Seigneurie, et la chose du monde qui faict plus mesler et mesconnoistre les races" (*Essais*, Pléiade edition, p. 267). "Il y a tant de liberté en ces mutations," he adds righteously, "que, de mon temps, je n'ay veu personne, eslevé par la fortune à quelque grandeur extraordinaire, à qui on n'ait attaché incontinent des titres genealogiques nouveaux et ignorez à son pere." And he pleads with his readers: "Ne desadvouons pas la fortune et conditon de nos ayeulx" (p. 268).

3. For the Bohier career, see C. de Mecquenem, "Antoine Bohier," in *Mémoires de la société historique du Cher*, 4th ser. 33 (1922): 1–47. For the Duprat career, see M. Boudet's studies, published in the *Revue de la Haute Auvergne* in the years 1927–31.

4. The detailed story of Bohier's campaign for the possession of Chenonceaux can be found in C. Chevalier, *Le Château de Chenonceaux* (Tours, 1882), pp. 17–22.

5. He appears as "honorable homme, marchant" in a contract of 14 April 1490, and on 11 November 1492 he is still only "honorable homme, Sire Jacques de Beaune"—*sire* being an indication of notability and prosperity but also of *marchandise*.

6. In all this, I am following Chevalier. The kind of loan described here is the most common and most successful device for capital investment in the sixteenth century. It deserves to be studied much more thoroughly than it has been so far. The only modern study is Bernard Schnapper's *Les Rentes au 16ᵉ siècle* (Paris, 1957), which is quite good but is concerned only with certain *rentes* in the Paris region in the early part of the century. *Rente* contracts fill every nook and cranny of the departmental and municipal archives of France. They are the nervous system of preindustrial capitalism in this country. Quite possibly the same could be said of the Castilian *censos* and *juros* so carefully analyzed in B. Bennassar, *Valladolid au siècle d'or* (Paris, 1967).

7. My 10 percent figure is an approximation. It was the legal maximum at the time of the Bohier-Marques transactions. In the course of the sixteenth century the rate settled at 8.33 percent, and after 1600 it slipped down to 6.25 percent. See Schnapper, "La Fixation du denier des rentes," *Revue d'histoire moderne et contemporaine* 4 (1957): 161–70.

8. The Micheau contract is cited in Paul Raveau, *L'Agriculture et les classes paysannes* (Paris, 1926), pp. 85–86. On the custom of elevating a shop sign into a resounding title, see ibid., p. 84.

9. E. LeRoy Ladurie, in his classic *Paysans du Languedoc* (Paris, 1966) has made it his business to trace this pattern for one region of France.

10. Raveau, *Agriculture*, p. 222.

11. Ibid., p. 282.

12. I do not take seriously the arguments of L. Merle, who takes issue

violently and uncritically with Raveau's conclusions. In his study, *Métairie et l'évolution agraire de la Gâtine poitevine* (Paris, 1958), Merle concedes that in the end it is the *bourgeoisie de robe* which reaps the benefits (pp. 92–93); but he insists that in the beginning, in the late fifteenth and early sixteenth centuries, it was the nobility which was most prominent in achieving concentration of landed property (aristocratic reaction), and he believes that as much as 60 percent of the land in the Gâtine region was in noble hands throughout. The confusion is the usual one. It revolves around Merle's unstated definition of nobility, which is too charitable by far. To accept the La Porte family, for example, as "puissants représentants de la noblesse poitevine" is to fall victim to the retroactive status elevation so dear to the old régime. We know nothing of the La Porte family before 1537, and the second known La Porte is an *advocat;* but he also happens to be very rich, as we shall have occasion to see, and one of his grandsons would, in time, become the most powerful man in the kingdom, namely Cardinal Richelieu. The half-dozen other examples given by Merle to back up his claim of noble domination are not impressive. La Poupelinière may be a large estate, and the marquis de Chilleau may cut quite a figure in the eighteenth century; but in our period these lands are in the hands of the Darrot family, of whom we know nothing before 1529. Other major *rassembleurs de terres* in the Gâtine, like Garnier, *juge au présidial de* Poitiers, or the merchant dynasty of the Myots—and most of the "nobles" cited by Merle—can stand as noble only so long as we have no other way to describe the families which have risen from the bourgeoisie. This line of thinking results in denying the social mobility which was clearly there.

13. Yvonne Bézard, *La Vie rurale dans le sud de la région parisienne, 1450–1560* (Paris, 1929), pp. 68–75.

14. The conquest of noble lands, in the region sampled by Bézard, seems to have been completed by the end of the fifteenth century. Of course, in time, bourgeois and gentry property has a way of becoming noble, only to give way to new waves of parvenus eventually. An amusing and well-documented story of this process is told in Chevalier's study of Chenonceaux. As for the conquest of peasant property, it is still going on in the seventeenth century, according to Marc Venard's findings in *Bourgeois et paysans au XVIIe siècle* (Paris, 1957). Schnapper's study, *Les Rentes,* seems to imply a two-stage conquest: the pattern of Parisian bourgeois and *officiers,* lending money first primarily to *laboureurs* and then suddenly to noblemen, is very striking.

15. Though not quite as high as their fancy could lead them to. See, for instance, the seventeenth-century flatterer whose genealogical boldness allows him to argue that the Gondi are descended from "a Roman called Gondus, father of Pope John VIII, who flourished circa A.D. 572" (cited in E. Tambour, *Les Gondi et le château de Noisy* [Paris, 1925]). For the real Gondi career, see, in addition to Tambour's study, A. Vachez, *Histoire de l'acquisition* (Lyon, 1891), p. 61, and, above all, Marie Henriette Jullien de Pommerol, *Albert de Gondi* (Geneva, 1953). It was Albert (1522–1602) who made the transition from banker to count and marshal of France. In the army-supply business in the 1550s, married in 1565 to a noblewoman of ancient family who refused to take his name, *chevalier* of the Order of the Holy Spirit and gentleman of the king's bedchamber, Gondi, who never used his real name in his public career, adopted a *nom de terre* when he acquired the Retz lands. He was first count of

Retz and eventually became duke of Retz (1581). His younger brother Pierre, after being bishop of Langres—possibly the wealthiest diocese in the kingdom—ended up a cardinal and bishop of Paris.

16. Vachez, *Histoire*, p. 61.

17. L'Estoile comments on the Gondi success story under the rubric: De iis qui ex humili loco ad summas fortunas evaserunt (*Journal de l'Estoile pour le règne de Henri III*, [1574–1589] Lefebvre, ed. [Paris: Gallimard, 1943], p. 39).

18. See L. Prunel, *Sébastien Zamet* (Paris, 1912). For another perspective, the Zamets in their guise as barons of Murat, see Gilbert Martin, *Montmarand*, 2 vols. (Moulins, 1963), 1:230.

19. That is the reasonable conclusion of Louis Audiat in his erudite monograph on Estienne's son, *Nicolas Pasquier* (Paris, 1876), which is in my view more trustworthy in all respects than the more recent writings of Paul Bouteiller and Dorothy Thickett. The excellent introduction by M. Balmas to his edition of Pasquier's *Monophile* (Milan, 1957) is also very much worth consulting.

20. The only reference I can think of in his published works is in an epitaph published in a collection of his early poetry (*La Jeunesse d'E. Pasquier* [Paris, 1610], p. 530): "Mon pere fichant en moy / Le tout de son esperance / Amoncela sans requoy / Or, bien, argent & chevance." That is to say: "My father, putting all his hopes in me, amassed gold, property, money, and lands without ceasing."

21. Pasquier's published letters involve 125 correspondents of this sort. The most accessible edition of his letters is that which occupies volume 2 of the *Oeuvres* (Amsterdam, 1723). I prefer the edition *Lettres d'Estienne Pasquier*, 3 vols. (Paris, 1619).

22. Pasquier, *Lettres*, 2:799–800, gives us a glimpse of Pasquier, returning from his estate, meeting a colleague, maistre Brulart, in Melun. Having teamed up, as they ride toward Paris, Brulart suggests a visit at Croixfontaine, nearby, with a colleague of his father's, maistre Cognet. Welcomed at Cognet's house, they stayed three days.

We also see (ibid., pp. 801–2) Pasquier spending his evenings with two academics, Dr. Beguin, headmaster of the Collège du Cardinal Lemoine, and Dr. Le Vasseur, principal of the Collège de Reims. They go for long walks together, among the suburban gardens; they play *boules* and stop to eat in taverns. "In the midst of all this, we spoke of nothing but serious literary matters."

23. On Pasquier's *lettres de noblesse* of 11 March 1574, see Louis Audiat, *Nicolas Pasquier* (Paris, 1876), p. 74. On Pasquier's general coolness toward nobility and the military career, remarks can be found scattered everywhere in his letters. Among innumerable examples, note his admiration for the great merchant Jacques Coeur, "a simple citizen" who was, at the same time, "another King Alexander" (*Lettres*, 1:161). To his son Pierre, off to war, he writes that, above all else, he fears that as a military commander he may oppress the common people, the civilian population, that is. "I beg you, and I command you with every power I have over you ... to spare the poor people.... When I recommend the people to you, I recommend you to yourself." "If you degenerate from your virtue ... I will disavow you entirely. Adieu." To his oldest son, Théodore, he writes to extol the virtue of being a lawyer (ibid., pp. 532 ff.), a profession or estate superior to almost all others and for which he had prepared his son since childhood.

24. For all this, see Audiat, *N. Pasquier.*

25. For all this, see ibid.

26. Nicolas Pasquier, *Le Gentilhomme* (Paris, 1611), pp. 34–41.

27. Ibid., pp. 69–76.

28. Ibid., pp. 83–89.

29. Ibid., pp. 91–95.

30. The Jesuit Garasse, an old family enemy, as quoted by Audiat, *N. Pasquier*, p. 255.

31. Pasquier, *Le Gentilhomme*, p. 47.

32. In his introduction to the *Mémoires* of his ancestor, Mathieu Molé (Champollion-Figeac, ed.,4 vols. [Paris, 1855]).

33. Montaigne, *Essais*, p. 116. Montaigne is also clear in his mind, and quite agreed with his friend E. Pasquier here, that "the proper form, and the only one and essential one of nobility in France, lies in a military career [*la vocation militaire*]" (*Essais*, p. 363).

Chapter 6. The Demigods of Our Age

1. He uses this phrase in his *Meslanges historiques* (Lyon, 1589), p. 600.

2. Ibid., pp. 293 ff.: "Ie ne puis ignorer que les familles Nobles de Bourgogne ne sont pas eternelles, non plus que celles des autres pays." "Remuer telles besongnes & maints autres secrets des races & maisons seroit chose fort desirée de plusieurs: mais desplaisante à maints autres."

3. Ibid., pp. 549–50: "à traict de temps ... ceux qu'on appelle sages en droict furent equiparez aux Nobles & font portion de ce que nous avons autre part estimé Noblesse Civile. En ceste sorte & soubs ce nom ils peuvrent estre dits Nobles: mais Gentilshommes non." "La Gentilhominité regarde le sang." "Le plus du mal consiste en ce que ... ces hommes sont devenuz capables de porter Fiefs Nobles: ils en ont si bien appris la practique & en acquierent tant iournellement, que les roolles des Bans et Rierebans ne sont farcis que de leurs noms...."

4. Ibid., p. 597: "Entre les hommes qui sçavent iuger de l'or, il sera fort bien recogneu pour or sophistiqué & non recevable."

5. Ibid., p. 554: "Or il est à remarquer que s'il advient (comme de vray il est advenu assez souvent) que quelque riche homme du tier Estat, vertueux en l'exercise de ses fonctions, face initier ses enfants au train des armes, en intention de convertir (avec permission du Prince) sa Noblesse Civile, en Noblesse qui s'acquiert par les armes, & que ce premier entrant au chemin de vray Noblesse s'allie par marriage avec une bien Gentilfemme: puis suyvant son institut, ses enfants & les enfants de ses enfants iusques au 4ᵉ degré des descendants, se maryent avec des Damoyselles Nobles & yssues de vrayment Gentilhommes de nom & d'armes: il ne faut plus douter que tels soyent Gentilshommes."

6. Ibid., p. 555: "Si l'estat des Nobles n'eust eu pour supplement les plus avancez au tier Estat, ... longtemps y a que l'ancienne Noblesse de sang eust prins fin."

7. See, for instance, A. Vachez, *Histoire de l'acquisition des terres nobles par les roturiers* (Lyon, 1899), p. 67.

8. See C. Chevalier, *Le Château de Chenonceaux* (Tours, 1882), for the Bohiers' architects, anonymous masters who flourished in the Loire Valley

towns long before the arrival of Italian artisans, and to whom we owe the finest châteaux, including Chambord and Azay-le-Rideau. Similar styles of building are in evidence in town houses, notably the Coeur town house in Paris on the rue des Archives.

9. See Abbé Reure, *Du Verdier* (Paris, 1897), for a description of the rebuilt castle where Du Verdier "came so often to play the feudal seigneur." The castle, still standing in 1896, was half-Gothic, half-Renaissance, quite small, with frescoes in the chapel (see *L'Art* 1 [1882]: 101) picturing Antoine du Verdier and his son Claude.

10. Granvelle's letter, cited in Lucien Febvre, *Philippe II et la Franche-Comté* (Paris, 1911), p. 115. The cardinal's grandfather had been a blacksmith and small-town notary. His father, Nicolas Perrenot, was a lawyer and eventually a *conseiller* in the *parlement* of the province. He had bought the seigneurie of Granvelle in 1527. Antoine, his oldest son, became bishop of Arras and eventually cardinal, while the Perrenot-Granvelle family, through alliances, became the undisputed bosses of the province.

11. See ibid., pp. 297 ff., on the successes of bourgeois land management and the failure of the nobility.

12. Drawing the portrait of the ideal *mesnager* or landowner, Olivier De Serres (*Théâtre d'Agriculture* [Rouen, 1603]) proclaims Science, Experience, and Diligence as the quintessence of his art (preface). He is addressing himself particularly to owners who live in town. He advises them, when looking for land to buy, to make use of forced sales "par authorité de Justice" if possible, "qui est la plus seure voye, en l'acquisition d'un bien du Roy, d'un bien d'Eglise" or, better yet, in the case of lands belonging to "un endebté & hypotequé: d'un furieux, d'un prodigue" (p. 9). The new owner will not make the mistakes of his bankrupt "furious, prodigal" predecessor and victim. He will exact nothing from his subjects except what is due to him, but this due will be exacted to the letter: "Ne leur quittera ne laissera courir chose aucune, tant petite soit elle, luy appartenant de ses fiefs ou rentes: & soit bled, vin, argent, chastaignes, poules, chapons, cire, huyle, espices, corvées, servitudes, hommages, & autres droicts & devoirs seigneuriaux, du tout exactement s'en fera faire la raison, sans rien rabatre": full accounting of all things due, and no mercy. De Serres's new seigneur, unlike his noble predecessor, "n'entrera jamais en querelle avec aucun, pour le peril de l'issue." He will be "humain et courtois, non cholere, ou vindicatif, en tout raisonnable ... exact payeur de ses debtes ... veritable, continent, sobre, patient, prudent, provident, espargnant, liberal, industrieux & diligent." Thus, "noblement il augmentera son bien"!

13. Du Verdier's, for example. See Reure, *Du Verdier*, p. 10.

14. From the anonymous *Anatomie des trois ordres de la France* (1615), p. 37: "Comme le crocodile, aussi tost que ses petits sont éclos, leur présente quelque chose à happer, & s'ils en font refus la mère les déchire et met en pièces. Aujourd'huy de mesmes les enfants ne sont pas parvenus à une pleine puberté, qu'ils sont instruicts aux finances & à la rapine."

15. "Ces vautours desguisez en robes longues" (Tahureau, *Dialogues* [Paris, 1572], p. 86 verso).

16. Cited in Reure, *Du Verdier*, p. 10: "De toutes choses y a satieté, fors que des lettres."

17. I am following the candid observations of his son André, recorded

privately in 1615, discovered and published by Cheruel together with the *Journal d'Olivier Lefevre d'Ormesson* (Documents inédits sur l'histoire de France) (Paris, 1860).

18. For this excursion into the affairs of M. de Morvillier, I am following Gustave Baguenault de Puchesse, *Jean de Morvillier* (Paris, 1869).

19. We return now to the *Journal d'Ormesson*.

20. In the Franche-Comté, at the time, the classic bourgeois daydream is to have "an uncle worth 15,000 livres of (annual) *rentes*," and solid wealth is defined as a total capital at the 60,000–80,000-livres level. See Febvre, *Franche-Comté*, pp. 325–26.

21. "La Richesse est une chose vile," according to Florentin de Thierriat in his *Trois Traictez* (Paris, 1606), p. 164.

22. *Anatomie des trois ordres*, p. 36.

23. G. Fagniez, ed., *Le Livre de raison de Nic. Versoris*, Mémoires de la Société de l'Histoire de Paris, vol. 12 (1885), pp. 99–222. (Semblançay's death, p. 200; the treasurer's death, p. 135.)

24. Here I follow Michel Mollat, *Le Commerce maritime normand à la fin du moyen âge* (Paris, 1952). The phrase "bourgeois aristocracy" as a description of Rouen's leading families is Mollat's (p. 477).

Chapter 7. Schools

1. Both the verse quoted at the head of this chapter and the following one were found in a handwriting practice notebook of the time and cited by Lucien Febvre, *Philippe II et la Franche-Comté* (Paris, 1911), p. 351.

> Vive la plume magnifique
> Le papier et le parchemin.
> Qui d'escrire scait la pratique
> Il peut bien aller chemin.

2. They could buy fiefs and they could arrange noble marriages for their daughters, but these were pyrrhic triumphs, achieved at the cost of being systematically betrayed and forgotten by their posterity. This is true, for example, of Pierre Landais, merchant-draper of Vitré in Britanny, who rose to power as the duke's treasurer, made staggering land acquisitions, built sumptuous houses and castles, and gave his daughter in marriage to a nobleman. One of his nephews became bishop of Rennes, another a cardinal. The Landais lands, through his daughter Françoise, refurbished the fortune of the L'Espervier family, so that Pierre's great-granddaughter was to be the mother of the famous Protestant leader François de la Noue, born in 1531, less than fifty years after Pierre Landais' violent and terrible death at the hands of a noble lynching party. Other descendants of the erstwhile merchant of Vitré married into the Duplessis-Richelieu family; and even the Grand Condé, in 1641, married a descendant of Landais. But which of his grandsons and nieces wished to remember the old man? What sort of glory lay in such humble, foolish sacrifices to posterity? And how could the prudent and competent bourgeois founders of such dynasties recognize themselves in their alienated descendance? On the career of Pierre Landais and his glorious descendance, see Abbé Paul Paris-Jallobert, "Le Château Landais à Vitré," *Revue de Bretagne* (1904), pp. 101–33.

3. Jean des Caurres, *Oeuvres morales et diversifiées* (Paris, 1584), p. 3: "Nous ne pouvons vivre sans lettre . . . il seroit plus facile de denombrer la sable des deserts d'Arabie & les vagues de la mer Ionique, que d'expliquer les commoditez qui procedent de l'escriture."

4. *Discours non plus melancoliques que divers* (Poitiers, 1557), pp. 61–63.

5. Ch. de Robillard de Beaurepaire, *Recherches sur l'instruction publique dans le diocèse de Rouen avant 1789*, 2 vols. (Evreux, 1872), 1:155–56.

6. Ibid., pp. 157 ff. This happened in 1556.

7. Ibid., p. 157.

8. Ibid., p. 58.

9. Ibid., p. 59.

10. Ernest Gaullieur, *Histoire du Collège de Guyenne* (Paris, 1874), p. 29.

11. Ibid., p. 43. The man in question is Jehan de Ciret, *advocat*, son of Ciret, *conseiller* in the *parlement*.

12. See L. Gerig, "Le Collège de la Trinité à Lyon avant 1540," *Revue de la Renaissance* 9 (1908): 73 ff.

13. See M. J. Baudel, "Les Ecoles d'Albi de 1380 à 1623," *Bulletin de la Société des Etudes Littéraires, Scientifiques et Artistiques du Lot* (1879), pp. 113–29.

14. Aurillac, Archives communales, GG^{27}, GG^{29}.

15. Max Quantin, *Histoire de l'enseignement secondaire et supérieur dans les pays du département de l'Yonne avant 1790* (Auxerre, 1877), pp. 23–59.

16. Ibid., p. 73, for Avallon, where the city council buys a house and chooses two instructors (with the chapter's approval). The school in Avallon is a fairly small-scale enterprise but stable enough in the sixteenth century. Typically the staff consists of a principal instructor, a second instructor, and an *abécédaire* at 25 livres yearly to teach the beginners. Typically, again, the school declines in the seventeenth century: by 1635 there is only one instructor, there are few pupils, and the building is falling apart. Fortunately for the city, a big endowment from le Président Odebert of the Dijon *parlement* (the Odeberts were a local *famille*) bails the school out of its troubles in the 1650s. Nevertheless, the civic energy is no longer there, and in the late seventeenth century the school is finally taken over by a religious order. In Joigny (p. 85), in Tonnerre (p. 91), in Chablis, and in Villeneuve-le-Roi (p. 103) the story is much the same.

17. See Paul Bénétrix, *Les Origines du Collège d'Auch* (Paris, 1908), p. 4. A visitor in 1578 notes: "Auch est une petite ville presque peuplée de prestres."

18. Ibid., pp. 8–47, 65, 72–73.

19. See ibid., pp. 80, 137, for the cases of the lawyer Verneilh, himself a member of Auch's municipal administration; of the lawyer Sancetz, treasurer of the *collège;* and of maistre Masse, principal, *licensié ès loix*, who gets married and eventually moves on to practice law in Toulouse.

20. Edict of Orléans of 1560, article 9.

21. P. S. Moufflet, *Notice sur le Collège de Saintes* (Saintes, 1886), pp. 8–9, cites the clergy's remonstrance of 1560, which agrees to the need "pourvoir à ce que cy après la jeunesse soict mieux instruite ès lettres, et que les patrons et collateurs puissent plus facilement trouver personnes capables."

22. Ibid., p. 9, citing the municipal deliberations of 1571 and 1572: the instructor threatens to leave because he is not getting the promised salary from the chapter's funds; in 1581 the school building is admittedly in poor condition, but the chapter simply refuses to pay up.

23. Ibid., pp. 16–18. Meanwhile, in Albi the struggle between city councillors and chapter over the execution of the edict of 1560 drags on until 1608 (Baudel, *Ecoles d'Albi*, p. 120).

24. Ibid., pp. 20–23.

25. Ibid., pp. 26–31. It is Jacques Guitard, sieur des Brosses, *président au présidial*, who offers 6,000 livres for capital improvements and an annual *rente* of 1,000 livres, in execution of his father's will. Guitard's donation is made with the intention that the city council should have full control of the *collège* and act as its trustees.

26. "Per favor de la causo publico et afin que chacung sio en libertat de acquerir scientio." Cited by F. Mireur, "Gratuité de l'enseignement à Barjols," *Bulletin de la Société des Etudes Scientifiques et Archéologiques de Draguignan*, vol. 28 (1910–11).

27. On this point see the recent and conclusive evidence of Codina-Mir.

28. Guitard of Saintes, for instance, ended up as dean of the cathedral chapter after retiring from a long career as a magistrate (Moufflet, *Collège de Saintes*, p. 27). On the social origins of the canons of Notre-Dame in Paris, see E. Deronne, "Les Origines des chanoines de N.D. de Paris, 1450–1550," *Revue d'histoire moderne et contemporaine* 18 (1971): 1–29.

29. Volume 1 of Imbart de la Tour's *Les Origines de la Réforme* (4 vols.; Paris, 1905), describes the new *collèges* as "usines intellectuelles qui fonctionnent à jet continu" (p. 451).

30. Ibid., p. 523: "Constructions scolaires, entretien des maîtres, dépenses pour le mobilier ou la librairie, réforme des études, toutes ces faveurs vont surtout aux 'grandes écoles' ou écoles de grammaire qui représentent la culture classique."

31. This is Imbart de la Tour's conclusion: "Ce n'était pas le peuple qui les fréquentait" (ibid.).

32. Aside from the thoughtful, intelligent book by Philippe Ariès, *L'Enfance et la vie familiale* (Paris, 1960), which is concerned only with the Parisian *collèges*, and the very meager and ill-informed book by George Snyders, *La Pédagogie en France aux 17e et 18e siècles* (Paris, 1965), there are no modern general treatments of French education before the coming of the Jesuits. Ariès is badly mistaken in thinking there was no organized primary schooling to speak of before the seventeenth century (*L'Enfance*, p. 318).

33. F. Mireur, "Documents sur l'enseignement primaire en Provence avant 1789," *Revue des Sociétés Savantes*, 7th ser. 3 (1881): 191–222. The documents presented by Mireur attest to the early existence of these schools. In most cases the schools clearly were established long before the first record to come to his attention, but in any case his researches point to the mid-sixteenth century as the period of development: Aups, 1541; Besse, 1582; Carces, 1577; Correns, 1568; La Garde Freinet, 1550; Garéoult, 1557; Nans, 1583; Pierrefeu, 1576; Puget Ville, 1572; Rougiers, 1566; Draguignan, 1566; etc.

34. M. Quantin, *Histoire du Tiers Etat à Tonnerre au milieu du 16e siècle* (Auxerre, 1887). A *collège* was founded in town in 1571, but already in 1550 maistre Jean Dugny, *parisien*, is *recteur des escolles*, while villages like Donnemoine (in 1567) and Epineuil (in 1553) have schools.

35. The document is cited in Gilbert Martin's excellent study, *Choses et gens du pays de Montmarand aux XVIe et XVIIe siècles*, 2 vols. (Moulins, 1963), 1:65–66.

36. Although it is true that even a very small town like Montmarand has its gentry, officials in the *siège de justice, procureurs, advocats,* who are at the same time the local landowners, like the Aufauvres (royal notaries, *procureurs du roy,* and owners of seigneuries), the Aumaistres, and the Berthollets. There are no *gentilshommes* living in town.

37. Quantin, *Tiers Etat,* cites Jean Petit, *vigneron,* who assigns the rent from a house he owns to provide for his son "estudiant a Paris" (A.D., Yonne, E 653, 3 September 1553). Of course, the son of maistre Jazu, *licensié en lois,* and royal *élu* of Tonnerre, also a student in Paris at the same time, is maintained in better style at the cost of 29 livres of *rentes* yearly; meanwhile, the tanner, Jean Cerveau, does very well by his wife's brother, who is also an "écolier, étudiant en l'université de Paris," and son of a merchant (A.D., Yonne, E 654, year 1556). Such cases can be found in every town in the kingdom.

38. Quantin, *Tiers Etat,* pp. 393–94.

39. Moufflet, *Collège de Saintes,* p. 19. The license is granted.

40. Mireur, "Enseignement primaire," p. 222.

41. Moufflet, *Collège de Saintes,* p. 10.

42. Ch. Bréard, *Histoire du Collège d'Eu* (Eu, 1879), pp. 34–35.

43. Cited by F. de Dainville, "Effectifs des collèges et scolarité aux 17ᵉ et 18ᵉ siècles dans le Nord-Est de la France," *Population* (1955), p. 469.

44. For small-town and village schools, almost at random, in addition to those already mentioned, see Ch. de Robillard de Beaurepaire, *Recherches en l'instruction publique dans le diocèse de Rouen avant 1789,* 2 vols. (Evreux, 1872), 1:37, 52, for schools in Eu, Blangy, Criel, Aumale, Quilleboeuf, Pont de L'Arche, etc.; on schools in Troyes and surrounding villages, see Roserot de Melin, *Antonio Caracciolo* (Paris, 1922), p. 182, citing A.D., Aube, G 4199, on schoolmasters in the 1530s in several villages.

45. François Perrin, *Les Escoliers* [1586] (Brussels 1866, reprint). It is a really dreadful play, but the sentiments attributed to the hardworking schoolboy hero are worthy of Samuel Smiles: "Je porte pieça une bride / Qui a tousiours guidé mes ans: / L'amour des lettres et le temps / Qui, perdu, jamais ne se retourne / J'ayme bien mieux suivre l'estude / Qui au milieu de mille maux / Pourra soulager mes travaux / Et me retirer de la crasse / Ou la sordide populasse / Et l'ignorant gist abbattu. / ... Car, quant à moy, de la science / Je veux l'entière cognoissance" (p. 37). "La lecture, support de la vie future" (p. 41).

46. In Saintes, the principal is in trouble with the city council because he stands accused of making poor children pay tuition fees and charging others "excessive" fees of 10 to 20 sols monthly (Moufflet, *Collège de Saintes,* p. 20).

47. Bénétrix, *Collège d'Auch,* pp. 149–53.

48. Ch. Godard, *Histoire du Collège de Gray* (Gray, 1887), p. 52, citing municipal deliberations at the turn of the century. Gray, near Dijon, happens to be outside the obedience of the French crown in the sixteenth century, but this hardly matters. In language, in culture, in institutions, in social structure, the County of Burgundy can hardly be distinguished from the Duchy of Burgundy next door—or from most other French provinces, for that matter. The rise of an educated, officeholding, seigneuries-owning gentry out of the good bourgeoisies of its towns occurs in Franche-Comté as in Bourgogne. See Lucien Febvre's classic book on the subject, *Philippe II et la Franche-Comté.*

49. A. Plieux, "Etude sur l'instruction publique à Lectoure," *Revue de Gascogne* 29 (1888): 324–37.

50. "Civis nobilis, vivit de suo" is the notation describing such children in a Jesuit *collège*. Cited in Dainville, "Effectifs des collèges et scolarité," p. 477.

51. See Philippe Ariès, *Enfance et vie familiale.*

52. To the *collèges* already mentioned, one may add, at random, those of Loudun and Saumur (A.D., Maine-et-Loire, E 3381–6); of Caen (Jacques Mauger, "Journal," in *Recueil de Journaux Caennais*, G. Vanel, ed. [Paris, 1904]); of Digne (F. Arnaud, *L'Instruction publique à Barcelonette* [Digne, 1894]); the Grandes Escoles of La Rochelle (Amos Barbot, "Histoire de La Rochelle," *Archives historiques de la Saintonge et de l'Aunis* [1886], 14:469); Dijon (founded by the notable Godran family, documents in the D series of A.D., Côte-d'Or); in Châlon (A.D., Saône-et-Loire, founded by Fleury, merchant, and his son Fleury, *advocat*); in Beaune (*Revue des Sociétés Savantes* [1874], pp. 144–48); in Aix-en-Provence (Louis Wolff, *Parlementaires provençaux*, p. 13); in Pontoise (Marcel Lebrun, *Histoire du collège de Pontoise* [Pontoise, 1923]); in Riez (Elisabeth Pellegrin, "Le Programme de l'école municipale de Riez en 1533," *Provence historique* 6 [December 1956]: 199–209); Amiens (Louis Lorquin, "Un Homme à la mode: François de Louvencourt," *Mémoires de la Société des Antiquaires de Picardie* 49 [1942]: 5).

53. This is the point made laboriously by George Snyders, *Pédagogie*, who overstates his case by writing as if the Jesuit *collèges* of the seventeenth century were *internats* (p. 16). He also overstates the case of the separation from the French language; compare Dainville, *Effectifs.*

54. The physical aspect of a typical *collège* is taken here from an *inventaire* of the *collège* of Auch, made in September 1584 (cited by Bénétrix, *Auch*).

55. Regulations of the Auch *collège*, cited by Bénétrix (ibid., p. 84).

56. Again, this schedule is from the regulations at Auch, cited by Bénétrix, but the schedules of other *collèges* were almost identical. On the general impression of a new order imposed through the school on urban society at large, see the similar conclusions of Ariès, *Enfance*, p. 352.

57. Following the description of the program by the principal, Elie Vinet, as published by L. Massebieau, *Schola Aquitanica* (Paris, 1886).

58. The *Schola Aquitanica* describes these exercises from the eighth up to the third class.

59. See, for instance, such textbooks as Robert Estienne, *Traicté de la grammaire françoise* (Paris, 1569), or Pierre de la Ramée, *Grammaire* (Paris, 1572).

60. Maistre Jean Des Caurres, of the Amiens *collège*, of whom a friend grandiloquently wrote, "en toy Socrate est faict Picard," made it his business to teach Greek, Latin, and French humanities at the same time. Although the verses of his student, François de Louvencourt, may seem a poor advertisement for Des Caurres's teaching, it is not always prudent to judge a master by his student.

> La le docte Cujas seul vray soleil du monde
> expliquait Julian d'une langue feconde
> J'y fus vingt et deux mois, puis prenant une license,
> Je reveins à Paris, premier barreau de France.

61. This is the advice given by Robert Estienne in his schoolbook, which is a

beginner's manual, written in French, for the learning of Latin: *Les Declinaisons des noms et verbes que doibvent sçavoir entierement par coeur les enfans ausquels on veult bailler entree à la langue latine, ensemble la manière de tourner les noms, pronoms, verbes, tant actifs que passifs, gerondifs, supins, et participes* (Paris, 1549). This textbook also contains treatises on the *Huict Parties d'oraison* and a teacher's manual, *La Maniere d'exercer les enfans à decliner les Noms et les Verbes.* Estienne's recommendations are entirely in accord with the practice described in Bordeaux and elsewhere. He recommends with great emphasis that the master "accoustumera aussi l'enfant à bien prononcer le Français et le bien escrire, autant que le Latin" (p. 165). The Jesuits continued this practice, insisting on a perfect command of the vernacular, according to F. de Dainville, *Naissance de l'humanisme moderne* (Paris, 1940), p. 16.

62. In addition to the ancient history which was officially part of the curriculum, French history was read to the students for recreation at the *collège* of Auch, for example. Science-teaching may have been rudimentary, but it found its place in the curriculum in the advanced classes. Nor could it have been entirely neglected in the schools where—as was frequently true—physicians or even distinguished natural scientists like Fernel or mathematicians like Vinet were on the staff. The teaching of law in a *collège* is encountered in Rouen in 1615 (BN, Nouv. acqu. fr. no. 3417, fols. 229–30), and I seem to remember that it figures as part of the curriculum in Dijon at the Collège des Godrans.

63. The Italian, Masse, principal at Auch, the Scot, Alexander Blair, principal at Orthez, and the Portuguese, Govea, at Bordeaux are examples among many. (See Bénétrix, *Collège d'Auch*, on Masse.) Blair, who does very well for himself at Orthez, is principal in 1590; he marries into the local gentry, lends money, buys land, and his son will become well assimilated in local gentry circles as Pierre *de* Blair (A.D., Basses-Pyrénées, E 2008).

64. We shall have occasion to document this claim again in other chapters of this book. Quantin's similar observation, made in 1877 (in his *Histoire de l'enseignement*), while describing the cultured notables of the city of Sens, is just as valid today. Describing a kind of *Festschrift* produced in 1617 in memory of a physician, Quantin seems to shake his head as he leafs through the pieces of Latin and French verse written by local lawyers, physicians, and other *nobles hommes* and is moved to observe that in his day (1877) such work could not be expected in Sens.

65. "Aux fins que la jeunesse ne perde son temps," say the city councillors in Auch, 22 October 1570, as they hire new teachers in response to student complaints. Cited by Bénétrix, *Collège d'Auch*, p. 107.

66. These papers can be found in the cartons numbered E 3381 to E 3386, in the A.D., Maine-et-Loire, in Angers.

67. A.D., Maine-et-Loire, E 3386.

68. A complete inventory of the Milsonneau household made in August 1588, including a full catalogue of the library, is to be found in A.D., Maine-et-Loire, E 3381.

69. Some glimpse of the further tribulations of the Bourneau boys, as they move on to Paris and begin establishing themselves in the capital's salons, can be gained in letters preserved in A.D., Maine-et-Loire, E 3386 and 3384.

70. Cited by Louis Lorquin, "Un Homme à la mode: François de Louvencourt," p. 49: "Depuis l'asge croissant vous m'avez fait apprendre / Les Arts,

qu'un jeune esprit pour voguer doit comprendre" (p. 56). "[Comme je l'es-
pere encor] d'estre un jour senateur" (p. 65).

71. Snyders, *Pédagogie,* citing a letter from Pontchartrain written in 1689,
shows the pressure for removing educational qualifications to the sale of
offices: "J'ai enfin obtenu que M. le Chancelier ne refuserait plus aucune
dispense d'âge ni de parenté, et même à l'egard des études, qui était le plus
difficile: il se réduit à demander six mois . . . . Sur ce pied, ce qui nous reste de
charges ne doit pas être difficile a débiter." This relaxation of standards mis-
leads Snyders into thinking that it is "still possible" to achieve office without
proven competence in the seventeenth century. The fact is that it now *becomes*
possible.

Chapter 8. Living Nobly

1. Even as early as 1502 there were handy anthologies, in French, like the
Tulles des offices (Cicero), edited by *honorable et prudent homme* David Miffaut of
Dieppe.

2. Antonio Guevara, *L'Horloge des princes,* translated into French from the
Castilian by Nicolas de Herberay (Paris, 1955). This book was a great favorite
of Montaigne's and of such other practitioners of the "noble life" as Gouberville.

3. From the preface of the *Lucan, Suetoine & Saluste en françoys* (1500),
which, together with Guevara's *Horloge* and *Tulles des Offices,* can be found on
the shelves of modest provincial private libraries. See A. Labarre, *Le Livre
dans la vie amienoise au 16ᵉ siècle* (Paris, 1971). The *Lucan, Suetoine & Saluste*
volume, which found its way into the study of maistre Coquerel of Amiens,
was most likely picked up on a business trip to Paris, where the book was
sold in Antoine Verard's shop in the Palais de Justice "along the first pillar
before the chapel where the mass of *messeigneurs* the *présidents* of the *parlement*
is sung."

4. Michel de Montaigne, *Essais* (Pléiade edition), p. 140.

5. Ibid.

6. Jean Des Caurres, *Oeuvres morales et diversifiées* (Paris, 1584), 272 verso,
276 recto.

7. This citation is taken from the amusing play by Claveret (Paris, 1665)
entitled *L'Escuyer; ou, Les Faux Nobles mis au billon.*

8. Jehan Louvet, *Journal,* in *Revue de l'Anjou,* 3 vols. (1854–56), 2:39, for the
banquet scene; pp. 5 and 7, for captured *gentilshommes;* p. 17, for the capture
of Captain Trelay; p. 23, for the militia's sortie under Apvril's command; p.
24, for the names and professions of the militia commanders in 1576.

9. Le Riche, *Journal* (Saint-Maixent, 1846), pp. 194, 246.

10. Perhaps the most outspoken advocate of a nobility of virtue, learning,
and wealth to supplant the old nobility is Turquet de Mayerne, who, in his
Monarchie aristodemocratique (Paris, 1611), describes French society as a mobile
class society in which the "*Noblesse* est produicte de l'Estat roturier" (p. 243).
The nobility's claim of being descended from conquering Frankish raiders
impresses the author even less than it would impress the Abbé Sieyès, eventually (pp. 245–47). True nobility, according to Turquet, "represente un ordre
singulier d'hommes façonnez & qui se façonnent, par continuelle instruction . . . aux grandes charges & plus honorables devoirs de la Republique"

(p. 248). He is willing to grant, exceptionally, that there might, on occasion, be found "hommes de Noble race" who are "bien instituez, modestes & aymans l'egalité de droict." But, in practice, his reading of the history of French society is that a "nouvelle Noblesse" was gradually replacing "l'ancienne corrompüe, ce qui est du droict des gens & du stil de Nature" (p. 249). Turquet is persuaded that a "Noblesse pauvre est inutile à l'Estat" (p. 255), and he sees an "estroite affinité" among wealth, virtue, and nobility (p. 257). Turquet is the exponent of a coherent political theory, whose perspective allows him to state categorically that "les races ne sont ny sources ny fondemens de la Noblesse" (p. 258), and that true nobility is founded in "l'oeuvre des hommes bien meritans de la republique" (p. 260).

11. See Montaigne, *Essais*, pp. 104, 105.

12. Montaigne, *Essais*, "Au Lecteur."

13. Pasquier, *La Jeunesse d'E. Pasquier* (Paris, 1610), p. 530.

14. Montaigne, *Essais*, p. 157.

15. Nicolas de Nicolay, *Navigations et peregrinations orientales* (Lyon, 1568), "dedication to the king."

16. Montaigne, *Essais*, p. 64.

17. "Il deplet à un homme bien né, / De fere un exercise à l'argent adonné" (cited by C. Juge, *Jacques Peletier du Mans* [Paris, 1907], p. 80).

18. As Pasquier explains, referring to Aristotle, whose position he embraces: the ideal is to "jouïr de la vertu en affluence de biens" (*Lettres*, 3 vols. [Paris, 1619], 1:97).

19. As Montaigne explains in passing: "Une condition oisifve et qui ne vit, comme on dit, que de ses rentes" (*Essais*, p. 369).

20. Pasquier, *Lettres* (1619), 1:71.

21. It is, among many others, the device of Antoine du Verdier, who was "born a bourgeois and died a *gentilhomme*," as his biographer explains (Abbé Reure, *Du Verdier* [Paris, 1897], p. 10).

22. Des Caurres, *Oeuvres morales*, p. 114.

23. All of which Pasquier appears to admire (*La Jeunesse*, p. 531).

24. In his *Police chrestienne* (Paris, 1568).

25. Nicolas Pasquier, *Lettres* (Paris, 1623), p. 700. This obsession with the virtues of saving comes close to the views expressed by Molière's famous miser. M. de Montaigne would not express such views in public.

26. Ibid., pp. 212, 614.

27. See his sententious rephrasing of Montaigne in *Lettres* (1623), p. 523.

28. Ibid., pp. 615 ff.

29. E. Pasquier, *Lettres* (1619), 2:159.

30. *Lettres* (1619) 1:644.

31. Ibid., pp. 69–76.

32. "Je te vien retrouver, mon ancien sejour," he addresses his house, lovingly. "Maison qui as esté par mon travail acquise, maison qui sur le bord de Seine es assise, dans Paris, ou je veux finir mon dernier jour . . . . Je trouve en ma maison mon port aupres de l'eau" (*La Jeunesse* [Paris, 1610], p. 516).

33. On the Hôtel Guénégaud des Brosses, 60 rue des Archives—owned in succession by the Gentien family, *conseillers du roy*; the Beauclerc family (from 1571), *receveurs généraux de finances*; by the Bordeaux family (from 1605), *trésoriers au parlement*; by Coiffier (1644), *surintendant des mines*; by Guénégaud des Brosses (1647), *trésorier de France, maistre des comptes*—see J. P. Babelon,

"L'Hôtel G. des Brosses," *Paris et Ile-de-France* 13 (1964): 75–112. On the Hôtel d'Assy, 58 *bis* rue des Francs-Bourgeois—one of the buildings which make up the block of former *parlementaire hôtels* where the National Archives are housed, and which was owned by a Briçonnet, *président* in the *chambre des comptes;* by a *premier président au parlement;* by a *trésorier général des fermes,* and his son, *premier président* at Aix; by Daurat, *conseiller au parlement;* by Chaillon, *receveur des finances*—see J. P. Babelon, "L'Hôtel d'Assy," *Paris et Ile-de-France* (1963), pp. 169–96.

34. This inventory is published by J. G. Espiner-Scott, *Documents concernant Claude Fauchet* (Paris, 1930), pp. 28–44. In the cellars are 20 écus' worth of claret, a salted pork, a pot of butter, a large jar filled with olive oil; in the kitchen, a large oak table, a buffet equipped with double locks, pots and pans, copper candlesticks, two horse collars; in the private interior courtyard, supplies of firewood. A gallery overlooking the courtyard is used as a veranda and is equipped for lunches al fresco. It includes a table, three matching stools, three oil paintings (landscapes) on the wall, and a copper watering can, handy for gardening. Inside is a living room furnished with expensive and well-made walnut furniture. There is a buffet, covered with a green cloth, plus a folding table, a bed, four chairs covered in tapestry with a pattern of fruit and leaves, other chairs and stools covered in black leather, a fancy checkerboard made of brazilwood and walnut, a green rug on the floor, and expensive oil paintings and old tapestries on the wall. In the master's study, above the living room, is the same kind of furniture, plus eight paintings, green tablecloths, and books on shelves; another room, with windows giving onto the street, has beds, tapestries, paintings, and more green rugs; there is a children's room, and several other rooms are furnished with beds, tables, and chairs and decorated with tapestries and paintings; the closets and chests are filled with a profusion of clothes and linens: damask and taffeta dresses, an exotic black nightgown of camelot (wool and silk), lined with white fox fur; sheets, tablecloths, napkins literally by the hundreds, silver dishes, and jewelry.

35. The inventory, dated 1557, of the Du Prat houses, as cited in Connataud and Megret, "Inventaire de la Bibliothèque des Du Prat," *Bibliothèque d'Humanisme et Renaissance* 3 (1943): 72–128.

36. Cited by E. Dupré Lasale, *Michel de l'Hospital,* 2 vols. (Paris, 1875, 1899), 1:107.

37. Ibid.

38. For the country pleasures of the *parlementaires* of Aix, see Louis Wolff, *La Vie des parlementaires provençaux au 16ᵉ siècle* (Marseille, 1924), pp. 83 ff. Wolff, who has also written a monograph of the life of the Aix *robe* circles in the eighteenth century, is quite clear in his mind about the intellectual quality of the sixteenth-century *parlementaires,* "very much superior" to that of their descendants in the eighteenth century.

39. I am citing a sonnet of Etienne de la Boëtie, Montaigne's dearest friend, *licensié* of Orléans University and *conseiller* at the Bordeaux *parlement.* See M. Allem, ed., *Anthologie poétique française, XVIᵉ siècle,* 2 vols. (Paris: Garnier-Flammarion, 1965), 2:92.

40. Jean-Antoine de Baïf, "A soi même," ibid., 2:139.

41. Nicolas Rapin, "Les Plaisirs du gentilhomme champêtre," ibid., 2:180–84.

42. Etienne Tabourot, "A M. de Chanlecy," ibid., 2:277.

43. Raoul Busquet, *Etude historique sur le Collège de Fortet* (Paris, 1907).

44. Chapotin, *Le Collège de Dormans-Beauvais* (Paris, 1870).

45. See Pierre Bonnin, *Ablon s/Seine* (Paris, 1890), pp. 23–26. In the sixteenth century a family like the Grassins, of Sens, *advocats* and *conseillers* at the *parlement*, are capable of founding a *collège* in Paris to serve their home town—on a much larger scale. Pierre Grassin in his will of 1569 leaves 30,000 livres for this purpose and eventually adds another 60,000, to be taken from his estate. His brother, whose nibblings here and there may have offset Pierre's generosity, nevertheless took his duties as the executor of the will seriously. He bought several houses in the rue des Amandiers in 1571 and set up the endowment with a portfolio of municipal bonds (*rentes* on the Hôtel de Ville) paying 2,851l. 12s. 11d. annually. Of this sum the principal's salary took 300l., and much of the rest went for scholarships to students from Sens. The *collège* also inherited the Grassins' library in 1584 and received further endowments from various allies and relatives of the founders.

46. Alexandre Cioranescu, *Amyot* (Paris, 1941), pp. 23–28.

47. Ibid., p. 127.

48. See Audiat, *Pasquier*.

49. See the detailed study by Marie Madeleine Mouflard, *Robert Garnier*, 3 vols. (La Ferté-Bernard, 1961; La Roche-sur-Yon, 1963, 1964).

50. Etienne Tabourot, "Les Touches," p. 12 recto–verso, in *Les Bigarrures du seigneur des accords* (Paris, 1608): "Braquemard se dit Gentilhomme / Ie croÿ qu'il est à sa façon / Il joue, il vit sur le bon homme / Il nourrit des chiens à foison / Il jure bien, il doit grand somme / Il n'y a meuble en sa maison / Et pour le confirmer en somme / Ses dents sentent la venaison."

As for the attempts to show that legal work is noble, they have a long history, among the high points being the official judgments rendered repeatedly by various courts, from the mid-sixteenth century onward, to the effect that the exercise of the profession of the *advocat* does not conflict with noble status. The same argument is made (but much later) in reference to the status of a notary at the Chastelet court of Paris—the Chastelet being the Paris equivalent of a *bailliage* or *présidial* court. In "Discours pour montrer qu'un Gentilhomme ne déroge point à sa noblesse par la charge de notaire au Chastelet de Paris," the hilarious, zany argument runs: "On y peut vivre sans interest, on y peut travailler gratuitement, un Notaire qui ne prendra rien des parties ne cessera pour cela d'estre Notaire: si donc il prend quelque chose, ce n'est pas par ancien vice de sa profession, c'est par un usage." This ineffective casuistry can be found side by side with more serious historical arguments, namely, that it is no new thing for a notary to have noble status: "On voit par des contracts fort anciens qui ont esté passez en Provence et en Dauphiné, des Notaires qui ont esté qualifiez *Nobilis vir*," as opposed to *honorabilis vir*. This is quite true, as is, no doubt, the case cited from the records of the law court at Vannes, confirmed by the *parlement* at Rennes in 1550, in which the notary Yves Courtois's claim to exemption from the taille is held up against the suit of the Vannes municipality. (The *Discours*, of uncertain date, can be found in the Archives Nationales, K716 no. 10, p. 7.)

51. On the question of the gentry's aptitude for gallantry, no doubt the most exhaustive discussion is to be found in *Alcippe ou du choix des galands* by the Sr. de Somaize (Paris, 1661). Should a lady choose "un homme d'espée et

homme de cour" or an "homme de robe et de la ville (ceux qui composent le reste des societez et qui sont les gens de justice, de finance et de robe)"? On the one hand, "il y a plus de gloire à estre aimée d'un courtisan que d'un homme de robe," but that is true only if one knows no other glory than that resulting from ostentation. The *homme de robe* has *mérite*, "the least of his presents can make the fortune of entire families"; besides, he represents a challenge, for it is not easy to make him fall in love, since he ordinarily professes indifference to gallantry, while the noble courtier is a *plumet* who will boast of his conquest to one and all and is easy to conquer anyway; further, the man of the *robe* is likely to be more faithful: "il use d'une civilité reglée et sans affectation, s'il parle il se fait escouter. S'il dit qu'il aime ... il ne parle plus, il agist, il ne promet pas, il donne"; finally, he is so well educated that it is "un advantage d'avoir conversation avec luy." I owe this reference to Professor Dorothy Karafiol.

52. *Journal de l'Estoile pour le règne de Henri III*, Lefebvre, ed. (Paris: Gallimard, 1943) p. 130.

53. The classic case is Rabelais's treatment of the Pichrocoline War.

54. Pasquier, *Letters* (1619), 1:224.

55. Ibid., p. 232.

56. Ibid., p. 224.

57. Ibid., p. 223.

58. Ibid., p. 278.

59. Ibid., p. 309.

60. Tallemant des Réaux, *Historiettes*, Mongrédien, ed., 4 vols. (Paris, 1932–34), 1:174.

61. Anonymous, *Discours des querelles* (Paris, 1594), p. 13.

62. Ibid., p. 54.

63. Ibid., p. 26.

64. Ibid., p. 28: "Ces hommes donc ainsi esleus, que nous appellons à present nobles ou gentilshommes, avoient pris en protection le public ... non à faire des extortions & violences ... comme la pluspart font au temps ou nous sommes."

65. The inscription still stands today. See the so-called Maison de François Ier rebuilt in 1958 in the garden of the *mairie* of Moret-sur-Loing (Seine-et-Marne).

66. According to Malherbe, writing from the court to his friend Peiresc, the legislation against dueling passed in the last year of Henri IV's life was effective (*Oeuvres*, Lalanne, ed., 5 vols. [Paris, 1863], 3:70).

Chapter 9. Monsieur de Gouberville

1. Pierre de Vaissière, in *Gentilshommes campagnards*, uses Gouberville, together with Olivier de Serres and Noël du Fail, as typical examples of the breed. We have already met the merchant-draper family of the De Serres of Villeneuve-de-Berg. As for Noël du Fail, he was a *conseiller* in the *parlement* of Rennes, in Brittany. As we shall see, Gouberville is also an unfortunate example in Vaissière's *apologia* for the French *gentilshommes*.

2. First publicized and transcribed by the Abbé Tollemer, principal of the *collège* at Valognes, near Cherbourg, a century ago, this *Journal manuscrit*

d'un sire de Gouberville et du Mesnil was first published in a summary form—
some 800 pages of paraphrase and quotation—by Tollemer (Valognes, 1873).
This summary was recently reprinted by the Mouton publishing house (Paris
and The Hague, 1972), under the title *Un Sire de Gouberville, gentilhomme
campagnard au Cotentin de 1553 à 1562*. The title "sire," no doubt an invention
of the Abbé Tollemer's, would have grated on the ears of contemporaries,
who reserved it specifically for merchants. The proper title should be sieur de
Gouberville. A purist would settle for nothing but Gilles Picot, sieur de
Gouberville, since Gouberville had not officially received permission to drop
his family name of Picot, in favor of his *nom de terre*, until some twenty years
after the composition of his diary. This *Journal* must absolutely be studied in
the unabridged and carefully edited text provided by Eugène de Robillard de
Beaurepaire, who published it for the *Société des Antiquaires de Normandie*
(Caen, 1892). An indispensable complement to Beaurepaire's text is the further volume of more than 300 pages, published by the Count de Blangy
(Caen, 1895), also for the Société. This second volume contains the diary for
the years 1549–52, which had not yet been discovered when Tollemer sum-
marized the part of the *Journal* he knew about. The references which follow
are either to Beaurepaire's volume (1) or to Blangy's (2).

3. *Journal*, 2:834–35: "Comme je montoys le degré de la chambre, Thomas
Lejuez et led. Garin contestoyent en paroles, et led. Juez appelloyt ledit
Gardin sot. Je dys aud. Lejuez qu'il se teust ou je le mettroys en L. s.
d'amende, et qu'il me fist veye [give way] que je peusse passer. Il me respon-
dit en grande arrogance, par ces motz: 'J'ay affere la aussy bien comme vous
pour les franchises de Vallongnes, je ne m'en tayré icy.' et par nous fut dict
aud. Juez: 'Je vous met en L. s. [50 sols] d'amende, et si vous ne vous taises,
elle doublera.' et par luy respondu: 'Je appelle de vous et vous accuse d'avoyr
esté au ravagement et saccagement des maisons et eglise de ceste ville. Je
demande l'ayde du peuple. Je le veux prouver a l'encontre de vous.' De quoy
je prins pour tesmoings le sr. de Tourlaville, le verdier de Cherbourg qui
presentz estoyent et plusieurs aultres, puys entré en la chambre ou nous
fusmes jusques à VII heures. Je couché chez Denys."

This confrontation occurred on the last day of October 1562. Violence was
in the air. As can be seen from Juez's remarks, Gouberville was suspected of
being a Protestant. His friend, the sieur de Tourlaville, with whom he had
lunched at Denys's inn just before the incident, was a known Protestant. (See
A. de Blangy, *Une Collation chez Madame de Clamorgan à Rouen* [Caen, 1890].)
Gouberville's reaction to provocation is a legalistic procedure, as we can
gather from the entire tone of this diary entry. His opponent, Juez, was also a
man of the law. The confrontation was all words and legal formulae: "I appeal
from you," "I accuse you," "I will provide evidence against you." These
lawyers' duels ended in threats of fines and the naming of witnesses in case
the matter should come to court.

4. The royal letters patent of 13 May 1570, approving the name change—of
which a copy is on file in the Archives Départementales of the Seine-
Inférieure—are published by Beaurepaire, *Journal*, 1:15: "ledit seigneur [the
king] approuve le cognom de Gouberville pris par Gilles de Gouberville,
escuier, sieur dudit lieu et du Mesnil, lieutenant en la vicomté de Vallongnes ... encore que Guillaume Picot et autres, ses predecesseurs, aient
toujours porté ledit surnom de Picot, permettant audit sieur Gilles et à ses

successeurs de continuer a l'advenir prendre ledit cognom de Gouberville au lieu de celuy de Picot." That this name change was a touchy matter for Gouberville and that his efforts to achieve the official name change were a lifelong preoccupation of his can be deduced from the fact that he discusses his efforts to collect the necessary papers "pour le changement de mon nom" as early as 1561 and enters these confidences in his diary using Greek characters, his unvarying practice when recording sensitive issues (*Journal*, 1:696).

5. *Journal*, 1:231–32. As a bourgeois of Cherbourg, Gouberville is exempt from tailles and *aides* anyway.

6. Ibid., p. 237: on Saturday afternoon, 21 December 1555, in Bayeux, Gouberville, accompanied by several relatives, goes to argue with le président de Mendreville and the *procureur général pour le Roy en la Cour des Aydes à Rouen*, "auxquels nous voulusmes monstrer lettres anciennes, de plus de 240 ans, comme nos predecesseurs dès lors estoyent nobles." But the *président* counters that Guillaume Picot was on his tax rolls for the year 1463.

7. Ibid., p. 291. Maistre Jacques Davy, *bailli* of the Cotentin, was the highest royal official in the *pays*. Nevertheless, le président de Mendreville fined him 8,000 francs and six years' wages, or so Gouberville is told toward the end of a day in August 1556. The Davys were to go far before the end of the century.

8. Ibid., p. 315. Gouberville receives 40 sols for one year's rent of one of the rooms of his house in Cherbourg; Gouberville performs his guard duty in Cherbourg as a matter of course: in the afternoon, "je m'en allé à Cherbourg ... pour ce que j'estoys du gué avant my nuyct et le landemain de la porte." In the course of his evening tour of duty "sur la muraille," he spends four sols for two pots of wine to offer his comrades. He sleeps over at a friend's house and finishes his tour of duty the next day, starting at six o'clock in the morning, when he is present at the opening of the city's gates. That day he spends another six sols in wine, to say nothing of the cost of stabling his horses (eight sols). After 4 P.M., having received the captain's leave, Gouberville rides home. Another time, we find Gouberville "en la boutique de Jehan L'Arbalestier" in Cherbourg, getting the captain to sign a certificate of residence in Cherbourg for him, to use in his attempts to be exempted from the noble duty of the *ban et arrière-ban* (ibid., p. 178).

9. Ibid., p. 226.

10. Ibid., pp. 230–31.

11. Ibid., p. 243.

12. Vaissière, *Gentilshommes*, p. 2.

13. Ibid., pp. 28, 18, 9.

14. *Journal*, 2:115–16.

15. Ibid., p. 59.

16. Ibid.

17. Ibid., pp. 59–60.

18. Ibid., 1:21, a volume of *Ordonnances* borrowed from the sieur Pierre Dosses in Cherbourg; 2:55, a book borrowed from Monsieur Trexot, *conseiller* at Valognes; 1:136, Gouberville acquires a volume of *Institutes*; 1:228, he inherits twelve books from his brother. Gouberville's reading is by no means confined to law books: he is an active borrower and lender of books of all kinds, as are his friends and colleagues. See, for example, *Journal*, 1:231, where he writes of returning a book on ancient medals (*Promptuayre des*

medailles) to maistre Bonnet, who reciprocates by returning Gouberville's copy of the *Diverses Lessons* of Pierre de Messie, which Gouberville in turn lends to his cousin, Monsieur de Hemevez. The *Diverses Lessons* was one of Montaigne's favorite books, and the interest in numismatics is entirely characteristic of the educated lawyers' and judges' world.

19. Ibid., p. 65: "je fys consultation à l'esleu Pinard, sçavoyr sy une femme veufve aveugle seroyt pour ce desrollee de la taille."

20. Ibid., 2:55; ibid., 1:164.

21. Ibid., 2:62.

22. Ibid., pp. 62–66.

23. Ibid., p. 127.

24. Ibid., p. 129.

25. Ibid.

26. Ibid., pp. 130–35. To begin with, on Saturday, 27 December (the year is 1550), Gouberville lunches with Le Prevost. That night he checks in at Le Prevost's house. Sunday morning he begins his cure by taking "10 dragmes de casse"; after lunching with his friend, the Captain Papillon and his wife, he plays cards all afternoon. Monday morning he takes his first "syrop," concocted by Le Prevost, and begins "une diette pour mon plaisir et pour tenir compagnee au dit capitaine." Each of the guests buys a "bonnet de nuyct" (nightcap) at 27 sols—no doubt on Le Prevost's advice—while Papillon takes some pills. On Tuesday Gouberville plays "triquetrac" with Le Prevost. This regime of harmless medicaments, slow lunches, and card games goes on day after day. The "compagnee" includes a sieur de Caumont, a seigneur Horace, Le Prevost's brother, maistre Robert, the *capitaine* Cadiot (eye troubles), Madone and his son Horacyo, and the *bailli* Marette. Maistre Pierre Lachere, bourgeois de Rouen, arrives "pour faire la diette, à raison qu'il estoyt trop repplet pour son age qui n'estoit que de XXVII ans"; another new patient is the sire Thomas Le Ties, an innkeeper, for a "douleur de teste"; soon they are joined by Thomas Noblet, who arrives with his wife and brother-in-law to "faire la diette pour la verole [smallpox]." The *diette* was an all-purpose regime, and Le Prevost's house functioned as a resort. While staying there, Gouberville and his acquaintances indulge in the behavior characteristic of tourists in a health resort, right down to the aimless but pleasurable buying of souvenirs: Gouberville has a souvenir ring made by a local jeweler (11s.), and he buys himself a fancy pair of shoes (14s.), a book of psalms in French (4s.), and five little metal boxes from Germany (7s. 6d.). At Le Prevost's, Gouberville is so struck by the usefulness of an "estuves de chambre"—which I take to be some sort of sauna-like steam bath—that he has workmen measure the *estuve*, "affin d'en faire unes pareilles quand nous serions au pays."

27. These *lettres de remission* are indeed an excellent source for the study of violent clashes between gentilshommes and bourgeois. Vaissière uses the JJ series of the Trésor des Chartes (Archives Nationales, JJ 241–63).

28. This phenomenon is analyzed in G. Proccacci, *Classi sociali e monarchia assoluta nella Francia della prima meta del sècolo XVI* (Turin, 1955).

29. Among innumerable examples, see the sale of Louis d'Harcourt's lands in 1561–62. The successful bid is made by Pierre Chevreuse, bourgeois de Paris, against Lefebvre, bourgeois de Paris; Du Val, *conseiller du roy*; a Parisian goldsmith-banker; and Anne de Montmorency (A.D., Calvados, E 298, cited by Proccacci).

30. A development described rather schematically by Proccacci: "Una considerevole porzione del Terzo Stato e dunque in effeti integrata nelle strutturi feudali esistenti" (p. 118).

31. Described, *inter alia,* in Lucien Febvre, *Philippe II et la Franche-Comté* (Paris, 1911), pp. 180–236..

32. The account of this dramatic incident can be found in the diary of maistre Estienne Baluze, himself a notable official at the Tulle court and related to most of the *familles* of the city to such an extent that I should think he would have found it difficult to bump into anyone on the town square that night who was not at least a second cousin. See *Le Livre de raison des Baluze,* Louis Guibert, ed. (Tulle, 1888), entry for 19 November 1607.

33. *Journal,* 2:111, won by maistre Jehan Le Pelletier's bid of 895 livres and celebrated at a dinner at Denys's inn.

34. Ibid., p. 61.

35. Ibid., 1:282.

36. Ibid., p. 356. This was in June 1557. Gouberville assembles the men of the parish on his own authority and marches off to the beaches, where they spend the night in readiness. He also undertakes to order the men of neighboring parishes to join his men. This is on 15 June. Three days later, the danger past, we find him at his cousin's side in Toqueville, writing up a last will and testament in due form. And while he thus performs as a notary, he receives the military command in writing, retroactively, addressed to the "captain or ensign de Gouberville," ordering him to the defense of the coast. The paper is filed away for future use.

37. Ibid., p. 208; a good twenty-five people are kept busy at harvest time. In the evening, "they were still dancing at midnight in the *salle.*"

38. Ibid., p. 186. "Je fys achever de touser nos moutons"; p. 194: "Jehan Caulvin vinst ceans pour avoyr ma laine. Nous ne peusmes accorder."

39. Ibid., 2:56.

40. Ibid., pp. 79–80.

41. Ibid., 1:25, Cantepye at the market; 1:33, in Barfleur, on business; 1:37, legal secretary's work; 2:79, works in fields; 2:80, goes to court in Valognes in Gouberville's stead; 2:9, "toute la matinée Cantepye ne bouge d'escrire de ma chambre"; 2:72, paper work in Cherbourg; 2:115, carrying butter to town; 1:17, on Cantepye's name and status; 1:12, Cantepye walks to Cherbourg, sent on an errand.

The phrase sieur de Gouberville says nothing about his social status. The only real question is whether he is termed *noble homme* or *escuyer* in the contracts before notary. The answer is that even as late as 1576, after his patented name change, and in front of the local notaries who are his cronies, Gilles Picot appears as *noble homme.* (Contract cited in full by Tollemer, *Journal* [summary], p. 832.)

42. *Journal,* 2:68.

43. Ibid., p. 178.

44. Ibid., p. 184. The festivities at Le Mesnil on the occasion of his *fête,* that is, on Saint Gilles's day, differ from other days only by the number of his guests. A sheep is slaughtered and his best friends come to dinner. These include Claude Cabart and his wife, Jehan Liot, the wife and daughters of Jacques Cabart, Chandeleur, Dauge—*sergeants, greffiers, procureurs* and their wives. Next morning Gouberville goes to Valognes (with Cantepye, Symmonet, maistre Guillaume Cabart, and maistre Gilles Cabart), and they all

lunch at the inn, together with the *receveur des tailles,* and other legal men of the *élection.* After lunch, still accompanied by his friends, Gouberville takes the long way home and stops at the baron de la Lutumyere's place for a drink.

45. Ibid., p. 185.

46. Ibid., 1:139.

47. Ibid., 2:191.

48. Ibid., 1:51.

49. Ibid., p. 96.

50. Ibid., p. 125.

51. Ibid., 2:10.

52. Ibid., p. 83.

53. Ibid., p. 99.

54. Ibid., p. 115.

55. Ibid., p. 70.

56. Ibid., p. 72. Having wasted much time on Saturday at Gouberville, what with his cousins who were hunting, M. de Gouberville gets home on Sunday and sends Cantepye to Cherbourg, "mettre au net les declarations qu'il me fallayt bailler au vicomte." The Mardi Gras celebrations do not stop him from working either (ibid., p. 76).

57. Ibid., p. 150, on M. l'escuyer Poton's hunting habits and the loan of the bitch Mitaine through the good offices of Françoys Damours. On Damours, see ibid., p. 208. He is the nephew of Marguerite Le Berger—who is the mistress of Gouberville's Uncle Jean, the curé, and probably also the daughter of Gouberville's tenant Le Berger.

58. Ibid., p. 181.

59. *Vicomte* in Normandy was not a noble title but an administrative office. The *vicomte* in Valognes was Thomas Laguette, no more noble than Gouberville but one of the three most powerful men in the *élection* of Valognes, at a time when Gouberville had much to lose.

60. Ibid., 1:235.

61. For this episode, all references are ibid., pp. 243–52.

62. The classic analysis of the old nobility's losses through bad land management is that given by Lucien Febvre (*Franche-Comté,* pp. 180–236). Febvre's conclusion, that competent managers among the old nobility were rare, is one which can plausibly be extended to most French provinces in the sixteenth century, as long as one does not lose sight of the frequent transfers of property from bankrupt seigneurs to new seigneurs who run a profitable estate. The new seigneur is almost always a "new man," but, as we know, his *qualité* is not always easily detected by modern observers—the *locus classicus* being Olivier de Serres, sieur du Pradel.

63. See the analysis of this phenomenon in E. Le Roy Ladurie, *Paysans du Languedoc,* 2 vols. (Paris, 1966).

64. *Essais* (Pléiade edition), p. 238, for instance.

65. *Journal,* 1:271.

66. Apple orchard tending: see Tollemer, *Journal* (summary), pp. 273 ff. He does his own pruning (*Journal,* 1:485) and no task on the farm is beneath him: "Tout le jour, je fys charier du fumier" (ibid., p. 485).

67. *Journal,* 1:119.

68. Ibid., 2:210. Girette was rented from her father for 46s. a year, plus

keep. Occasionally Gouberville has trouble with his women: "Les femmes de la maison avoyent esté en discord," he records, on one occasion, writing in code (ibid., 1:485).

69. See Tollemer, *Journal* (summary), pp. 28–40, for a summary of the question of wages and servants. In the spring of 1554, Jehan Hoston, who is entitled, *en principe*, to 6 francs a year, is given a heifer worth 50s. instead. Jehan Groult ends up with only 20s. in cash, while Tiphane Groult (Jehan's sister, perhaps) does get her money: 46s. for a year's service. Gaultier Birette, on the other hand, is given a mare, with her new foal, in lieu of wages; and since the worth of the horses is said to exceed the wages owed, and since they graze on the master's lands, the field hand, Birette, *ends up paying 46s. to his master*, "declaring himself content." Who is getting the best of whom? The annual wages of the men, as negotiated at the July fairs, ran as high as 7 or even 9 or 10 livres, but also, for boys and shepherds, to as little as 20 sols. The women were paid less: 45–50s., usually, and some skirts or dresses, or fabric, in addition. A generous premium—as much as 20s.—should be added for the conclusion of the bargain at the fair.

70. Tollemer, *Journal* (summary), p. 368.

71. Ibid., pp. 377–80.

72. Ibid., p. 381.

73. Ibid., p. 383.

74. Ibid., p. 384.

75. Ibid., p. 385.

76. Ibid., p. 399.

77. *Journal*, 2:81.

78. Ibid., p. 57.

79. Ibid., 1:614.

80. Ibid., p. 264.

81. A nice example of the profits which come his way because of his office is the following transaction, revealed in a contract of 1576 published by Tollemer (*Journal* [summary], pp. 831–34). Gouberville buys three acres of royal land and obligates himself in exchange for a *rente* of 18d. per annum. He never pays a penny of this *rente*. Eventually he sells one of the three acres to his neighbor Drouet, who is glad to have it, on condition that Drouet (1) pay all the arrears of the *rente* already due on all three acres to the royal treasury, (2) continue to pay the full 18d. a year from then on, and (3) pay Gouberville 35 livres in cash. In this transaction Gouberville clears a profit of 35 livres and remains proprietor of two acres of land without ever having spent a penny. This is a case of speculation, no doubt typical, in which the position of the *officier* and his political alliances are used in lieu of capital. It is in this sense that office is a valuable investment.

82. Le Roy Ladurie, in his introduction to the Tollemer reprint, page xliv, suggests that Gouberville spends more in cash than he receives in cash. I have my doubts about that.

83. This question puzzles Le Roy Ladurie.

84. This contradiction is inherent but unnoticed in Le Roy Ladurie's introduction. See p. xliv on the "losses" of this seigneur, who is said to understand nothing of the spirit of capitalism and is convicted of being a poor businessman; and see p. xvi on his being *gros richard*.

Chapter 10. Wealth

1. The livre, in which most of the calculations in this book are expressed, does not really exist. It is a money of account, a theoretical denomination, whose relationship to real coins, such as the gold écu, keeps changing. The livre is subdivided into an equally imaginary twenty sols. A real écu, in Cherbourg, in the mid-sixteenth century, is worth roughly 2.5 livres. Twenty years later, L'Estoile notes that it is worth 4l. 5s. in Paris.

2. Gouberville, *Journal*, 2:78. These gentlemen showered each other with gifts: small gifts, like the curé's white rose, and more substantial ones, like M. de Saulsemenil's present of "12 oranges, 2 pomegranates, and a bottle of muscadet".

3. Ibid., 1:289. Gouberville records such a gift, made in his presence in Barfleur harbor.

4. See chap. 2, p. 10.

5. See chap. 3, p. 18.

6. Marcel Couturier, *Recherches sur les structures sociales de Châteaudun, 1525–1789* (Paris, 1969), pp. 219–20, offers occasional glimpses of how bourgeois, *rentier,* and *officier* families hit by bad luck retain their *famille's* inherited social status despite their malheurs, as depicted in the tax-roll remarks for 1695–96. The Mesnager brothers, last descendants of a family which had been noted for its lawyers and *officiers* in the sixteenth century, have no possessions; they are unmarried and "malheureux," but do not lose their *qualité,* even though they cannot pay a penny in taxes. On the other hand, the tax rolls include a rubric for fallen bourgeois: "filles qui regulierement doivent être dans la classe des fileuses parce qu'elles vivent chetivement et sans servante avec tres peu de bien et travaillent partie en secret."

7. Jacques Lavaud, *Desportes* (Paris, 1936), estimates Desportes's revenues at 22,000 livres in 1600. To be sure, abbeys are ephemeral properties, in no way comparable to land, *rentes,* and offices, which can easily be transmitted to the next generation.

8. Cioranescu, *Amyot* (Paris, 1941), p. 39.

9. For all this, see ibid.

10. "O bien heureux qui peut passer sa vie / Parmi les champs, les forets et les bois / L'ambition son courage n'attise / Il ne se plait a vider sa foi / Mais, en vivant content de sa fortune, Il est sa cour, sa faveur et son roi."

11. See George E. Diller, *Les Dames des Roches* (Paris, 1936).

12. Among others: the daughter's lover, Guersens, who studied at the *collège* Du Plessis in Paris in the 1560s, did his law course in Poitiers, married for a dowry, bought an office of *conseiller* in the *parlement* at Rennes, was eventually named royal professor in Paris, given letters of ennoblement in 1581, and died two years later, of the plague. The poet Nicolas Rapin and his nephew, Raoul Cailler, *advocat* at the *parlement* in Paris; the playwright Guillaume Le Breton, of Nevers, who studied law in Poitiers; the dean of the Faculty of Medicine at Poitiers University, Pierre L'Anglois; the physician and canon, Guillaume Sacher de Saint-Secondin (cf. Le Riche, *Journal* [Saint Maixent, 1847]).

13. Diller, *Des Roches,* p. 54.

14. Ibid., p. 13.

15. Ibid., p. 175.

16. See Lucien Pinvert's introduction to Grévin, *Théâtre complet et poésies choisies* (Paris, 1922).

17. Here I follow V. L. Saulnier's excellent monograph, "Etude sur Béroalde de Verville," *Bibliothèque d'Humanisme et Renaissance* 4 (1944): 209–326.

18. Ibid., p. 243.

19. See his autobiographical *Palais des Curieux* and his *Sagesse*, written in 1593, the year he achieved material success in the form of the canon's prebend.

20. Michel de Montaigne, *Essais* (Pléiade edition), p. 555, on Jacques Peletier's visiting him; p. 344, on Jacques Amyot. While Monsieur de Montaigne may feel much contempt for bad *collèges* (which *abrutissent* their pupils (p. 164) and for half-baked teachers (*savanteaux*) (p. 139), he reserves the highest praise for great teachers life Turnèbe, who had nothing *pédantesque* about him. "Que le port de sa robe et quelque façon externe qui pouvoit n'estre pas civilisée à la courtisane": a certain clumsiness of dress and manners, eternal characteristics, it would seem, of the intellectual, but these, in Montaigne's eyes, are "choses de neant," if one is to believe him (p. 139).

21. Estienne Pasquier, *Lettres*, 3 vols. (Paris, 1619), 1:434.

22. Denis Richet, "Une Famille de robe à Paris du 16ᵉ au 18ᵉ siècle: Les Séguier" (unpublished thesis, cited by permission of the author).

23. Ibid., p. 51: "Un président au Parlement, bientôt chevalier, a beau différer en beaucoup de points d'un marchand laboureur, sa gestion et ses procédés sont fondamentalement les mêmes."

24. That is to say that the principal was paid off, presumably, by 1573; for the next 67 years, at least, Seguier collected 1,000 livres a year of pure interest, so that by 1640 the interest paid on the original loan of 12,000 livres amounted to more than five times the capital—which says a great deal about the great nobility's inability to get out from under their debts.

25. Richet, "Une Famille," pp. 56–57.

26. Ibid., pp. 81–86.

27. Ibid., pp. 97–98, for these estimates of the Séguiers' investment returns, which agree with what we have seen elsewhere.

28. About 200,000 livres, according to Richet (ibid., p. 72).

29. And for good reason: at "their old seigneurie" of L'Estang la Ville, the lease of 140 *arpents* of lands brings in no more than 100 livres annually, while a single sale of 106 trees from the estate nets 760 livres in 1560; at Sorel, five *arpents* of timber are farmed out for 3,150 livres a year, while the ploughlands—over 100 *arpents*—bring in barely more than 1,000 livres (ibid., p. 91).

30. Ibid., p. 87. The obligations of the *fermiers* and other dependents on the Séguier lands are spelled out in detail, as was customary. Thus, the crops due to the seigneur were to be delivered to his Parisian *hôtel* at the expense of the *fermier* (p. 93); several additional hauls were usually provided for in the contracts—three or four times a year—while it was specified that the farmer and his horses would be lodged and fed at the seigneur's expense upon arrival in Paris (p. 94).

31. Ibid., p. 115.

32. L'Estoile's comment that Séguier gave his daughters away in marriage "very advantageously when it comes to wealth, having no other concern," is cited ibid., p. 106.

33. Titling themselves *escuyers* before any of the other Séguiers, the Séguiers de la Verrière contracted ruinous marriage alliances with noble families, tried their hand at the military life, and, in the end, found themselves not only poorer but of lesser *qualité* than their uncles and cousins in the *parlement*. See ibid., p. 66.

34. They remain "marqués dans le choix des gendres, l'établissement des fils et la gestion de leur fortune, par des préoccupations dont la dominante est encore bourgeoise" is the way Richet puts it (ibid., p. 117).

35. Ibid., p. 114.

36. At least in the sixteenth century (ibid., p. 92).

37. See J. P. Babelon, "L'Hôtel d'Assy," *Paris et Ile-de-France* 13 (1963): 169–96.

38. The Hôtel de Sully, built by the financier Gallet, the Hôtel de Breton-villiers, built by the financier Le Ragois, or the Hôtel de Sens, serving the Confitures de Saint James.

39. Tallemant des Réaux (son of a financier, and sensitive to such matters) makes himself the echo of this reaction to Séguier's candid signpost (cited in Babelon, *Demeures parisiennes sous Henri IV et Louis XIII* [Paris, 1965]).

40. Ibid., p. 42.

41. Ibid., pp. 15–18.

42. Babelon, "Hôtel d'Assy." "Survived" may be hardly the word for it, though. The Hôtel d'Assy, worth 40,000 in 1641, brought 160,000 in 1723.

43. To piece together the edifying history of the Nicolays, one consults the documents collected by M. de Boislisle in his *Histoire de la maison de Nicolay*, 2 vols. (Nogent-le-Rotrou, 1875) (in folio, rare).

44. Ibid., vol. 1: *Titres, correspondances, et pièces diverses*, p. 27.

45. Among the property titles in his safe we find documents entitling him to: 300 livres on the *grenier à sel* of Pont-Saint-Esprit; 100 livres on the same; "un achat de la part du peage a sel que prenait M. Antoine de Meseyrac sur la Riviere du Rosne"; another *achat* of the *péage* "que prenet tous les ans sus le viatge noble Guiron de Aguilhac"; the rights "que monsr de Balmefort prent au pont d'Ardeche, prest St. Just"; the rights "sus les bateaulx vendues par noble Loys de Barjac"; those of Antoine de Joys, of Saint-Esprit, on the *péage du sel* of Bourg-Saint-Andéol; and so on.

46. "Ung instrument de une pension que messire J. et A. Faure funt a noble Jehan Nicolay de 3 florins et dimi sus une terre"; a pension "sus une meyson dans la ville de Donzera"; an "acquisition de ung florin pancionel de Micheau"; another pension of 6 florins "sus une terre et pres"; a pension of 8 gros from Fabri "sus une terre" near Donzere; another pension of 2 florins from the same; a pension of 1 florin on a house in Donzere "a la place publique;" a pension of 12 gros on a house; another worth 7 sols 6 deniers from Fabri; 30 gros from Radulphe on a house; 22 sols 6 deniers from Reddon on two houses; "5 livres de pension tous les ans que Jehan Nicolay achepter de J. Bonot, sur 2 terres;" 5 sols from Reynaudi on a house; 15 sols from Cesteron on a house; 5 florins on a house; 15 sols on another house; 2 livres 6 deniers "sus une botique a la place"; 10 sols on a house; 32 sols on a house; 22 sols with collateral unspecified; 4.5 florins on a house; 6 livres, collateral unspecified; two more pensions, one for 28 sols, the other for 6 livres; a pension, in kind, of two barrels of oil "tous les ans," bought from the munici-pality of Saint-Julien, and a "cartiera de sel sus le peage," bought from noble Loys de Barjac; 4 sols of pension on a *vigne*; and so on.

47. Full description of the house and its furnishings in the *Inventaire* of 1527 published in Boislisle, *Titres*.

48. The contracts are published ibid., pp. 157–58.

49. See ibid., p. 172, for the documents concerning this negotiation.

50. The inventory of the *hostel seigneurial* of Goussainville, made in 1554, is published ibid. The *comptoir*, in addition to the chair, the two *pupitres*, and the ivory *escritoire*, contained two alabaster sculptures and sixty books in French and Latin.

51. On the Ile de la Cité, see the excellent study of J. L. Bourgeon, "L'Ile de la Cité pendant la Fronde: Structure sociale," *Paris et Ile-de-France* [*Mémoires*] 13 (1963): 23–144, which introduces us to the dense world of the Cité, clustered around the Palais de Justice, in 1648. Here we shall find the great gentry families living in separate splendor on the rue de Harlay and the Place Dauphine in the opulent three-story stone buildings which set them aside from the crowded mass of merchant and artisan streets, with their narrow wood-and-plaster houses, two minutes' walk away, in the center of the island. Another favorite retreat of the gentry is to be found in the superbly comfortable canons' houses clustered around Notre-Dame cathedral. These are small *hôtels*, with private gardens, which rent out at 1,300 livres a year. A Séguier, bishop of Meaux, lives in one of these, worth 25,000 livres. A fairly typical gentry household in 1648 is that of Jacques Hilaire, *advocat* at the *parlement;* he rents a house in front of Notre-Dame for 1,414 livres a year. Hilaire shares his house with a cousin of his, also *advocat* at the *parlement.* In addition to Hilaire's law clerk, there are two butlers, a driver, and two maids. The house has seven rooms, including an office-study on the first floor, which houses Hilaire's library—close to 600 volumes appraised at 1,537 livres, in which history and law books dominate. There is a stable in the courtyard. Altogether, a private world and an opulent one; but space is at a premium. One can see that Hilaire might have toyed with the idea of buying or renting a far more capacious house in the Marais.

52. Aymard's letter of 1551, Anne's testament of 1553, given in Boislisle, *Titres*, pp. 190–95.

53. Ibid., p. 215.

54. Ibid.

55. Boislisle, *Titres.*

56. The copious correspondence concerning this catastrophe is published ibid.

57. Antoine's sister Jeanne had married Jehan du Tillet in 1567, bringing a dowry of 30,000 livres. The marriage ceremony was performed by Du Tillet, bishop of Meaux (ibid., p. 269). His other sister, Renée, married an Hennequin, *président*, and a Luillier, *président*, in succession. Her son, Antoine, the future bishop of Rennes, was baptized in 1538 in the presence of his godfather, an Hennequin, who was *controlleur général d'Outre-Seine* (ibid., p. 254). Antoine's younger brother, Thibault, married Catherine Luillier, whose mother was an Hennequin. This marriage, of 1560, established young Thibault. Catherine's dowry consisted of properties in Soissons; *rentes* of 500 livres a year; her mother's inheritance, worth 11,000 livres (partly in cash, and partly in the form of a *rente* of 741 livres annually); and a gift, to be taken from her father's estate after his death, of 10,000 livres. Thibault, now established, bought an office of *conseiller* in the *parlement* (in 1561); on the occasion of his entrance into that august body, he is described as "personne

honneste et amplissime familie." Unfortunately he was to die shortly after these *amplissime* beginnings (for documents concerning Thibault see ibid., pp. 258–60).

58. The documents are published ibid.

59. Rosny's letter is given ibid., p. 280: "estant yssue du lieu d'ou elle est sortye, elle eust bien trouvé ung party aussy avantaigeulx, et n'en peust jamais entrer une de meilleure part en vostre race, et estoit recherchée de gentilhomme d'antienne maison"; and, later: "sy je la veulx veoir, il fault que je l'aille veoir à Paris despendre 500 escus à chascun voiage qui ne peuvent estre sy tost remis en ma bourse comme vous."

60. Fifteen years after her marriage, we find her writing to her sister and insisting that she return her money, "celon la coutume de Normandie, au denié dis."

61. Ibid., pp. 280 ff.

62. Jean Aymard Nicolay, the great-grandson of Marie Billy, seems to have been determined to make up for his great-grandfather's mistake. Born in 1658, *président*, like all the Nicolays, he married Marie Catherine Le Camus in 1690. After her death, at the age of 53, he finally realized his lifetime ambition of forming an alliance with the Lamoignon family, as he explains candidly in a letter written in 1705 to his sister: "La chose du monde . . . que j'ay toujour le plus souhaitée, comme vous sçavez, a été l'alliance de M. de Lamoignon" (ibid.).

63. See Pierre Goubert, *Beauvais et le Beauvaisis* (Paris, 1960), p. 328, on these "fortunes vieilles, fortunes rentières," which "tendaient à se stabiliser, parfois à decroître." See ibid., p. 218, for analysis of the ruin of the *gentils-hommes* caused by their inefficient management.

64. Here again, excellent information in the Beauvaisis, where at least one-third of the country nobility are "pauvres honteux," while half of the so-called noble lands in the *bailliage* are in the hands of thirteen big landowners, mostly *parlementaires* and ex-financiers like Hanyvel (ibid., p. 212).

65. Ibid., p. 214: "Les grands noms de Beauvaisis . . . figurent presque tous sur la liste," Tristan's acquisitions being made, "presque toutes, aux dépens de nobles endettés."

66. Ibid., pp. 214–15.

67. Le Clerc, "Un Fief de l'abbaye de St. Magloire: La Seigneurie de Vau-détard à Issy," *Mémoires de la Société de l'histoire de Paris* (1882), pp. 287–309.

68. Romain Baron, "La Bourgeoisie de Varzy au 17e siècle," *Annales de Bourgogne* 36 (1964): 179. Bogue, *advocat au parlement*, Dupin *bailli*, and Billetout *marchand* in partnership. Dupin's investment alone runs to 10,000 livres (ibid., p. 182).

69. Ibid., p. 203. In seventeenth-century Varzy, "il était extrêmement difficile aux bourgeois d'accéder eux-mêmes à la noblesse. Les charges [offices] n'étaient pas suffisantes pour conférer le titre d'écuyer alors que l'on faisait la chasse aux usurpateurs. Au siècle précédent l'accession à la noblesse semble avoir été plus facile."

70. *Mémoires de Jean Maillefer (1611–1684), marchand bourgeois de Reims*, H. Jadart, ed. (Reims, 1890).

71. Ibid., pp. 6–7: "Pour feu mon pere, il estoyt marchand de soye. Je fus mis aux estudes, je fis ma 7e, 6e jusques à la 3e classe, pendant lesquelles j'eus un prix de composition en grecq . . . . J'avois grande inclination aux estudes,

et souvent comme nos Régens nous dictoient nos themes en françoys, je les composois en latin sans escrire le françoys, mais je fus retiré de classe à l'âge de 14 ans...."

72. Robert Angot, *Les Nouveaux Satires* (Rouen, 1637), p. 100:

> Celui seme à present sur l'onde
> Qui fonde au Barreau son dessein ...
> Que n'est tu donc en la boutique
> A gaigner la piece d'argent?

73. Maillefer, *Mémoires,* p. 8: "Les plaisirs de l'esprit sont purs, agreables, durent tousjours; on va la teste levee, la conscience ne reproche rien."

74. Ibid., p. 12. In Lyon he learned "à coucher une lettre par escrit pour le fait du commerce, à dresser des comptes, à régler et tenir des livres par raison, à tenir une caisse et donner le crédit ... ce fust là où je vis les ouvertures de fort belles affaires et que je recogneue que le commerce en gros avoit des chesnes et quelque chose de noble et d'atrayant qui ne se trouvoit pas dans le detail ... dans lequel il faut effectivement faire des défferences que le gros n'obleige pas."

75. Ibid., p. 33: "Je n'estois pas à la boutique, come n'y ayant ny attachement, ny désir de m'y attacher. J'estois dans une chambre enfermé que je lisois."

76. Ibid., p. 34. Jean disposed then of an inherited capital of some 26,000 livres.

77. Ibid., p. 35: "Je luy mandois que sy la condition de marchand dans laquelle elle m'avoit veue ... luy desplaisoit, que j'estois une table d'attente sur laquelle elle pourroit tracer ce que elle voudroit, que mes parens mesme avoient plus d'inclination pour m'achepter une charge que pour me mettre à la marchandise."

78. Ibid., p. 37.

79. Ibid., p. 41.

80. Ibid., p. 40.

81. As Malherbe notes in a letter to Pereisc: "Il y a des fous de robe longue aussi bien que de courte," in *Oeuvres,* Lalanne, ed., 5 vols. (Paris, 1863), 3:56.

82. Jean Papon, *Instrument du premier notaire* (Lyon, 1576). Speaking of "rentes vulgaires à prix d'argent" constituted on a person's goods, Papon notes that "cette façon d'usure couverte" has been practiced for a long time and is perfectly legal (p. 21). It is one of two "new and honest means of lending money at interest, so colored that one cannot criticize it" and practiced nowadays openly "sans scrupule & sans aucune reprehension" (p. 20).

83. Bernard Schnapper, "La Fixation du denier des rentes et l'opinion parlementaire au 16ᵉ siècle," *Revue d'histoire moderne et contemporaine* 4 (1957): 163.

84. The crown's efforts to limit interest rates on *rentes* to 6.67 percent, in 1567, were successfully resisted by the *parlement.* Another attempt made in 1572 failed as well. It was only after 1601 that the crown succeeded in overriding the objections of the *parlement:* the early seventeenth-century *rente* contracts are mostly written at the low legal maximum rate of 6.25 percent (ibid., p. 168).

85. The portfolio of *rentes* signed over by Amyot in exchange for the Courtempierre property consists of a *rente* of 1,183 écus paid by a partnership consisting of Vivetier, chancellor of France, Gondi, duke of Retz, and

Boureaulx, canon of Notre-Dame, which was originally contracted for on 14 November 1566; a *rente* of 400 écus to be paid by a partnership consisting of Messire G. de Souvre and *honorables hommes* Dargouges and Marchant, *bourgeois* of Paris, contracted for only three years earlier, in 1582; a new *rente* of 300 écus to be paid by the comte de la Suze and *honorables hommes* Gauron and Camus, *advocats* of the city of Coulommiers, contracted for in June 1585; a *rente* of 250 écus to be paid by Saint-Gelays, *capitaine,* and Nicolas de Neuville, seigneur de Villeroy; and two small *rentes,* one of 206 sols to be paid by Messire d'Orgemont and another of 312 sols by Messire Lusson, professor of medicine.

86. His wife's dowry—she was the daughter of a *président* at Aix—consisted of a low-interest *rente* on the municipality of Brignoles, 3,000 écus invested at 6.25 percent. Meanwhile, Malherbe owed 300 or 400 écus, on disastrous terms, to his brother-in-law, Fauconnier, a wily *trésorier:* "Le contrat fait avec ledit Fauconnier contient 400 écus et quelque de principal, mais la vérité est que je n'en reçus que 300 livres [that is, only about 100 écus, or 25 percent of the acknowledged debt]." If one is to believe Malherbe, he is paying an annual interest of 10 percent on a loan of 400 écus, of which he never received more than a small portion in cash. The rest was already owed to Fauconnier because of a loan he had made to Malherbe's father for the purchase of a house. (We saw the father, le sieur Digny, already in difficulty with Gouberville because of outstanding loan payments.) Fauconnier was obviously under no illusion about Malherbe's financial condition when he made the loan, for he insisted on a cosigner, cousin Pierre, who in turn would cosign the loan only in exchange for a promissory note signed by Malherbe's father! The circle is complete.

87. These letters to Bodin are published by A. Ponthieux, "Quelques documents inédits de Jean Bodin," *Revue du 16ᵉ siècle* 15 (1928): 56–99.

88. While Bodin cannot collect his *rentes* from the marquis, he himself is in no position to resist the demands of Jean-Jacques de Mesmes, *conseiller* at the *parlement,* another demigod he comes into distant contact with through the Trouillart alliance (De Mesmes was married to the grand-niece of Françoise Trouillart's Le Cirier mother). The De Mesmes do not overlook small debts, and the tone of their requests is peremptory. The example here is a reminder, in 1592, concerning a *rente* of 25 livres and its arrears, for a balance due of 68⅔ livres (ibid., p. 93).

89. "Car l'Etat et le beau temps que vous voyez ne tiendra pas." Nicolas, it appears, did not follow the advice. He ended up as *controlleur des finances* at Calais and was jailed in 1596. He was accused of irregularities in his accounts, and his possessions were confiscated (ibid., p. 69).

90. Armand Garnier, *Aubigné,* 3 vols. (Paris, 1928), 1:96, for the first marriage; p. 151, for the management of the estates; p. 147, for his later years.

Chapter 11. Religion

1. The chapter at Rodez, for instance, whose prebends are valued at a modest 500–800 livres annually, is made up almost exclusively of such notable bourgeois (see Raoul Bousquet, *Enquête sur les commodites du Rouergue en 1552* [Toulouse, 1969], p. 98).

2. See E. Deronne, "Les Origines des chanoines de Notre-Dame de Paris, 1450–1550," *Revue d'histoire moderne et contemporaine* 18 (1971): 1–29. The author of this well-documented study stresses (1) the national character of the chapter's recruitment—only 85 of a total of 473 canons are Parisians, (2) the domination of the chapter by the "nouvelle élite sociale," composed of the "grande bourgeoisie qui accéda à la noblesse," the "classe des gens de robe," the "grande bourgeoisie parlementaire," which "gardait le souvenir de son origine commune et n'avait pas oublié les secrets de ce négoce qui lui avait donné la direction des affaires du royaume," and (3) the new mentality and culture which distinguished the sixteenth-century canons from their medieval predecessors: they had degrees in law rather than in theology.

3. Among countless examples: Antoine Le Cirier moves from the canon's prebend to the bishopric of Avranches in 1561 (ibid., p. 17), and Philibert Babou, son of the mayor of Tours, grandson of a notary of Bourges, is dean of the cathedral chapter at Tours and will soon be bishop of Angoulême and, eventually, cardinal (*Dictionnaire de Biographie française*).

4. Imbart de la Tour, *Les Origines de la Réforme*, 4 vols. (Paris, 1905), 1:346–47.

5. *Mémoires du clergé*, 9:22–40.

6. Cited by the Abbé Duchâteau in his *Histoire de diocèse d'Orléans* (Orléans, 1888), p. 223.

7. The Florentine ambassador thought so in 1597. Cited by L. Prunel, *Zamet* (Paris, 1912), p. 11. Financiers like Zamet could put together massive loans to the crown and advance enormous sums to the church as well. Zamet maintained such good relations with the papacy that he could put his treasure in the nuncio's safekeeping in times of trouble. Small wonder that his son inherited a very rich abbey at the age of three. Sébastian junior was invested with the bishopric of Langres, one of the most profitable in the kingdom, at the age of twenty-six. The pope, predictably, waived the usual and onerous fee. For the career of the younger Zamet, see Prunel, *Zamet*. For the bishopric of Langres and its income, see the "Déclaration des eveschés et abbayes du royaume," BN Ms fr. 23 338, which gives a figure of 25,000 livres for its annual revenue, the third-highest figure in the kingdom.

8. Sébastian Zamet's claims on the treasury are obvious, as are the claims of *généraux des finances* like the Briçonnets, Bohiers, Beaunes, and of financiers and bankers like the Duprats or the Strozzi among so many others. On Laurent Strozzi, bishop of Béziers and banker to the queen, see Bellaud-Dessalles, *Les Evêques italiens de l'ancien diocèse de Béziers* (Paris, 1901). On Duprat's contribution to royal finances, see Albert Buisson, *Le Chancelier Antoine Duprat* (Paris 1935). On the Bohiers' generalship of finances and various bishoprics, see C. de Mecquenem, "Antoine Bohier," in *Mémoires de la société historique du Cher*, 4th ser. 33 (1922): 1–47.

9. Thus, for example, one can follow the Duprats' long rise to the highest honors in the church by starting with maistre Pierre du Prat, *licensié ès lois*, who manages the affairs of the diocese of Saint-Flour for the absentee bishop a century before the Duprats acquire bishoprics. See Marcellin Boudet, "Du Prat," *Revue de la Haute-Auvergne* (1927–28).

10. In 1579 Desportes and Ronsard, in partnership, invest a sum of 333 écus in the form of a *taxe de vacation* payment, in their unsuccessful bid for the

abbey of Saint-Aubin-des-Bois. When their bid is turned down, they get their money back (Jacques Lavaud, *Desportes* [Paris, 1936], p. 259).

11. Thus Desportes, who intrigues for years to get his hands on two abbeys in the diocese of Chartres, has old family interests in the Chartres clerical world. His acquisition of the two abbeys is a commercial transaction which plays out an old family strategy. The poet does his duty to the family when he resigns his canon's prebend in Chartres for the benefit of his nephew (ibid., p. 316).

12. Cited ibid., p. 375. Henri III may have been less astute than his successor, but he too was stopped by no considerations of rank or propriety in disposing of ecclesiastical appointments. He did not always have the good grace to wait for an abbé's death in a financial emergency, even when the abbé was the Cardinal d'Armagnac: "Write a dispatch immediately," he orders Villeroy in 1584, "make it very pressing and without ambiguity and full of all the reasons you can find, and make it clear that I will not suffer anyone to have possession except the one I wish. I will not suffer it" (ibid., p. 320). The Cardinal d'Armagnac, replying plaintively to the king's brutal order to resign the abbey of Aurillac, insists on his "astonishment."

13. For details of Bertaut's career, see Georges Grente, *Jean Bertaut* (Paris, 1903).

14. Typical in this respect is the Daulhou family of Rodez, merchants and bankers (papal provisions, wheat, copper, and sheepskins). Hugues Daulhou, son of a merchant, *consul* of the city, and *banquerius,* is a shrewd real-estate operator who collects the tithe for the diocese in 1520 and, by 1534, contracts for the collection of the diocese's *temporal* revenue in the name of the absentee bishop, a grandee of the Armagnac house. (See Bousquet, *Rouergue,* for the Daulhou careers and finances.)

15. On the very special role played by *officiers,* lawyers, and the notables in such sales, see V. Carrière, *Introduction aux études d'histoire écclésiastique locale,* 3 vols. (Paris, 1936), 3:419–30.

16. Ibid., p. 430, it is suggested that these sales were arranged at ridiculously low prices through conspiracies.

17. The observation is made by the Venetian ambassador, Correro, in *Relations des ambassadeurs vénitiens,* cited by Carrière, *Introduction,* 3:145.

18. As they are described in the *cahier* prepared by the deputies of the nobility for the Estates-General of 1561. Cited by J. Laférrière, *Le Contrat de Poissy* (Paris, 1905).

19. This *cahier du Tiers* of 1561 (BN Ms fr. 3970) is analyzed by Laférrière, ibid., pp. 115 ff.

20. The dirty tricks of this election campaign are preserved in the records of the lawsuit which followed in August 1498 (Archives Nationales, X⁷a 4839, fol. 339r–341r), cited in Augustin Renaudet, *Pré reforme et humanisme à Paris (1494–1517)* [1916] (Paris, 1953), p. 237.

21. Guillaume Briçonnet's reforming activities are sketched in Imbart de la Tour, *Origines,* 3:110–15.

22. The evidence for both desires is plentiful. Having cited the *cahiers* of the Third Estate as evidence of the gentry's most ambitious scheme for possession of all the church's wealth, we might cite the same source for their wish for reform. In 1560, as well as in later assemblies, the leaders of the Third Estate express a desire for "more virtuous and learned clerics ... more fre-

quent sermons, more regular episcopal visitations, and closer surveillance by the bishops of public sinning, blasphemy, nonobservance of Sundays, immoral pleasures, and dangerous books" (cited in Jean Orcibal, *Duvergier*, 2 vols. [Louvain, 1947–48], 1:13).

23. I am following Orcibal's reading of the municipal deliberations of 11 July 1575 and 13 November 1587, which I have not seen. According to Orcibal, Duvergier's supervisory duties specifically required him to make sure that all the children went to the *collège* (I have some trouble believing this) and that only one or two children should be left to serve the priests and monks (ibid., p. 99).

24. Ibid. Orcibal cites the minutes of the meeting, according to which Duvergier is asked "faire consulter si les bourgeois et autres habitants de la ville peuvent differer de payer les dimes, vu que l'evesque ne fait precher à ses depens ni le chapitre bailler la prebende preceptorale."

25. Ibid., p. 101.
26. Ibid., p. 99.
27. Ibid., p. 101.
28. Ibid.
29. Grente, *Bertaut*, p. 59.
30. As does Morvillier in naming the scholar Gentian Hervet to a *cure* in 1556 (see Gustave Baguenault de Puchesse, *Jean de Morvillier* [Paris, 1869], p. 108) or Briçonnet in naming François Vatable to a *cure* and a canon's prebend in 1523 (Imbart, *Origines*, 3:115).
31. Imbart, *Origines*, 3:60.
32. Ibid., p. 81, citing Erasmus; see also p. 75.
33. Ibid., pp. 324, 335, 336, 127.
34. See A. Labarre, *Le Livre dans la vie amienoise au 16ᵉ siècle* (Paris, 1971), for the inventory of the library of Antoine de Coquerel.
35. This is in the splendid 240-book library of Jean Forestier, *licensié ès loix* and *advocat du roy* at the *présidial* court in Amiens, in 1553 (ibid.).
36. In Grenoble, the *recteur des escolles* teaches the Gospel in 1529; in Nîmes, Bible study is required on Sundays at the public school; in Toulouse, the students hear regular lectures on Saint Paul; in Valence, the regulations governing the newly founded *collège* in 1542 require the reading of the Gospel to the students during mealtimes, "so that the entire book will have been read to them in the course of the year." The same regulations expressly forbade theological discussions. No wonder *collège* teachers are suspect to the orthodox. Putting a son in charge of the *régents* was a grave risk. Father Coton, the most influential French Jesuit of his time, remembered being put to study with a pedagogue in Roanne who soon turned out to be a secret Protestant. Coton came from a typical gentry background, which may explain his eventual successes. His father had been among the deputies of the Third Estate in Orléans in 1559. When Coton reached power, he obtained letters patent which proclaimed that his father had been a person "never having been subject to the taille nor ever having derogated from nobility." Coton himself went through a classic *cursus*, having studied law at Bourges under Cujas (J. M. Prat, *Recherches historiques et critiques sur la Compagnie de Jésus*, 5 vols. [Lyon, 1876–78], 1:2–5).
37. The diaries of provincial lawyers and magistrates record the uneasiness and the tension felt in notable circles as early as 1532, when "a great number

of people, doctors of law, *licensiés, procureurs,* and others, suspected of being Lutherans" were apprehended in Toulouse, as Jean du Pouget, *advocat* in Cahors, notes in his diary. Among those caught in Toulouse, du Pouget notes sadly (switching from French to Latin, *par prudence?*), there was Jean de Caturco, *licensié,* "qui fuerat mihi contemporaneus Tholose in studio et lectura." Within the city of Cahors, one observer notes the flight of Guillaume Leclerc, "advocat bien fameux," who left for Geneva, in 1556 and was burned in effigy. Among those who stayed, some suffered a worse fate when the masses turned against the local Protestants in 1561; among the victims was the *conseiller* Borie. In Angers, the meticulous social observer, Jehan Louvet, notes the *qualité* of the Protestants in town: Bouja, *receveur des tailles,* lynched; maistre Mellet, *advocat,* lynched; Noireulx, *advocat,* lynched; the wife of the *advocat* Sigonneau, killed by the mob. Bonvoisin, *juge de la prevosté,* and Grimauldet, *advocat du roy,* are Huguenots. (Although they are imprisoned, they are eventually freed through the pressure exercised by their brother-in-law, the *advocat* Le Fevre.) The local Protestant minister, Jousselin, is an *advocat.* And the Richard family, mayors of Angers, *nobles hommes* and rich, are among the first targets of the mob. When royal commissioners arrive to implement the edict of pacification in 1571, Louvet notes that one of the three commissioners, Goureau, sieur de la Proustiere, *maistre des requestes,* was the brother of the *prevost* of Angers and, although "he went to mass for appearances' sake," he was "grandement Huguenot" in his soul. When the bishop of Angers drew up a list of suspects, it contained the names, according to Louvet, of seven *advocats,* three *conseillers,* two *élus,* one *receveur des tailles,* and nine merchants. See Louis Greil, *Le Livre de main des Du Pouget (1522–1598)* (Cahors, 1897), pp. 8, 69, 72; and Louvet, *Journal,* 1:264–302; 2:6.

38. Imbart, *Origines,* 3:244, 257.

39. See ibid., p. 246, for letters sent by the *parlement* to the Queen Regent in April 1525 (citing Archives Nationales, X^{1a} 1527, fol. 322), placing the blame on "aucuns particuliers" who have embraced Luther's doctrine "à laquelle ils ont adjousté leurs opinions et erreurs."

40. Ibid., pp. 247–55.

41. Ibid., p. 334, summing up: "Ces magistrats lettrés, érudits, épris d'antiquité et de culture classique, pourront être opposés au changement de religion: ils n'en sont pas moins acquis à la révolution intellectuelle."

42. "Maistre Matthieu, mon ami, je vous recommande mon fils que voilà ... pour le regard de la Religion, je ne veux pas que vous me l'ostiez de ceste Eglise; je vous le defends. Mais aussi je ne veux pas que vous me le nourrissiez aux abus et superstitions d'icelle" (cited in Garnier, *Aubigné,* p. 50).

43. Estienne Pasquier, *Lettres,* 3 vols. (Paris, 1619), 1:62, 273, 278, 318, 216, 223, 210.

44. Pasquier observes, in 1561, that the Catholic party within the *parlement* had mustered a majority of only three votes in the last discussion of a royal edict concerning the rights of Protestants. This had now grown to an edge of twenty-four votes, as the Paris *parlement* resists the registration of a new edict of toleration. Pasquier understands the Catholic position as one which had been strengthened by the militancy of the Protestants. The magistrates, in his judgment, "have learned from the new actions and insolences of the others

[the organized Huguenots] how important it was, for the mass of the population, to conserve everything about the ancient religion" (ibid., p. 214). This is also essentially the conclusion of Imbart de la Tour: "If the Reformation failed, in the end, in France, it is because the peasant, attached to his farm, rooted in his memories, remains the man of tradition."

45. Imbart, *Origines*, 4:251.

46. Pasquier, *Lettres* (1619), 1:186.

47. Ibid., p. 232, 224.

48. Ibid., p. 179.

49. Gouberville, *Journal*, vol. 1, introduction, and p. 91: "Comme je revenoys d'Argougelles a Russy je trouvai le contrerolleur Noel de Bayeux et Me Jehan France qui se pourmenoyent aux champs. Nous devisames ensemble jusqu'a ce que nous vinssions a la rue d'Argouges. Comme nous parlions de la relligion et des opinions qui sont aujourd'huy entre les hommes en grande controverse et contradiction, le dict France dist par ces propres mots: Qui me croira, on fera un Dieu tout nouveau qui ne sera ni papiste, ni huguenot, affin qu'on ne dye plus: un tel est lutherien, un tel est papiste, un tel est heretique, un tel est huguenot." Maistre France's robust ecumenism, no doubt informed by book learning, is probably, at the same time, not too far away from peasant common sense. One thinks of the learned master Rabelais but also of the anonymous peasant who, at about the same time, is accused, near Troyes in Champagne, of having said that "le bonhomme Dieu est trop vieil, il ne sat plus qu'il y fait. Il gaste tout, noz vignes et noz poyres sont perdues. Il en fault faire un autre" (A.D., Aube, G 4201, fol. 35; cited by J. Roserot de Melin, *Antonio Carracciolo* [Paris, 1923], p. 194).

50. "Mémoire touchant l'édit de janvier 1562," in La Boétie, *Discours*, Bonnefon, ed. (Paris, 1922), pp. 136–39.

51. Le Riche, *Journal* (Saint-Maixent, 1846), pp. 155, 294, 334, 351.

52. Imbart, *Origines*, 3:436: "En dépit des efforts de Calvin pour l'attirer, malgré des adhésions retentissantes, nombre de gens en place, ayant pignon sur rue, renonceront malaisément à abondonner leur office, leur école ou leur négoce." In Geneva, among the French exiles, "l'élite n'est qu'une minorité." If need be, observes Imbart de la Tour, such men will send their wives and children, while they remain in France. (I am reminded of the case of Nicolas Vignier, for example, royal physician and historiographer, rich, notable, well connected, whose wife and children lived in Heidelberg while he returned to Paris to make his peace with the authorities.)

53. In his *Petit Traicté montrant que c'est que doit faire ... un homme fidele connaissant la verité de l'Evangile quand il est entre les Papistes* (1543), analyzed by Imbart, *Origines*, 4:429 ff. "God wants us entirely," preached Calvin, "in our body as well as in our spirit." The abbé of Saint-Cyran, son of Jean Duvergier, would say much the same thing eventually: "Dieu veut avoir la totalité" (Orcibal, *Duvergier*, p. 598). This hard line proved to be not only uncomfortable but, in fact, intellectually unattractive to the more notable sympathizers in France, among whom it does nothing but "trouble consciences and create horror and consternation," according to Calvin's correspondent in the *parlement* of Paris, Adam Fumée.

54. Imbart, *Origines*, 3:427, characterizes the state of mind of those whom Calvin at times denounced as Nicodemites as being an "état d'esprit qui

prétendait garder la hiérarchie, le culte, bref la structure et la vie extérieure du Catholicisme, tout en acceptant les idées essentielles de la réforme." On Calvin's being forced to make concessions, see ibid., p. 430.

55. "A curious compromise dear to the élites," writes Imbart (*Origines*, 4:428).

56. Cited in Roserot, *Antonio Carracciolo*, p. 37.

57. Imbart, *Origines*, 4:474.

58. Roserot, *Carracciolo*, pp. 201, 219, 229, 298–99.

59. Ibid., pp. 300–301.

60. Roserot (ibid.) speaks of a "parti des modérés" and cites the presence in the Pithous' own house of a manual for secret reformers apparently written in what Calvin called the Nicodemite spirit. The book's title was *Le Calendrier qui dispense l'homme fidele et lui permet de se trouver à la messe et aux vespres catholiques à cause des Psaumes, des Prieres, de l'Evangile, de l'Oraison dominicale et autres telles choses bonnes qu'on y dit et chante quoiqu'il y ait du vice meslé.*

61. Gustave Carré, *L'Enseignement secondaire à Troyes* (Paris, 1888), pp. 42–76. It may be worth noting, in comparison, that in Bayonne the leadership of the city council was so strongly set against the Jesuits that even when, in 1654, a Jesuit principal was imposed on the *collège* by royal order, so much trouble was stirred up against him that he was forced to leave town (Orcibal, *Duvergier*, p. 112).

62. It was Estienne Pasquier who had represented the university in its lawsuit against the Jesuits' right to teach in Paris. Many years later Pasquier remained the favorite target of the Jesuits' attacks, even after his death. The high point of this vendetta was reached with a 1,000-page denunciation of Pasquier's libertinism by Father Garasse, S.J., in 1621, the year of Pithou's death. It was this same Garasse, one of the Society's most avid libertine-hunters, who was in his turn attacked, in 1626, by Jean Duvergier, abbé of Saint-Cyran, Jansenius's closest collaborator and son of the Duvergier who had fought off the bishop and the cathedral chapter of Bayonne a generation earlier.

Chapter 12. Adrift

1. This is the thesis of Lucien Goldmann, in his *Le Dieu caché* (Paris, 1955); see especially pp. 117 ff. Goldmann analyzes an ideology "affirmant l'impossibilité radicale de réaliser une vie valable dans le monde" as a "tragic vision" which defines the behavior of a social group between 1637 and 1677. The social group, as Goldmann defines it, is that of the *robins* or *officiers* (p. 132). Jean Duvergier, known as the abbé of Saint-Cyran, was the founder of the Jansenist movement and the son of Jean Duvergier of Bayonne. Lemaître was an *advocat* at the *parlement*. His mother was an Arnauld. He was a protégé of the chancellor Séguier.

2. Estienne Pasquier, *Lettres*, 3 vols. (Paris, 1619), 1:69–76.

3. Ibid., pp. 95–97.

4. Ibid., pp. 98–100.

5. Ibid., 2:474.

6. Ibid., p. 406.

7. Ibid., 1:644.

8. Ibid., 2:403.

9. Nicolas Pasquier, *Lettres* (Paris, 1623), p. 615.

10. Goldmann, *Dieu*, p. 133.

11. N. Pasquier, *Lettres* (1623), p. 703.

12. Ibid., p. 705: "La Noblesse abastardie d'une nonchalante paresse."

13. Pasquier does not use the word *classe*, but it will soon come into usage. I find it in Furetière, *Roman bourgeois* (1666), p. 921, for example, where it is used to describe categories of the population differentiated by the amount of their income. It is understood that one can "monter d'une classe." Furetière, himself an *advocat* and *procureur fiscal* by profession, is very sensitive to social climbing. Thus he aptly describes one of his characters, an *advocat*, as "un homme amphibie" who wore the lawyer's *robe* in the morning, at the *palais*, but dressed as a nobleman at night (ibid., p. 907). I am citing from the Pléiade edition (Paris, 1958).

14. N. Pasquier, *Lettres*, p. 706.

15. Ibid., p. 707.

16. See Paul Porteau's honest bewilderment in his *Montaigne et la vie pédagogique de son temps* (Paris, 1935). Porteau discovered that Montaigne's attack on the *collèges* proceeded, clearly, from some deep bias. The gentry's favorite gentleman expressed himself on the subject with "disconcerting violence."

17. *Essais* (Pléiade edition), p. 135.

18. Ibid., p. 136.

19. Ibid., p. 137.

20. Ibid., p. 140: "Si cette fin de s'en enrichir, qui seule nous est proposée par le moyen de la Jurisprudence, de la Medecine, du pedantisme, et de la Theologie encore, ne les tenoit en credit, vous les verriez [les écoles] sans doubte aussi marmiteuses qu'elles furent oncques."

21. Ibid., pp. 140–41.

22. E. Pasquier, *Lettres*, 2:472–74.

23. Montaigne, *Essais*, p. 360.

24. Ibid., p. 233.

25. Ibid., p. 311, "sorcelleries et effets magiciens"; p. 304, "nous prions par usage et par coustume . . . ce n'est en fin que mine."

26. Ibid.: "Aux vices leur heure, son heure à Dieu."

27. Ibid., p. 305.

28. Ibid.

29. Ibid., pp. 305–6: "Ce n'est pas l'estude de tout le monde."

30. Ibid., p. 306.

31. Goldmann, *Dieu*, p. 37. His formulation strikes me as a brilliant guess: "The two closely linked concepts of community and universe were replaced by two others: the reasonable individual and infinite space."

32. *Essais*, p. 225.

33. Ibid., p. 242.

34. Ibid., p. 235.

35. Ibid., p. 117.

36. Garasse, *La Doctrine Curieuse des beaux esprits de ce temps ou pretendus tels* (Paris, 1623); Saint-Cyran, *Somme des fautes et faussetés capitales contenues en la Somme theologique de François Garasse* (1626).

37. Garasse, *Doctrine*, p. 230.

38. Ibid., p. 237.

39. Ibid., pp. 984, 991. Garasse attributes such deceptions to "le bonhomme Pasquier," but he does not dare attack Montaigne.

40. Ibid., p. 1016. One is struck speechless, of course, in reading the worthy controversialist, not only at the notion of "offending God mortally," but at the dangers he must have subjected himself to in the line of duty. But then we are reassured: "I protest in all conscience that I have never read as much as 4 lines in succession of the dangerous Rabelais."

41. Ibid., p. 174.

42. Ibid., p. 173. This is an old refrain of the Ligueur publicists against the rich *officiers*, who have "ne Dieu, ne Religion" (cited in Miriam Yardeni, *La Conscience nationale en France pendant les guerres de religion* [Louvain and Paris, 1971], p. 247). "Ces parlementaires sont pis qu'Hérétiques," says the Ligueur mayor of Dijon, bitterly (cited by J. Garnier in his editor's introduction to Gabriel Breunot, *Journal* 3 vols. [Dijon, 1866]).

43. Ibid., p. 169.

44. "In the year of Our Lord 1574, at the age of 38, . . . Michel de Montaigne, impatient with his servitude in the *parlement* and in public offices, in the full vigor of his age, retired . . . . May Fate allow him to perfect this ancestral home . . . which he has consecrated to his liberty, to his tranquillity, to his leisure," reads the inscription in Montaigne's library (*Essais*, p. xvi).

45. Jean Orcibal, *Duvergier*, 2 vols. (Louvain, 1947–48), 1:543, who quotes, among other sources, a letter of Chapelain, written in December of that year: "M. Lemaistre's motives . . . are absolutely saintly . . . . No sorrows, no failures, no apprehension of the future brought him to think of retreat. On the contrary, he retired at the highest point of his success and of public esteem, when he could obviously expect the further growth of both." Nicolas Fontaine, who claims to have been familiar with Lemaistre and his friends and family, reports that Lemaistre told him that his decision to retire from the *palais* was as difficult for him as would be "a king's decision to renounce his kingdom" (*Mémoires pour servir à l'histoire de Port-Royal*, 2 vols. [Cologne, 1738], 1:35).

46. The letter is published in Fontaine, *Mémoires*, 1:36: "Je suis encore plus eloigné de prendre les Ordres de la Prêtrise & de recevoir des bénéfices que de reprendre la condition que j'ai quittée," he explains, although he is determined "de n'avoir plus de commerce, ni de bouche ni par écrit, avec le monde qui m'a pensé perdre & de passer ma vie dans la solitude comme si j'étois dans un Monastère." To his father, Lemaistre wrote: "Je ne quitte point le Palais pour me mettre dans l'Eglise . . . . Je me retire dans une maison particulière, pour vivre sans ambition." He emphasizes that "ce n'est pas foiblesse d'esprit d'embrasser la vertu chrétienne, puisqu'une personne qui n'a point passé jusqu'ici pour foible ni pour scrupuleux, & qui est encore le même qu'il étoit lorsqu'il eut l'honneur de vous voir la dernière fois, se résout de changer ces belles qualités d'Orateur & de Conseiller d'Etat, en celle de simple serviteur de Jesus Christ."

47. Jean-Antoine de Baïf, in *Anthologie poétique française, XVIᵉ siècle*, M. Allem, ed., 2 vols. (Paris, 1965), 2:139–40. Pauline Smith, in her monograph *The Anti-Courtier Trend in Sixteenth-Century French Literature* (Geneva, 1960), pp. 160 ff., observes a considerable increase in the number of poems "built upon the contrast of court and country life" after 1560.

48. Nicolas Rapin, *Anthologie poétique française*, 2:178.

49. Jean de la Taille, ibid., p. 229.

50. Desportes, ibid., p. 265.

51. Tabourot, ibid., p. 277.

52. Durant, ibid., pp. 305–7.

53. Louis Turquet, *La Monarchie aristo-démocratique* (Paris, 1611), p. 262.

54. "Le peuple est un barbare Gameleon qui toujours hait l'estat présent," says André Maillard, of the Cour des Aydes (cited in Yardeni, *Conscience*, p. 261). "C'est comme une matiere premiere, grossiere et mal polie," explains another writer; and, for Hurault, "le peuple est le vague."

55. "Tous y sont déguisés," complains Jean de la Taille (*Anthologie*, 2:229). "Vouloir tant seulement estre ce que je suis," is Tabourot's definition of tranquillity. The "homme amphibie" is dissected by Furetière, himself a lawyer, in *Roman bourgeois* (1666; Pléiade edition, Paris, 1958), p. 907. At the *parlement* of Rouen, the newer generation of magistrates, as observed by contemporary diarists, began to dress in noble fashion by the end of the sixteenth century. Cloakrooms were installed in their chambers for the quick changes required by this new breed of amphibious dandies. When they took their official and legal robes off to play tennis, "on voyait leurs chausses bouffantes, bouillonnées et descoupées, pourpoincts et autres habits de couleur exquise et estrange" (E. Gosselin, "Des Usages et moeurs de MM. du Parlement de Normandie," *Revue de la Normandie* [1868], pp. 551, 598).

56. The poet Malherbe seems to me a typical example of this tension between the requirements of noble appearance and the desire to be free of this servitude. Insanely insistent about the spurious "nobility" of his family, he becomes a comic figure at court. The comedy lies in the insufferable contradictions which push him to true eccentricity. He is quoted as saying that it was "madness to brag about being of ancient nobility: the more ancient, the more dubious." He is reported as telling one of his nephews, who was not doing well at school that he might as well choose valor as his profession—that is, take up the *épée*—since he was good for nothing else. At the same time, he was so ludicrously sensitive about his own *soi-disant* nobility that when beggars addressed him hyperbolically as "Mon noble gentilhomme," he perceived a slight in this redundant greeting and would lose his temper, explaining, "if I am a *gentilhomme*, I must be noble" (Tallement des Réaux, *Historiettes*, Mongrédien, ed., 4 vols. [Paris, 1932–34], 1:171–83). In a letter to Peiresc, in 1610, Malherbe admits sourly, "You know that at this court one does not speak of people of that kind [of the long robe]. Our gallant courtiers would have it that such men can find no grace among the ladies" (Malherbe, *Oeuvres*, Lalanne, ed., 5 vols. [Paris, 1863], 2:122).

57. Malherbe, *Oeuvres*, 2:183. To a man of the *robe*, of very good status, who shows Malherbe his verse, Malherbe remarks: "Have you been condemned to hang or to write verse as an alternative? Unless that is it, I don't see how one could excuse [your attempts at writing]."

58. "Je desire singulierement qu'on nous juge chacun à part soy," Montaigne reminds us emphatically (*Essais*, p. 225); "Ie suis Parisien par adoption & de tous autres pais esquels il y a à apprendre," exclaims maistre Bigot of Rouen (in E. Pasquier, *Lettres* [1619], 1:98); and Monsieur de Montaigne is quick to remind us that Socrates was a citizen of the world "whose imagination was fuller and vaster, who embraced the universe as his city and included all humanity [*tout le genre humain*] in his learning, in his social commerce, and in his affection" (*Essais*, p. 156).

59. The exclamation is attributed to La Boétie, cited by Paul Bonnefon in the

introduction to his edition of La Boétie's *Discours de la servitude volontaire* (Paris, 1922), p. 16. Etienne de la Boétie was born in Sarlat, an administrative town of some importance in the Périgord, in 1530, the son of the *lieutenant particulier*. He received his *license* in civil law at Orléans in 1553 and began a career as *conseiller* in the *parlement* of Bordeaux in the same year. His mother was Protestant and the daughter of a *président* in the *parlement*.

60. Jacques Amyot, *Plutarch*, fol. 233 verso.

61. Montaigne, *Essais:* "un noble et un villain, un magistrat et un homme privé, un riche et un pauvre . . . ne sont differents par maniere de dire qu'en leurs chausses" (p. 252). "Pourquoy, estimant un homme, l'estimez vous tout enveloppé et empaqueté? . . . Vous n'en donnerez à l'adventure pas un qua-train, si vous l'avez despouillé. Il le faut juger par luy mesme, non par ses atours" (p. 251). "Ce ne sont pourtant que peintures, qui ne font aucune dissemblance essentielle" (p. 252). On the emperor: "Voyez le derriere le rideau, ce n'est rien qu'un homme commun. . . ." (p. 253). "Les avantages principesques sont quasi avantages imaginaires" (p. 257). "La subjection essentielle et effectuelle ne regarde d'entre nous que ceux qui s'y convient et qui ayment à s'honorer et enrichir par tel service; car qui se veut tapir en son foyer, et sçait conduire sa maison sans querelle et procès, il est aussi libre que le Duc de Venise . . .; un Seigneur retiré et casanier, nourry entre ses valets; et voyez aussi le vol de son imagination; il n'est rien plus Royal" (p. 257). Citing Amyot's *Plutarch,* he raises the question: "Le plus heureux estat d'une police seroit où, toutes autres choses estant esgales, la precedence se mesureroit à la vertu, et le rebut au vice" (p. 259).

62. Ibid., p. 23: "Domination populaire," he says, speaking of the Athenians, " . . . me semble la plus naturelle et equitable."

63. Ibid., pp. 212–13.

64. Ibid., p. 213: "Tout cela ne va pas trop mal: mais quoy, ils ne portent point de haut de chausses."

65. "Faire Justice, aymer verité, priser aequalité" is the anonymous annotation in a good sixteenth-century script, inscribed on the flyleaf of a copy of Guevara's *Mepris de la Court* (Lyon, 1543) in the collection of the Newberry Library in Chicago.

66. Montaigne, *Essais:* "Les paisants simples sont honnestes gens, et honnestes gens les philosophes, ou, selon nostre temps, des natures fortes et claires, enrichies d'une large instruction de sciences utiles" (p. 299). And he speaks of his own efforts to find his way back to his "premier et naturel siege" (p. 300).

67. Estienne de la Boétie, *Discours sur la servitude volontaire ou le contr'un* (Paris, 1947), p. 27.

68. Montaigne had read La Boétie's *Servitude* in manuscript before he met the author, and it was this *discours* which prompted him to seek La Boétie's friendship. The *Servitude* was never published during the author's lifetime. An unauthorized and incomplete version was printed in 1574. Montaigne, as executor of his friend's literary estate, refused to allow the publication of the *Servitude*. To attenuate the impression that his friend's discourse was a seditious tract, Montaigne explained in print that it was the work of a very young man, a student exercise. This, it seems, is not quite true. The work may indeed have been written by a gifted young man. But it was revised in later

life and may come closer to expressing La Boétie's views—and perhaps Montaigne's—than it was prudent to admit in print. (See the introduction in Paul Bonnefon's edition of the *Oeuvres complètes d'Estienne de la Boétie* [Paris, 1892].)

69. La Boétie, *Servitude* (1947 ed.): "Il ne faut pas faire doute que nous ne soions tous naturellement libres" (p. 29). "Cela est, comme je croy, hors de doute que, si nous vivions avec les droits que la nature nous a donné et avec les enseignemens qu'elle nous apprend, nous serions naturellement obeissans aus parens, subjets à la raison, et serfs de personne" (p. 26). "Les bestes, ce maid'Dieu! si les hommes ne font trop les souds, leur crient, VIVE LIBERTÉ!" (p. 30). "La premiere raison de la servitude volontaire, c'est la coustume.... Ils disent qu'ils ont esté tousjours subjets, que leurs peres ont ainsi vescu; ... mais pour vrai, les ans ne donnent jamais droit de mal faire, ains agrandissent l'injure" (pp. 47–48). " ... ceus là qui, ayans l'entendement net et l'esprit clairvoiant, ne se contentent pas, comme le gros populas, de regarder ce qui est devant leurs pieds, ... ce sont ceus qui, aians la teste d'eus mesmes bien faite, l'ont ancore polie par l'estude et le sçavoir: ceus là, quand la liberté seroit entierement perdue et toute hors du monde, l'imaginent et la sentent en leur esprit ... " (p. 49). (Compare with Montaigne's "philosophes," who are "natures fortes et claires, enrichies d'une large instruction de sciences utiles.")

70. The eighteenth-century vogue of the *Servitude* is inseparable from Montaigne's own reputation. Beginning with Coste's edition of the *Essais* (Geneva, 1727), the *Servitude* was included as a matter of course in succeeding editions.

71. As a matter of fact, the preservation of a good text of the *Servitude* is largely due to the président Henri de Mesmes's intention of refuting La Boétie's views, for which purpose he kept a manuscript copy in his private library. This copy is now in the Cabinet des Manuscrits of the Bibliothèque Nationale, Fonds Français, p. 839. (See the preface to the Bonnefon edition of La Boétie's *Oeuvres complètes*.)

72. Montaigne, *Essais*, p. 182: This *discours* "court pieça és mains des gens d'entendement, non sans bien grande et méritée recommandation."

73. "Hors de Paris on n'est pas civilisé," explains maistre Pierre de la Martellière, *advocat*, in a brief in 1612 (cited by Dupont Ferrier, *Collège de Clermont*, 3 vols [Paris, 1921], 1:54, n. 4).

74. G. Lefebvre, *Etudes Orléanaises*, 2 vols. (Paris, 1962), 1:187.

75. Cited in H. Taine, *Origines de la France contemporaine*, 10 vols. (Paris, 1906), 1:73.

76. This well-informed observation is made by Chrestien Guillaume de Malesherbes (a member of the Lamoignon family). He explains that Montesquieu, finding himself snubbed by the nobility, was seized by "a kind of mania" to be treated as a noble which made him an apologist for the nobility in his philosophical works: "Quand on lit ses ouvrages avec cette clef, il est aisé de s'en apercevoir," adds Malesherbes, shrewdly. These remarks were made in a letter in 1766, cited by Pierre Grosclaude, *Malesherbes et son temps: Nouveaux documents inédits* (Paris, 1969), p. 55.

77. Cited by J. P. Brancourt, "Un Théoricien de la société au 18e siècle: Le Chevalier d'Arcq," *Revue historique* 508 (October 1973): 356. Brancourt also

observes that this perspective was common among the *noblesse* in the eighteenth century.

78. One of the most notorious instances being the war ministry's regulations of 1781, requiring proof of four quarters of nobility on the father's side for a candidate for even the most junior post in the army. As David Bien's recent analysis shows, these regulations were clearly not directed at bourgeois—a requirement of one quarter of nobility would have sufficed to exclude them. As a knowledgeable observer noted at the time, "Une telle ordonnance humilioit la Magistrature, les gens opulens, et une foule de familles honorables dans les provinces." See David Bien, "La Réaction aristocratique avant 1789: L'Exemple de l'armée," *Annales* 29 (January–February 1974): 23–48, especially 41–42.

79. The Joly fortunes were solidly established in the sixteenth century, following a series of typical provincial gentry careers: tax collectors in Burgundy in the fourteenth century; *lieutenants* in their *bailliages, docteurs en droit, advocats* at the Dijon *parlement* by 1511; seigneurs of the land of Fleury, near Corbeil; *advocats* in the Paris *parlement* before the end of the sixteenth century; *conseillers* in the *parlement* of Rennes by 1629 and in Paris by 1697; *procureurs généraux* in the *parlement*, from father to son, between 1717 and 1790, without interruption. The Jolys de Fleury nevertheless failed to claim nobility (Paul Bisson de Barthelemy, *Les Joly de Fleury* [Paris, 1964], p. 15).

80. A point still made as late as 1789, apropos of the selection of deputies for the forthcoming meeting of the Estates-General by an anonymous pamphleteer, in a work entitled *Réflexions d'un gentilhomme orléanois*. "La noblesse ne gît pas dans les parchemins," he explains. That is, no *lettres patentes*, no edicts, can make one noble. Not in official documents, but rather "dans le coeur, dans l'esprit, dans la façon de penser de ceux de notre ordre" is nobility to be found. It is not a legal but a social quality. The confusion between the two is said to be desired by social climbers from the *officier* world and by the treasury as well. It must be rejected by the true nobility, and the surest way to keep usurpers out of the deputations is to elect only "*simple gentilshommes*"; *présidents* and *trésoriers du roy* do not become "*simple gentilshommes.*" They are rich and endowed with large estates. They can masquerade as abbés, bishops, barons, counts, and marquis, but they are not likely to be hiding in the rustic household of a simple *traisneur d'espée*. The pamphlet is cited by Lefebvre, *Etudes Orléanaises*, 1:187.

81. See M. Vovelle and D. Roche, "Bourgeois, rentiers, propriétaires," *Actes du 84ᵉ Congrès National des Sociétés Savantes* (Paris, 1960), pp. 419–52. In the Marais neighborhood in Paris, the category of *bourgeois vivans noblement* was a particular and specific social category, as seen by contemporaries, making up from 7 to 15 percent of the population. In Chartres, the category of bourgeois made up 5.6 percent of the population.

82. Grosclaude, *Malesherbes . . . documents*, p. 42. In contrast, the chevalier d'Arcq, writing from the point of view of the *noblesse de race*, opposes equality on the ground that "l'égalité générale parmi les citoyens détruit nécessairement la monarchie" (Brancourt, "D'Arcq," p. 357).

Index